Nothing Ventured

How Venture Capital Built America's Greatest Companies

J.F. Perkins

Copyright and Legal Disclaimer

LEGAL DISCLAIMER AND IMPORTANT NOTICES

Investment Disclaimer This book is for informational and educational purposes only and does not constitute investment advice, financial advice, trading advice, or any other sort of advice. The content of this book should not be construed as a recommendation to buy or sell any security or make any investment decision.

Venture capital investing involves substantial risk of loss and is suitable only for sophisticated investors who can bear the loss of their entire investment. Past performance does not guarantee future results. All investments carry the risk of loss, and there can be no assurance that any investment strategy will be successful.

The author and publisher are not registered investment advisors, financial planners, or securities dealers. Readers should consult with their own professional advisors before making any investment decisions.

Accuracy of Information While the author has made every effort to ensure the accuracy of the information contained in this book, the author and publisher make no warranties or representations as to the accuracy, completeness, or timeliness of the content. The information is provided on an "as is" basis and may contain errors, omissions, or inaccuracies.

The venture capital industry is dynamic and constantly evolving. Company valuations, fund performance, and market conditions change rapidly. Information that was accurate at the time of writing may become outdated or incorrect.

Sources and Attribution This book is based on extensive research including public documents, SEC filings, published interviews, academic papers, industry reports, and other publicly available sources. Where possible, multiple sources have been consulted to verify information.

Some information is based on interviews conducted specifically for this book. Interview subjects spoke on the condition of anonymity in some cases, and their identities are protected where requested.

The author has made every reasonable effort to trace copyright holders and obtain permission for the use of copyrighted material. If any copyrighted material has been inadvertently used without proper attribution or permission, the author and publisher will be pleased to make the necessary corrections in future editions.

Company Information All company names, valuations, financial data, and business information are based on publicly available sources and are believed to be accurate as of the date of publication. However, this information may change, and readers should verify current information independently.

References to specific companies, venture capital firms, or individuals should not be construed as endorsements. The inclusion or exclusion of any company or individual does not reflect any judgment about their quality, performance, or suitability for any purpose.

Forward-Looking Statements This book contains forward-looking statements and projections about future trends, technologies, and market developments. These statements are based on current expectations and assumptions that are subject to risks and uncertainties. Actual results may differ materially from those projected.

Forward-looking statements should not be relied upon as predictions of future events, and readers should not place undue reliance on such statements.

Personal Opinions The views and opinions expressed in this book are those of the author and do not necessarily reflect the official policy or position of any company, organization, or institution mentioned. Any analysis, commentary, or interpretation represents the author's personal perspective based on available information.

No Professional Relationship The author's inclusion of information about specific venture capital firms, companies, or individuals does not imply any professional relationship, endorsement, or recommendation. The author may have professional relationships with some entities mentioned in the book, but such relationships do not influence the objective presentation of historical information.

Limitation of Liability In no event shall the author, publisher, or their respective affiliates be liable for any direct, indirect, incidental, special, or consequential damages arising out of or related to the use of this book, even if advised of the possibility of such damages.

Privacy and Confidentiality The author has respected all confidentiality agreements and has not disclosed any proprietary or confidential information. All information included in this book is either publicly available or has been specifically authorized for publication.

International Considerations This book focuses primarily on the U.S. venture capital industry, though it includes global perspectives where relevant. Laws, regulations, and business practices vary by jurisdiction, and readers outside the United States should consider local conditions and seek appropriate professional advice.

Educational Purpose This book is intended for educational purposes and to contribute to the historical record of venture capital and innovation. It is not intended to provide specific guidance for investment decisions, business strategies, or professional advice of any kind.

This disclaimer is subject to change and may be updated in future editions of this book.

Table of Contents

Introduction

The Risk Takers

"The significant problems we face cannot be solved at the same level of thinking we were at when we created them."

Albert Einstein's observation about the nature of human progress captures the essence of what makes venture capital unique among all forms of investment. While most investors seek to minimize risk and preserve capital, venture capitalists do exactly the opposite, they actively seek out uncertainty, embrace failure as a learning tool, and commit their resources to entrepreneurs who insist the world can be fundamentally different than it is today.

This book tells the story of how this counterintuitive approach to investing became one of the most powerful forces in modern economic history. From its humble beginnings in post-World War II America to its current status as a global engine of innovation, venture capital has funded the companies that have reshaped how we live, work, communicate, and understand our place in the universe.

The Paradox of Venture Capital

At first glance, venture capital seems almost designed to fail. The statistics are sobering: most venture-backed companies fail entirely, never returning a penny to their investors. Of those that survive, most generate modest returns that barely compensate for the risks taken. Only a tiny fraction, perhaps one in ten achieve the extraordinary success that creates transformative value and generates the returns that make venture capital viable as an asset class.

Yet this apparent failure is actually the source of venture capital's remarkable success. By accepting, indeed, by planning for high failure rates, venture capital creates space for the kind of experimentation and risk-taking that established companies and traditional financing sources cannot support. This willingness to fail enables the occasional spectacular success that more than compensates for the inevitable losses.

Consider the mathematics: if nine out of ten investments fail completely, but the tenth investment returns 100 times the initial investment, the overall portfolio still generates exceptional returns. This "power law" distribution, where a small number of extraordinary successes drive the majority of returns is unique to venture capital and explains why the industry can prosper despite, or perhaps because of, its high failure rate.

But venture capital's impact extends far beyond financial returns. The companies it has funded have created millions of jobs, generated trillions of dollars in economic value, and produced innovations that have fundamentally altered human civilization. The personal computer, the internet, mobile technology, social networking, search engines, e-commerce, and countless other transformative technologies were brought to market through venture capital funding.

The Human Element

While venture capital is often discussed in terms of financial structures, investment strategies, and portfolio construction, its true essence lies in human relationships and judgment. At its core, venture capital is about identifying exceptional people with breakthrough ideas and providing them with the resources needed to build transformative companies.

This human element sets venture capital apart from other forms of investing that can rely more heavily on quantitative analysis and established metrics. When a venture capitalist evaluates a startup, they are making judgments about factors that cannot be easily measured: the quality of the founding team, the size of the market opportunity, the defensibility of the competitive position, and the probability of successful execution over many years of development.

The best venture capitalists combine pattern recognition developed through years of experience with intuitive insights about people, markets, and technology trends. They must be able to see potential where others see only uncertainty, to identify signals amid overwhelming noise, and to maintain conviction in their judgments despite the inevitable setbacks and skepticism that accompany breakthrough innovation.

This dependence on human judgment also means that venture capital outcomes are highly dependent on the quality of the people making investment decisions. The most successful venture capital firms are those that have consistently attracted and developed investors with exceptional judgment, network effects, and the ability to add value beyond just providing capital.

The Network Effect

One of venture capital's most powerful characteristics is its network nature. Unlike other forms of investing where investors typically compete with each other for scarce opportunities, venture capital often benefits from collaboration and information sharing. The most successful venture capitalists tend to co-invest frequently, share deal flow, and collectively support portfolio companies through multiple rounds of financing.

This network effect creates value for entrepreneurs, who gain access not just to capital from individual investors, but to entire ecosystems of expertise, relationships, and resources. A company backed by prominent venture capitalists gains credibility that can help with customer acquisition, employee recruitment, partnership development, and subsequent fundraising.

The network effect also explains why venture capital has remained geographically concentrated despite the global nature of technology and markets. Silicon Valley's continued dominance in venture capital is not primarily due to lower costs or regulatory advantages, but rather to the density of relationships between entrepreneurs, investors, employees, and service providers that creates a self-reinforcing ecosystem of innovation.

As venture capital has expanded globally, successful new centers have typically emerged around similar network effects, concentrations of technical talent, successful entrepreneurs who become angel investors, experienced venture capitalists, and supporting infrastructure that can nurture startup development.

The Evolution of Innovation

The story of venture capital is also the story of how innovation itself has evolved. In the immediate post-war period, most technological breakthroughs emerged from large corporate research laboratories or government-funded programs. Companies like Bell Labs, IBM Research, and various defense contractors employed thousands of scientists and engineers working on long-term research projects.

Venture capital enabled a different model of innovation, one where small teams of entrepreneurs could pursue breakthrough ideas without the constraints and bureaucracy of large organizations. This shift toward entrepreneurial innovation proved remarkably effective, generating more rapid development cycles, greater willingness to pursue risky approaches, and more direct connections between technological capabilities and market needs.

The venture capital model also enabled innovation to become more democratic and accessible. Rather than requiring employment at large corporations or government agencies, ambitious individuals could start their own companies and compete directly with established players. This democratization attracted talent and energy to innovation while creating competitive pressure that accelerated technological progress.

Over time, the venture capital approach to innovation became increasingly sophisticated. Early venture capitalists often had limited technical expertise and relied primarily on financial analysis and business judgment. Modern venture capital firms employ partners with advanced degrees in relevant technical fields and maintain extensive networks of advisors who can evaluate breakthrough technologies.

The Platform Shifts

Perhaps venture capital's greatest successes have come from identifying and capitalizing on "platform shifts", fundamental changes in technology infrastructure that enable entirely new categories of products and services. The personal computer, the internet, mobile technology, cloud computing, and artificial intelligence represent platform shifts that created opportunities for venture capital investment across multiple industries and application areas.

The key insight about platform shifts is that they create opportunities not just for individual companies, but for entire ecosystems of innovation. When the personal computer platform emerged, it enabled venture capital investment in hardware companies, software companies, peripheral manufacturers, and various service providers. The internet platform created opportunities across e-commerce, media, communications, and enterprise applications.

Identifying platform shifts before they become obvious to all investors requires a combination of technical understanding, market insight, and timing judgment that exemplifies venture capital's highest skills. The most successful venture capital firms have been those that recognized platform shifts early and deployed capital systematically across the companies that could capitalize on new technological possibilities.

Platform shifts also explain why venture capital returns tend to be cyclical, with periods of exceptional performance corresponding to major technological transitions. The firms and investors who correctly identify and position themselves for platform shifts can generate extraordinary returns, while those who miss these transitions may struggle with more modest opportunities.

The Global Expansion

While venture capital began as a uniquely American phenomenon centered in Silicon Valley, it has evolved into a global system of innovation funding. Today, significant venture capital ecosystems exist in China, Europe, Israel, India, Southeast Asia, and other regions around the world.

This global expansion has created both opportunities and challenges. Entrepreneurs now have access to larger pools of capital and can choose investors based on expertise and strategic fit rather than just geographic proximity. International competition has also accelerated innovation and created pressure for continued improvement in venture capital practices.

However, the globalization of venture capital has also created new complexities related to regulatory differences, cultural variations, and geopolitical tensions. Cross-border venture capital investment requires sophisticated understanding of different legal systems, business practices, and market dynamics.

The emergence of venture capital as a tool of national competitiveness has also created strategic considerations that extend beyond pure financial returns. Countries recognize that venture capital ecosystems are essential for participating in the global innovation economy and maintaining economic competitiveness.

The Responsibility Factor

As venture capital has become more powerful and influential, questions about its responsibilities and obligations have become more prominent. The companies funded by venture capital now employ millions of people, serve billions of customers, and influence economic and social trends in ways that attract public attention and regulatory scrutiny.

This increased influence brings both opportunities and obligations. Venture capital has the potential to help address humanity's greatest challenges, climate change, healthcare, inequality, and education through the companies it chooses to fund. However, it also bears responsibility for the unintended consequences and negative externalities that can result from rapid technological change.

The most thoughtful venture capitalists are increasingly considering not just financial returns, but also environmental impact, social consequences, and governance practices when making investment decisions. This evolution toward more holistic evaluation criteria reflects both changing investor expectations and recognition that sustainable long-term success requires consideration of multiple stakeholder interests.

The Structure of This Book

This book traces the evolution of venture capital from its origins to its current global influence and future possibilities. The narrative is organized both chronologically and thematically, following major developments in venture capital while also exploring the key companies, technologies, and investment approaches that have defined different eras.

Part I examines venture capital's origins in the post-World War II economic boom and the early pioneers who established the basic structures and approaches that continue to define the industry. Part II explores the foundation years when venture capital funded the semiconductor industry and early computer companies that created the technological infrastructure for the digital revolution.

Part III covers the scaling era of the 1980s and 1990s when venture capital funded the companies that brought computing to mainstream markets while beginning to explore new frontiers like biotechnology and telecommunications. Part IV examines the internet revolution and the dramatic boom and bust cycle that tested venture capital's assumptions and approaches.

Part V explores the modern era of venture capital, including the emergence of Google, Facebook, and the mobile revolution that created new models for venture capital success. Part VI covers venture capital's evolution with new models, players, and approaches that have democratized access to startup funding.

Part VII looks toward the future, examining artificial intelligence, global competition, and the emerging technologies that will define venture capital's next chapter.

Throughout this narrative, the book emphasizes the human stories behind venture capital's success, the entrepreneurs who risked everything to pursue breakthrough ideas, the investors who supported them despite uncertain odds, and the broader ecosystem of talent, expertise, and resources that made transformative innovation possible.

The Lessons Ahead

The history of venture capital offers numerous lessons for entrepreneurs, investors, policymakers, and anyone interested in understanding how innovation occurs and how breakthrough technologies become successful companies. These lessons include insights about timing, team building, market development, competitive strategy, and the complex interplay between technological possibility and commercial viability.

Perhaps most importantly, the venture capital story demonstrates that the future is not predetermined, that through human creativity, intelligent risk-taking, and sustained commitment, we can build companies and technologies that solve important problems and improve the human condition.

The companies funded by venture capital have repeatedly proven that what seems impossible can become inevitable, that small teams can compete with large incumbents, and that breakthrough innovations can create value that extends far beyond their immediate commercial applications.

As we face current challenges including climate change, inequality, healthcare access, and the need for continued economic growth, the venture capital model offers a proven approach for channeling resources toward solutions. The combination of entrepreneurial vision, patient capital, and systematic innovation support that defines venture capital may be essential for addressing the complex challenges of the 21st century.

The Continuing Story

While this book covers venture capital's history from its origins to the present, the story is far from over. Indeed, some of the most important chapters may yet to be written. The artificial intelligence revolution, the development of quantum computing, advances in biotechnology and space technology, and the urgent need for climate solutions all represent opportunities for venture capital to continue its role in enabling transformative innovation.

The entrepreneurs and investors who will write these future chapters are already at work in laboratories, startup offices, and venture capital firms around the world. They are united by the same fundamental belief that has driven venture capital throughout its history, that the combination of human ingenuity and intelligent risk-taking can create a future that is better than the present.

This book is their story, and ours. It is the story of how venture capital became the engine of innovation that has transformed the world, and how it continues to shape our collective future through its willingness to support the unreasonable ambitions of entrepreneurs who refuse to accept the world as it is and instead insist on building the world as it should be.

The greatest venture capital successes have always begun with someone who was willing to take risks that others considered foolish, to pursue visions that others deemed impossible, and to persist through setbacks that would have discouraged more reasonable people. In a very real sense, all progress depends on such unreasonable optimism.

This is the story of the risk takers and the extraordinary companies they built.

Part I: The Genesis (1940s-1970s)

Chapter 1

Seeds of Innovation

The story of venture capital begins not in the glass towers of Sand Hill Road or the garages of Palo Alto, but in the crucible of World War II. As American bombers thundered across European skies and Allied forces stormed the beaches of Normandy, a quiet revolution was taking place in laboratories and research facilities across the United States. The marriage of government funding, academic research, and industrial innovation during the war years would plant the seeds for an entirely new form of capitalism, one that would reshape the American economy and create some of the world's most valuable companies.

The War Machine as Innovation Catalyst

The scale of technological advancement during World War II was unprecedented in human history. In just six years, American scientists and engineers developed radar systems that could track enemy aircraft, proximity fuses that revolutionized artillery, synthetic rubber to replace supplies cut off by Japanese expansion, and ultimately, the atomic bomb that ended the war. The Manhattan Project alone employed over 130,000 people and consumed resources equivalent to the entire American automobile industry.

What made this possible was not just American ingenuity, but a fundamental shift in how innovation was funded and organized. For the first time in peacetime, the federal government became the primary source of research and development capital, pouring billions of dollars into universities, private companies, and hybrid research organizations. The Office of Scientific Research and Development, led by Vannevar Bush, coordinated this massive effort, creating new models of collaboration between government, academia, and industry that would outlast the war itself.

Dr. Bush understood that this wartime innovation infrastructure could not simply disappear when peace returned. In his influential 1945 report "Science, The Endless Frontier," he argued that continued government investment in basic research was essential for national security and economic prosperity. "Scientific progress is one essential key to our security as a nation, to our better health, to more jobs, to a higher standard of living, and to our cultural progress," Bush wrote. His vision would lead to the creation of the National Science Foundation and establish the federal government as a permanent patron of American research.

However, Bush also recognized that government funding alone could not commercialize the technologies emerging from this research. There was a gap between laboratory discoveries and marketable products, a gap that would require new forms of private capital willing to take extraordinary risks on unproven technologies. This gap would become the hunting ground for venture capitalists.

The Technology Spillover Effect

The end of World War II unleashed a torrent of technologies seeking civilian applications. Radar technology, developed for tracking enemy aircraft, found new life in air traffic control and weather forecasting. Jet engines, which had powered the fastest warplanes, began carrying commercial passengers. Electronic computing machines, used to calculate artillery trajectories, started processing business data and scientific calculations.

Perhaps most significantly, the transistor emerged from Bell Laboratories in 1947, building on wartime research into semiconductors and solid-state physics. John Bardeen, Walter Brattain, and William Shockley's invention would eventually replace vacuum tubes and enable the miniaturization of electronics, but in 1947, its commercial potential was far from obvious. Bell Labs, as part of the regulated telephone monopoly AT&T, had little incentive to aggressively commercialize the transistor beyond telecommunications applications. This created opportunities for entrepreneurs willing to explore new applications and business models.

The challenge was that these emerging technologies required substantial capital investment and carried enormous technical risks. Traditional banks, focused on securing loans with tangible assets, were ill-equipped to evaluate semiconductor manufacturing processes or judge the market potential of electronic computers. Insurance companies and other institutional investors were legally restricted from making speculative investments. Meanwhile, wealthy individuals who might have the capital to invest often lacked the technical expertise to evaluate these opportunities.

This financing gap was not just theoretical, it was actively constraining innovation. Across the country, brilliant engineers and scientists who had worked on wartime projects were leaving large corporations to start their own companies, but many promising ventures died for lack of capital. The few that survived often had to accept unfavorable terms from wealthy individuals or family offices that did not understand the businesses they were funding.

The Birth of Professional Risk Capital

Into this gap stepped a handful of visionary financiers who recognized that the commercialization of advanced technology required a new approach to investment. Unlike traditional bankers or investment managers, these pioneers needed to combine financial sophistication with technical expertise, patience with ambition, and structured thinking with entrepreneurial intuition.

The first institutional venture capital firm in America was J.H. Whitney & Company, founded in 1946 by Cornelius Vanderbilt Whitney. Whitney, heir to the Vanderbilt fortune and a successful businessman in his own right, had served in the Army Air Forces during the war and witnessed firsthand the rapid pace of technological development. He established his firm with the explicit goal of providing "venture capital" to promising new businesses, coining a term that would define an entire industry.

Whitney's approach was methodical and professional. Rather than making ad hoc investments based on personal relationships or hunches, the firm developed systematic processes for evaluating opportunities, conducting due diligence, and supporting portfolio companies after investment. Whitney hired experienced business executives to serve as partners and advisors, creating a bridge between the financial community and the emerging technology sector.

The firm's early investments reflected the technological opportunities of the post-war era. Whitney backed Spencer Chemical Company in its development of new plastics and synthetic materials, invested in early television broadcasting equipment manufacturers, and supported aerospace companies developing civilian applications for military technologies. While not all of these investments succeeded, Whitney demonstrated that professional investors could generate attractive returns by backing innovative companies in emerging industries.

More importantly, Whitney established many of the practices that would become standard in venture capital. The firm typically invested in multiple rounds, providing additional capital as companies reached development milestones. Whitney partners took active roles in portfolio companies, serving on boards of directors and providing strategic guidance. The firm maintained a diversified portfolio, understanding that high-risk investments required a statistical approach to generate consistent returns.

The Professor Who Changed Everything

While Whitney was establishing venture capital on the East Coast, an even more influential figure was beginning his career on the other side of the continent. Georges Doriot, a French-born professor at Harvard Business School, would become known as the "father of venture capital" for his role in creating American Research and Development Corporation (ARD) and his decades of teaching and mentoring future venture capitalists.

Doriot's path to venture capital was unconventional. Born in Paris in 1899, he had served in the French army during World War I before emigrating to the United States to study at Harvard. After earning his MBA, he joined the Harvard Business School faculty in 1926, where he taught manufacturing and became known for his engaging lectures and practical approach to business education. During World War II, he served as deputy director of the U.S. Army's Research and Development Division, where he oversaw the development of military equipment and supplies.

This wartime experience convinced Doriot that America was on the verge of a technological revolution that would create enormous investment opportunities. In 1946, the same year Whitney founded his firm, Doriot collaborated with MIT president Karl Compton and other Boston business leaders to establish the American Research and Development Corporation. Unlike Whitney's firm, which was structured as a traditional partnership funded by family wealth, ARD was organized as a publicly traded corporation that raised capital from institutional investors including insurance companies, universities, and foundations.

ARD's mission was ambitious: to bridge the gap between scientific research and commercial application by providing capital and guidance to technology companies. The firm's prospectus stated its goal as "the development of new enterprises based on scientific research which have long-term growth and profit possibilities." This focus on science-based businesses, rather than traditional industries or financial plays, distinguished ARD from other investment organizations of the era.

Doriot brought a unique philosophy to venture investing that would influence generations of practitioners. He viewed venture capital not merely as a financial transaction, but as a collaborative partnership between investor and entrepreneur. "Someone, somewhere, is making a product that will make your product obsolete," he often told his portfolio company

CEOs, emphasizing the need for continuous innovation and strategic thinking.

His investment approach was methodical and patient. Doriot insisted on thorough due diligence, often spending months evaluating potential investments and getting to know management teams. He preferred to make concentrated investments in a small number of companies rather than spreading capital across many opportunities. Most importantly, he took a long-term view, holding investments for years or even decades while companies developed their technologies and built market positions.

Early Successes and Lessons Learned

The first major validation of the venture capital model came in the 1950s with several breakthrough successes that demonstrated the potential returns from backing innovative technology companies. ARD's investment in Digital Equipment Corporation (DEC) became legendary in venture capital circles, not just for its financial returns but for what it revealed about the power of patient capital and strategic guidance.

DEC was founded in 1957 by Kenneth Olsen and Harlan Anderson, two MIT engineers who had worked on the Whirlwind computer project. Their vision was to build smaller, more affordable computers that could be used by individual researchers and departments rather than requiring the massive installations and specialized operators that characterized mainframe computers of the era. However, the conventional wisdom in the computer industry was that there was a market for perhaps a dozen computers worldwide, making DEC's vision seem quixotic.

Doriot saw something different. His wartime experience had convinced him that computers would become essential tools for business and scientific research, and his technical advisors helped him understand that advances in transistor technology were making smaller computers technically feasible. More importantly, Doriot was impressed by Olsen's technical competence and business acumen. After extensive due diligence, ARD invested $70,000 in DEC in exchange for 78% of the company.

The partnership between ARD and DEC exemplified Doriot's approach to venture capital. Rather than simply providing money and waiting for results, ARD partners worked closely with Olsen to develop business strategies, recruit key personnel, and navigate the challenges of building a technology company. Doriot insisted that DEC focus on building a sustainable business rather than chasing quick profits, even when this meant passing up lucrative short-term opportunities.

This patience was rewarded spectacularly. DEC pioneered the minicomputer market, developed innovative products like the PDP series computers, and grew to become the second-largest computer company in the world after IBM. When DEC went public in 1968, ARD's initial $70,000 investment was worth over $37 million, representing a return of more than 500 times the original investment. This success not only validated the venture capital model but also created a new class of millionaires among DEC's employees, many of whom would go on to start their own companies and become venture investors themselves.

Other early venture successes reinforced the lessons from DEC. High Voltage Engineering Corporation, backed by ARD in 1946, developed specialized equipment for scientific research and industrial applications. Ionics, another ARD portfolio company, commercialized new techniques for water purification and chemical separation. These companies shared common characteristics: they were based on advanced technologies, served specialized markets that incumbents had overlooked, and benefited from patient capital that allowed them to develop their products and build market positions over time.

The Infrastructure of Innovation

The success of early venture capital firms like Whitney and ARD demonstrated that professional risk capital could generate attractive returns, but it also revealed the importance of supporting infrastructure for technology entrepreneurship. Successful venture investing required more than just capital, it demanded technical expertise, industry connections, legal frameworks, and cultural acceptance of risk-taking and failure.

Universities played a crucial role in this ecosystem. Institutions like MIT, Stanford, Harvard, and Caltech served as sources of both technology and talent, conducting research that led to commercial applications and training the engineers and scientists who would start technology companies. The close relationships between venture capitalists and university researchers created informal networks that helped identify promising technologies and evaluate investment opportunities.

Legal and accounting professionals also adapted to serve the needs of technology companies and their venture investors. Law firms developed expertise in intellectual property protection, complex corporate structures, and securities regulations. Accounting firms learned to value intangible assets like patents and technical expertise. Investment banks created new mechanisms for taking venture-backed companies public, providing exit opportunities for early investors and entrepreneurs.

Perhaps most importantly, a culture of entrepreneurship began to emerge that celebrated risk-taking and tolerated failure. Unlike in many other countries where business failure carried permanent social stigma, American culture increasingly viewed failed entrepreneurs as experienced executives who had learned valuable lessons. This cultural shift was essential for venture capital, which required a steady flow of talented entrepreneurs willing to leave secure corporate positions to start risky new ventures.

Setting the Stage for Silicon Valley

By the late 1950s, the fundamental elements of the venture capital industry were in place. Firms like Whitney and ARD had demonstrated that professional investors could generate attractive returns by backing technology companies. The legal and regulatory frameworks for venture investing had been established. Universities were producing both the technologies and the talent needed for new ventures. Most importantly, a generation of successful entrepreneurs and investors had emerged who would serve as mentors and role models for the next wave of innovation.

The stage was set for the next chapter in venture capital history, which would unfold in the orchards and suburbs south of San Francisco. There, the intersection of academic research, military spending, entrepreneurial ambition, and venture capital would create the most powerful innovation ecosystem the world had ever seen. But that transformation built directly on the foundation established by the pioneers of the 1940s and 1950s, who first recognized that the commercialization of advanced technology required a new form of capitalism, one that combined financial sophistication with technical expertise, patience with ambition, and systematic thinking with entrepreneurial intuition.

The seeds planted in those early decades would grow into towering trees that would shelter and nurture companies like Intel, Apple, Google, and thousands of others that would reshape not just the American economy, but the entire world. The venture capital industry that emerged from the wreckage and opportunity of World War II would prove to be one of America's most successful and influential innovations, creating trillions of dollars in value and transforming entire industries. But it all began with a handful of visionaries who recognized that in the gap between laboratory bench and marketplace lay the opportunity to fund the future.

Chapter 2

Silicon Valley's Birth

The transformation of a sleepy agricultural valley south of San Francisco into the world's most dynamic center of technological innovation didn't happen overnight. It was the result of a unique convergence of visionary leadership, institutional support, entrepreneurial rebellion, and the emerging venture capital model that would define American innovation for generations to come. The story of Silicon Valley's birth is inseparable from the story of venture capital itself, as both evolved together in a symbiotic relationship that would reshape the global economy.

The Stanford Foundation

At the heart of Silicon Valley's emergence stood Stanford University and one man's extraordinary vision. Frederick Emmons Terman, often called the "Father of Silicon Valley," understood something that few academics of his era grasped: the immense potential that lay in bridging the gap between university research and commercial application. As a professor of electrical engineering and later provost at Stanford, Terman didn't just teach students, he actively encouraged them to start companies and stay in the area to build an industrial ecosystem around the university.

Terman's philosophy was revolutionary for its time. While most prestigious universities maintained a distinct separation between academic research and commercial enterprise, he actively promoted what would later be called "technology transfer." He encouraged his graduate students to work with local companies, facilitated consulting relationships between faculty and industry, and most importantly, provided both intellectual and practical support for student entrepreneurs who wanted to commercialize their research.

The timing of Terman's vision was fortuitous. The post-World War II economic boom had created unprecedented demand for new technologies, particularly in electronics and communications. Military spending during the Cold War provided substantial funding for research and development, much of which flowed through universities like Stanford. Terman recognized that this government investment could serve as the foundation for a broader commercial ecosystem if properly channeled.

One of Terman's earliest and most significant successes came with two of his students: William Hewlett and David Packard. In 1938, with Terman's encouragement and a $538 loan, the two engineers started Hewlett-Packard in a Palo Alto garage. The company's early success in producing electronic test equipment validated Terman's thesis that Stanford could serve as an incubator for technology companies. More importantly, HP's growth created a model that other Stanford graduates would follow, establishing a pattern of university-to-startup migration that became central to Silicon Valley's culture.

But Terman's influence extended far beyond individual companies. In the 1950s, as Stanford's provost, he spearheaded the creation of Stanford Research Park, one of the first university-affiliated industrial parks in the world. By leasing Stanford land to technology companies, the university created a physical space where academia and industry could interact more closely. Companies like Varian Associates, Lockheed, and later Xerox established facilities in the research park, bringing thousands of engineers and scientists to the area and creating a dense network of technical talent.

The research park model was revolutionary because it solved several problems simultaneously. For Stanford, it provided a steady revenue stream from land that had previously generated little income. For companies, it offered access to university research, graduate students, and faculty expertise. For the broader community, it created high-paying jobs and established the area as a center of technological innovation. Most importantly for the future of venture capital, it concentrated a large number of technically sophisticated entrepreneurs and potential investors in a small geographic area.

The Semiconductor Revolution

While Terman was building the institutional foundation for Silicon Valley, a technological revolution was brewing that would provide the perfect vehicle for venture capital investment. The invention of the transistor at Bell Laboratories in 1947 had opened up entirely new possibilities for electronics, but translating this laboratory breakthrough into commercial products required significant capital and entrepreneurial vision.

The semiconductor industry was uniquely suited to the venture capital model for several reasons. First, semiconductor companies required substantial upfront investment in research and development, specialized equipment, and manufacturing facilities before generating any revenue. Traditional sources of business financing, such as bank loans, were inadequate for companies with no tangible assets and uncertain prospects. Second, the potential returns were enormous if successful, semiconductors promised to revolutionize everything from computers to telecommunications to consumer electronics. Third, the industry was characterized by rapid technological change, creating opportunities for new entrants to disrupt established players through superior technology.

The arrival of semiconductor technology in Silicon Valley can be traced to one pivotal decision by William Shockley, co-inventor of the transistor and Nobel Prize winner. In 1955, Shockley left Bell Labs to start Shockley Semiconductor Laboratory in Mountain View, California, drawn partly by the area's growing reputation as a technology center and partly by his desire to be closer to his aging mother. Shockley's company attracted some of the brightest young engineers and physicists in the country, eager to work with the legendary inventor on the cutting edge of transistor technology.

However, Shockley's managerial style proved problematic. He was brilliant as a scientist but difficult as a boss, prone to paranoid suspicions about his employees and erratic decision-making about the company's technical direction. By 1957, eight of his key employees had grown so frustrated with his leadership that they began secretly planning to leave and start their own company. This group, Robert Noyce, Gordon Moore, Julius Blank, Victor Grinich, Jean Hoerni, Eugene Kleiner, Jay Last, and Sheldon Roberts would become known as the "traitorous eight," a nickname that reflected both Shockley's bitter reaction to their departure and their subsequent legendary status in Silicon Valley history.

Arthur Rock and the Birth of Venture Capital

The departure of the "traitorous eight" from Shockley Semiconductor created a pivotal moment in both semiconductor history and the development of venture capital. The eight engineers had world-class technical expertise and a clear vision for building better semiconductor products, but they lacked the capital necessary to start a company. Their story intersected with that of Arthur Rock, a young investment banker from New York who was about to help create the modern venture capital industry.

Rock worked for Hayden, Stone & Co., a Wall Street investment firm, when he received a call in 1957 from Eugene Kleiner, one of the eight defectors from Shockley's company. Kleiner was looking for financial backing to start a new semiconductor company, and he had been referred to Rock through a mutual contact. Rock was intrigued by the opportunity, but he faced a significant challenge: traditional Wall Street firms had little experience with technology startups, and the established financing models weren't well-suited to the kind of company the eight engineers wanted to create.

Rock's solution was innovative and would become a template for venture capital deals. Rather than trying to raise money for the engineers to start an independent company, a difficult proposition given their lack of business experience and the unproven nature of the semiconductor market Rock convinced Sherman Fairchild, son of IBM founder George Fairchild and a wealthy technology enthusiast, to provide backing for a new subsidiary of Fairchild Camera and Instrument Corporation.

The deal structure Rock negotiated was revolutionary. Fairchild Camera would provide $1.4 million in funding for the new company, Fairchild Semiconductor, in exchange for ownership. However, the eight founders would receive stock options that could make them millionaires if the company succeeded. This alignment of interests between investors and entrepreneurs, with both parties benefiting from the company's success became a fundamental principle of venture capital.

Perhaps even more importantly, Rock negotiated a provision that if Fairchild Semiconductor met certain performance targets, the founders could exercise their options to gain control of the company. This gave the entrepreneurs a path to independence and ownership, addressing one of the key concerns that had driven them away from Shockley in the first place.

The Fairchild Semiconductor deal demonstrated several principles that would become central to venture capital. First, it showed that technology startups could attract significant investment if they had the right combination of technical expertise, market opportunity, and investor confidence. Second, it established the importance of equity compensation in aligning the interests of investors and entrepreneurs. Third, it demonstrated that professional investors could add value beyond just providing capital, helping to structure deals and solve problems that entrepreneurs couldn't address on their own.

Fairchild's Golden Age

Under the leadership of Robert Noyce, Fairchild Semiconductor quickly became one of the most successful and influential companies in Silicon Valley. The company's technical achievements were extraordinary, they developed the first commercially viable integrated circuit, pioneered new manufacturing processes, and created products that found applications across a rapidly expanding electronics industry. But perhaps even more important than Fairchild's direct contributions was its role as a training ground for entrepreneurs and executives who would go on to create dozens of other companies.

Fairchild's success validated the venture capital model in several ways. The company's rapid growth demonstrated that technology startups could generate enormous returns for investors. Its need for multiple rounds of financing as it expanded showed how venture capital could support companies through various stages of growth. Its eventual acquisition by Schlumberger for hundreds of millions of dollars proved that venture-backed companies could create substantial wealth for both entrepreneurs and investors.

But Fairchild's most lasting contribution to Silicon Valley may have been cultural. The company developed a more egalitarian and entrepreneurial culture than was typical in large corporations of the era. Engineers were encouraged to experiment and take risks, informal communication was valued over rigid hierarchies, and stock options gave employees a direct stake in the company's success. This culture would become characteristic of Silicon Valley companies and would prove particularly attractive to the kind of technically talented individuals who thrived in the venture capital ecosystem.

The "Fairchild Mafia," as the network of former Fairchild employees came to be known, went on to found or lead dozens of semiconductor and technology companies throughout the 1960s and 1970s. Intel, AMD, National Semiconductor, and numerous other companies traced their origins to Fairchild alumni. This pattern of successful entrepreneurs becoming investors and mentors for the next generation of startups became a defining characteristic of Silicon Valley's ecosystem.

The Kleiner Transformation

Eugene Kleiner's journey from engineer to venture capitalist exemplified the evolution of Silicon Valley's financial ecosystem. As one of the "traitorous eight," Kleiner had experienced firsthand both the technical excitement and financial rewards of building a successful technology startup. After Fairchild's success, he found himself drawn to the possibility of helping other entrepreneurs achieve similar success.

In 1972, Kleiner partnered with Tom Perkins, a Harvard Business School graduate with experience in both engineering and finance, to form Kleiner Perkins (later Kleiner Perkins Caufield & Byers). Their partnership represented a new model for venture capital, combining deep technical expertise with sophisticated financial and business knowledge. Kleiner brought credibility with entrepreneurs and the ability to evaluate technical risks and opportunities, while Perkins contributed business strategy expertise and connections with potential customers and strategic partners.

The formation of Kleiner Perkins marked a crucial evolution in venture capital. Earlier venture investors like Arthur Rock operated primarily as deal-makers, identifying opportunities and structuring investments. Kleiner Perkins pioneered a more hands-on approach, working closely with portfolio companies to help them develop strategies, recruit talent, and navigate the challenges of rapid growth. This model of "value-added" venture capital became the standard for the industry and helped explain why venture-backed companies often outperformed their competitors.

Kleiner Perkins also demonstrated the importance of specialization in venture capital. Rather than investing across all industries, the firm focused primarily on technology companies, particularly those related to semiconductors, computers, and telecommunications. This specialization allowed the partners to develop deep expertise in these areas and build networks of relationships that could benefit their portfolio companies. It also helped them identify trends and opportunities earlier than generalist investors.

Geographic Clustering and Network Effects

The concentration of venture capital activity in Silicon Valley wasn't accidental, it reflected powerful economic forces that would become central to understanding how innovation ecosystems develop. The clustering of technology companies, venture capital firms, universities, and supporting services in a small geographic area created what economists call "network effects" and "agglomeration benefits."

The network effects were particularly powerful in venture capital because the industry depends heavily on relationships and information flow. Venture capitalists need to identify promising entrepreneurs and technologies before their competitors. Entrepreneurs need to find investors who understand their markets and can provide not just capital but also strategic advice and business connections. Both groups benefit from being part of a dense network where information travels quickly and relationships develop naturally through frequent interaction.

Stanford University remained at the center of this network, providing a steady stream of technically trained graduates, many of whom either started companies or joined existing startups. The university's continued emphasis on practical application of research, encouraged by Frederick Terman's legacy, meant that academic discoveries were quickly translated into commercial opportunities. Faculty members often served as advisors to startups or even co-founders of companies based on their research.

The concentration of talent also created a unique labor market that proved particularly conducive to venture capital investment. Engineers and executives could move between companies relatively easily, allowing startups to recruit experienced talent and enabling the rapid transfer of knowledge and best practices across the industry. This mobility also meant that successful entrepreneurs often became investors or advisors to other startups, creating a virtuous cycle of experience and capital.

The Cultural Foundation

Perhaps the most important and least tangible aspect of Silicon Valley's birth was the development of a distinctive culture that embraced risk-taking, celebrated entrepreneurship, and viewed failure as a learning experience rather than a career-ending catastrophe. This culture didn't emerge accidentally, it was shaped by the specific circumstances of the area's development and the values of its early leaders.

The military's role in funding early technology development contributed to a culture of ambitious technical projects and comfort with uncertainty. The university environment fostered intellectual curiosity and collaboration. The venture capital model encouraged risk-taking by providing both financial support and guidance for entrepreneurs. The success of companies like Hewlett-Packard and Fairchild demonstrated that starting a technology company could lead to both financial rewards and professional recognition.

This culture became self-reinforcing as Silicon Valley attracted ambitious entrepreneurs and investors from around the world. The area's reputation for innovation and opportunity drew talented individuals who might have pursued more conventional careers elsewhere. The presence of role models, successful entrepreneurs who had built great companies inspired others to take similar risks. The availability of venture capital meant that good ideas could find funding even when they challenged established industries or business models.

The cultural foundation established during Silicon Valley's birth would prove to be its most durable competitive advantage. While other regions could copy the area's institutions, infrastructure, and policies, replicating its culture of entrepreneurship and risk-taking proved much more difficult. This cultural foundation would support waves of innovation in personal computers, software, internet technologies, and beyond, making Silicon Valley the world's most successful and enduring innovation ecosystem.

As the 1970s dawned, Silicon Valley had established the basic elements that would define it for decades to come: world-class research universities, successful technology companies, sophisticated venture capital firms, and a culture that celebrated entrepreneurship and innovation. The stage was set for the next phase of development, as venture capital would begin to institutionalize and expand beyond its early informal networks to become a major force in American business and economic growth.

Chapter 3

Institutionalizing Risk

By the late 1960s, venture capital had proven its worth through spectacular successes like Fairchild Semiconductor and the emerging ecosystem of Silicon Valley startups. However, the industry remained a relatively informal collection of wealthy individuals, family offices, and ad hoc partnerships operating without standardized structures or regulatory frameworks. The transformation of venture capital from an entrepreneurial experiment into a professional investment industry required fundamental changes in how these firms organized themselves, raised capital, and operated within the broader financial system. This institutionalization process would unlock enormous pools of capital and establish venture capital as a permanent feature of the American economy.

The Partnership Structure Revolution

The early venture capital industry faced a fundamental organizational challenge. Most early venture investors operated as informal syndicates or used corporate structures that weren't well-suited to the unique characteristics of venture investing. Corporate structures subjected investment gains to double taxation and didn't provide the flexibility needed for the long-term, illiquid investments that characterized venture capital. Traditional investment partnerships were designed for liquid securities that could be easily valued and traded, not for startup equity that might take five to ten years to generate returns.

The solution came through the adaptation of a centuries-old business structure: the limited partnership. While limited partnerships had been used in various forms since medieval times, their application to venture capital created a nearly perfect alignment between the needs of investors (limited partners) and venture capitalists (general partners).

Under the limited partnership structure, venture capital firms raised funds from institutional and individual investors who became limited partners. These limited partners provided the capital but had no role in day-to-day investment decisions or portfolio company management. The venture capitalists became general partners, contributing a small percentage of the fund's capital (typically 1-3%) but taking full responsibility for investment decisions and portfolio management.

The economic terms of these partnerships became standardized around what came to be known as the "2 and 20" model, though early venture funds often had different fee structures. General partners typically received an annual management fee of around 2% of committed capital to cover operating expenses and salaries, plus 20% of any profits generated by the fund (known as "carried interest" or "carry"). This structure ensured that venture capitalists had substantial upside participation in successful investments while limited partners bore most of the downside risk.

The limited partnership structure solved several critical problems simultaneously. For limited partners, it provided a way to invest in venture capital without taking on the unlimited liability that general partners faced. It also allowed institutional investors like pension funds and university endowments to make venture capital investments without directly engaging in what might be considered "business activities" that could jeopardize their tax-exempt status.

For general partners, the limited partnership structure provided a clear framework for raising capital and established their compensation through management fees and carried interest. Equally important, it created legal separation between the venture capital firm and its portfolio companies, protecting both the firm and its limited partners from potential liabilities associated with startup investments.

William Draper Jr., often considered one of the founding fathers of modern venture capital, played a crucial role in popularizing the limited partnership structure. In 1958, he established Draper, Gaither & Anderson as one of the first venture capital partnerships organized along these lines. The firm's success demonstrated that the limited partnership model could attract institutional capital while generating attractive returns for both limited and general partners.

The ERISA Revolution

The most significant catalyst for venture capital's institutionalization came from an unexpected source: the Employee Retirement Income Security Act (ERISA) of 1974. Designed primarily to protect workers' pension benefits, ERISA included provisions that would fundamentally transform venture capital by unlocking the largest pool of investment capital in the American economy.

Before ERISA, pension fund investments were governed by restrictive "prudent man" rules that effectively limited trustees to investing in low-risk securities like government bonds and blue-chip stocks. These rules made it virtually impossible for pension funds to invest in venture capital, regardless of the potential returns, because venture investments were inherently speculative and illiquid.

ERISA revolutionized pension fund investing by replacing the restrictive prudent man standard with the "prudent expert" rule, also known as the modern portfolio theory standard. Under this new framework, pension fund trustees were required to evaluate investments not in isolation but as part of a diversified portfolio. This change meant that high-risk, high-return investments like venture capital could be considered prudent if they improved the overall risk-return profile of the pension fund's portfolio.

The impact was transformative. American pension funds controlled trillions of dollars in assets, and even a small allocation to venture capital represented enormous capital flows. In 1978, the Department of Labor clarified the "prudent expert" rule in a way that explicitly allowed pension funds to invest in venture capital partnerships, removing any remaining regulatory uncertainty.

The timing of ERISA's passage was particularly fortuitous for venture capital. The 1970s had been a difficult period for stock market returns, with the S&P 500 generating negative real returns for much of the decade. Pension fund trustees were increasingly interested in alternative investments that could provide diversification and potentially higher returns than traditional stocks and bonds. Venture capital, with its promise of generating returns through direct investment in innovative companies, offered an attractive alternative to public market investing.

The first pension funds to invest in venture capital were typically more adventurous institutions with sophisticated investment teams. The Oregon Investment Council was an early pioneer, making its first venture capital commitment in 1975. Other public pension funds, including those in California and New York, soon followed. Corporate pension funds, often managed by more conservative trustees, were initially slower to embrace venture capital but eventually became major investors as the asset class proved its worth.

The influx of pension fund capital had profound effects on the venture capital industry. Fund sizes increased dramatically, from typical funds of $10-20 million in the early 1970s to funds of $50-100 million or more by the end of the decade. This growth allowed venture capital firms to make larger investments in individual companies and to support companies through multiple rounds of financing as they grew.

Perhaps more importantly, the involvement of institutional investors brought new levels of professionalism and accountability to venture capital. Pension funds required detailed reporting on portfolio performance, standardized accounting practices, and regular communication about investment strategies and results. This institutional oversight helped establish best practices across the venture capital industry and contributed to its growing credibility as a professional investment discipline.

Tax Policy and Investment Incentives

The development of favorable tax treatment for venture capital investments provided another crucial pillar supporting the industry's institutionalization. The tax code's treatment of investment gains and losses significantly influenced both the willingness of individuals and institutions to invest in venture capital and the economic attractiveness of venture capital as a career.

The capital gains tax rate became a particularly important policy lever. During the 1970s, the maximum capital gains tax rate reached as high as 49%, making venture capital investments less attractive from a tax perspective. High tax rates on capital gains reduced the after-tax returns that investors could expect from successful venture investments, potentially discouraging participation in the asset class.

Recognizing the connection between capital gains taxes and entrepreneurial activity, policymakers began advocating for lower capital gains tax rates. The argument was straightforward: lower taxes on investment gains would encourage more investment in innovative companies, leading to faster economic growth and job creation. This logic proved particularly compelling during the economically challenging 1970s, when policymakers were searching for ways to stimulate innovation and competitiveness.

In 1978, Congress reduced the maximum capital gains tax rate from 49% to 28%, providing a significant boost to venture capital returns. The impact was immediately apparent in both fundraising and investment activity. Venture capital firms found it easier to attract both limited partners and general partners, as the improved after-tax economics made the asset class more attractive to investors and venture capital careers more lucrative for professionals.

The 1978 tax reduction also coincided with other policy changes that benefited venture capital. The Small Business Investment Incentive Act of 1980 relaxed certain regulatory restrictions on small business investments and simplified the process for companies to raise capital from private investors. These changes made it easier for venture capital firms to invest in early-stage companies and for entrepreneurs to raise capital from multiple sources.

Perhaps even more significant was the clarification of the tax treatment of carried interest. Venture capitalists' profit participation in their funds needed to be treated as capital gains rather than ordinary income to make venture capital careers economically viable. The tax code's treatment of partnership profits provided this favorable treatment, but periodic challenges from the Internal Revenue Service created uncertainty that could have undermined the industry's growth.

Congressional and regulatory support for favorable carried interest treatment reflected a broader recognition of venture capital's economic importance. Policymakers understood that venture capitalists' compensation structure aligned their interests with those of entrepreneurs and limited partners, and that this alignment was crucial to the industry's effectiveness. The carried interest structure ensured that venture capitalists were rewarded only when they generated profits for their investors, creating powerful incentives for successful investing.

Regulatory Framework Development

The Securities and Exchange Commission (SEC) played a crucial role in venture capital's institutionalization by developing regulatory frameworks that provided clarity and legitimacy while avoiding overly burdensome restrictions that could have stunted the industry's growth. The SEC's approach reflected a sophisticated understanding of venture capital's unique characteristics and its potential contribution to economic growth and innovation.

One of the most important regulatory developments was the clarification of venture capital's status under federal securities laws. Venture capital investments clearly involved the sale of securities, bringing them under SEC jurisdiction. However, the traditional securities law framework, designed for public markets, wasn't well-suited to private equity investments in startup companies.

The SEC addressed this challenge through a series of rules and interpretations that created appropriate regulatory frameworks for venture capital while preserving the flexibility that made the industry effective. Rule 506 of Regulation D, adopted in 1982, provided a safe harbor for private placement offerings that allowed venture capital firms to raise capital from accredited investors without registering with the SEC or complying with the extensive disclosure requirements applicable to public offerings.

This regulatory approach recognized that venture capital investors were sophisticated parties capable of evaluating investment risks without the extensive protections required for public market investors. Accredited investor requirements ensured that venture capital remained limited to wealthy individuals and institutions with sufficient resources to bear investment losses, while private placement rules preserved the confidentiality and flexibility that venture capitalists needed to operate effectively.

The SEC also provided important guidance on venture capital firms' obligations as investment advisers. The Investment Advisers Act of 1940 required most professional investment managers to register with the SEC and comply with various regulatory requirements. However, venture capital firms argued that their unique business model, involving long-term, illiquid investments and close working relationships with portfolio companies made them fundamentally different from traditional investment advisers managing public securities portfolios.

The SEC ultimately provided regulatory relief for smaller venture capital firms through various exemptions while requiring larger firms to register as investment advisers. This balanced approach ensured appropriate oversight of the industry while avoiding regulatory burdens that could have prevented venture capital firms from operating effectively or discouraged talented professionals from entering the field.

Banking regulations presented another area where venture capital firms needed regulatory clarity. Traditional banking laws restricted banks' ability to invest in or control commercial enterprises, rules that could potentially apply to venture capital activities. However, regulators recognized that venture capital investments served different economic functions than traditional banking activities and generally provided interpretations that allowed banks to participate in venture capital either directly or through subsidiaries.

Professionalization and Standards

The institutionalization of venture capital required the development of professional standards, best practices, and industry organizations that could support the growing community of venture capital professionals. This professionalization process helped establish venture capital as a legitimate investment discipline and career path while creating mechanisms for sharing knowledge and maintaining industry standards.

The National Venture Capital Association (NVCA), founded in 1973, played a central role in this professionalization process. The NVCA brought together venture capital firms to advocate for supportive public policies, develop industry standards, and promote venture capital as an important component of the American economy. Through its legislative advocacy, the NVCA helped secure favorable tax treatment and regulatory frameworks that supported industry growth.

Perhaps equally important, the NVCA served as a forum for sharing best practices and developing industry standards. Venture capital firms had historically operated as independent entities with their own proprietary approaches to evaluating investments and managing portfolios. The NVCA provided a mechanism for sharing non-competitive insights about fund structures, due diligence processes, and portfolio management techniques.

The development of standardized fund documents and investment terms represented another important aspect of professionalization. Early venture capital partnerships often used customized legal documents that reflected the particular preferences and circumstances of individual firms and investors. As the industry grew and institutional investors became more important, there was increasing demand for standardized documents that reduced legal costs and facilitated comparison across different venture capital opportunities.

Legal firms specializing in venture capital played a crucial role in developing these standards. Firms like Wilson Sonsini Goodrich & Rosati in Silicon Valley became centers of expertise in venture capital law, developing template documents and investment structures that became widely adopted across the industry. This standardization reduced transaction costs and legal risks while making it easier for entrepreneurs and investors to understand and negotiate venture capital investments.

The emergence of specialized service providers reflected and supported venture capital's professionalization. Accounting firms developed expertise in venture capital fund accounting and portfolio company valuation. Investment banks created practices focused on venture-backed companies, particularly around initial public offerings and merger and acquisition transactions. Executive search firms specialized in recruiting talent for both venture capital firms and their portfolio companies.

Industry Infrastructure and Data

The institutionalization of venture capital required the development of industry infrastructure that could support professional investment decision-making and performance measurement. This infrastructure included data providers, research organizations, and industry publications that helped venture capitalists make informed investment decisions and limited partners evaluate venture capital opportunities.

Venture Economics, founded in 1961, became the leading provider of venture capital industry data and research. The firm collected information on fund performance, investment activity, and industry trends that became essential tools for both venture capitalists and limited partners. This data allowed the industry to benchmark performance, identify trends, and communicate its value proposition to potential investors and policymakers.

The availability of industry data was particularly important for institutional investors who needed to justify their venture capital allocations to trustees and beneficiaries. Pension funds and other institutions couldn't simply rely on anecdotal evidence of venture capital's success; they needed quantitative data showing how venture capital performed relative to other asset classes and how individual venture capital firms compared to their peers.

Industry publications like Venture Capital Journal provided forums for sharing deal information, industry analysis, and best practices. These publications helped create a sense of professional community among venture capitalists while providing limited partners with information about industry developments and investment opportunities.

The development of industry conferences and networking events further supported venture capital's professionalization. Events like the NVCA annual meeting brought together venture capitalists, entrepreneurs, and limited partners to discuss industry trends, share insights, and build relationships. These gatherings helped establish venture capital as a distinct professional community with shared interests and standards.

International Expansion and Competition

As American venture capital institutionalized and demonstrated its effectiveness, other countries began developing their own venture capital industries. This international expansion created both opportunities and challenges for American venture capital firms while validating the venture capital model as a global phenomenon rather than a uniquely American innovation.

European countries were among the first to adapt the American venture capital model, though they faced different regulatory and cultural environments that required modifications to the basic structure. The United Kingdom, with its developed financial markets and entrepreneurial culture, proved particularly receptive to venture capital. British venture capital firms like 3i (formerly ICFC) began operating along lines similar to their American counterparts, though with some differences in focus and investment approach.

Continental European countries faced greater challenges in adapting venture capital due to different legal systems, tax regimes, and cultural attitudes toward entrepreneurship and risk-taking. However, government initiatives in countries like France and Germany provided support for emerging venture capital industries, recognizing their potential contribution to economic development and technological innovation.

The emergence of international venture capital created opportunities for cross-border collaboration and competition. American venture capital firms began making investments in foreign companies, particularly in sectors where they had developed expertise. European and Asian venture capital firms similarly began investing in American startups, bringing additional capital and expertise to the American market.

This international dimension added complexity to venture capital's regulatory environment, as cross-border investments raised questions about tax treatment, securities regulation, and currency risk. However, it also validated venture capital as a globally relevant investment approach and created opportunities for knowledge sharing and best practice development across different markets and cultures.

The Foundation for Growth

By the end of the 1970s, venture capital had successfully transformed from an informal collection of wealthy investors into a professional investment industry with standardized structures, regulatory frameworks, and institutional backing. The limited partnership structure provided an effective mechanism for raising capital and aligning incentives between investors and venture capitalists. ERISA's passage unlocked enormous pools of pension fund capital that would fuel industry growth for decades to come. Favorable tax treatment made venture capital investments attractive to both limited partners and general partners. Supportive regulatory frameworks provided clarity and legitimacy without imposing burdensome restrictions.

This institutional foundation positioned venture capital to play an increasingly important role in American economic development. The industry had proven its ability to identify and support innovative companies that could generate substantial returns for investors while creating new products, services, and industries that benefited the broader economy. The combination of patient capital, entrepreneurial expertise, and professional management that characterized mature venture capital firms provided a powerful engine for converting technological innovation into commercial success.

The institutionalization of risk that occurred during the 1970s created the platform for venture capital's explosive growth in subsequent decades. With access to pension fund capital, supportive regulatory frameworks, and professional standards, venture capital firms were positioned to participate in and help create the waves of innovation that would transform the American economy. The personal computer revolution, biotechnology industry, internet boom, and subsequent technological developments all benefited from the institutional infrastructure that had been established during venture capital's formative years.

As the 1980s began, venture capital stood ready to demonstrate its effectiveness on a scale that would exceed even the most optimistic projections of its founding pioneers. The institutionalization of risk had created not just an investment industry, but a mechanism for translating American entrepreneurial energy and technological capability into sustained economic growth and innovation leadership.

Part II: The Foundation Years (1970s-1980s)

Chapter 4

Intel Inside the Revolution

In the summer of 1968, two of Silicon Valley's most respected engineers walked away from secure, well-paid positions to start a company that would fundamentally reshape the global economy. Robert Noyce, the charismatic co-inventor of the integrated circuit, and Gordon Moore, the brilliant scientist whose predictive insights would become known as "Moore's Law," left Fairchild Semiconductor with nothing more than a one-page business plan and an audacious vision: to build a company that would mass-produce computer memory using silicon technology. Their startup, Intel Corporation, would become not only one of the most successful venture capital investments in history but also a paradigm for how patient capital, visionary leadership, and revolutionary technology could combine to create entirely new industries.

The Intel story illuminates venture capital's transformative power like few others. It demonstrates how venture investors could identify and support technologies that would reshape multiple industries, how they could recruit world-class management talent to complement entrepreneurial vision, and how they could provide the patient capital and strategic guidance necessary to build companies of enduring global significance. Perhaps most importantly, Intel's success established venture capital's credibility as a mechanism for funding the most ambitious technological ventures, paving the way for generations of entrepreneurs who would follow.

The Vision Takes Shape

The origins of Intel can be traced to Robert Noyce's growing frustration with Fairchild Semiconductor's corporate culture and strategic direction. Despite Fairchild's technical successes and Noyce's leadership of the semiconductor division, the parent company's East Coast management seemed increasingly disconnected from the rapid pace of innovation in Silicon Valley. Corporate bureaucracy was slowing decision-making, and

Noyce believed that Fairchild was missing crucial opportunities in the emerging computer memory market.

Gordon Moore shared Noyce's frustrations but brought a different perspective to their partnership. Where Noyce was the visionary entrepreneur and natural leader, Moore was the careful scientist and strategic thinker. His famous observation that the number of transistors on a computer chip doubled approximately every two years, later known as Moore's Law, reflected his deep understanding of semiconductor technology's trajectory and potential. Moore recognized that the exponential improvement in semiconductor performance would eventually make computers smaller, faster, and more affordable, creating massive new markets for semiconductor components.

The two men's complementary skills and shared vision created the foundation for what would become Intel. Their business plan, reportedly written on a single page, outlined a company focused on semiconductor memory products for the emerging computer industry. At the time, computer memory was dominated by expensive and bulky magnetic core technology that was difficult to manufacture and limited in performance. Noyce and Moore believed they could develop silicon-based memory chips that would be faster, more reliable, and ultimately less expensive than existing alternatives.

The timing of their departure from Fairchild was influenced by broader changes in the semiconductor industry. The Vietnam War had created strong demand for military electronics, driving growth in semiconductor markets and validating the commercial potential of integrated circuits. Simultaneously, the emergence of minicomputers from companies like Digital Equipment Corporation was creating new demand for semiconductor components from customers who understood and valued superior performance.

But perhaps most importantly, the venture capital industry had matured to the point where ambitious entrepreneurs could realistically expect to find funding for revolutionary technologies. The success of companies like Fairchild had demonstrated that venture investors could generate substantial returns from semiconductor investments, while the growing sophistication of venture capital firms meant that entrepreneurs could find investors who understood both the technology and the market opportunity.

Arthur Rock's Strategic Investment

Robert Noyce's reputation in Silicon Valley was such that when he decided to start a new company, finding venture capital proved remarkably straightforward. Arthur Rock, who had orchestrated the original Fairchild Semiconductor deal a decade earlier, immediately recognized the opportunity. Rock understood that Noyce and Moore represented exactly the kind of entrepreneurial team that venture capital was designed to support: world-class technical experts with deep industry knowledge and proven track records of innovation and execution.

Rock's investment decision reflected several key principles that would become central to successful venture capital investing. First, he focused on the quality of the entrepreneurial team rather than detailed market projections or elaborate business plans. Noyce and Moore's track records at Fairchild demonstrated their ability to develop breakthrough technologies and build successful businesses around them. Second, Rock recognized that the semiconductor industry's rapid growth and technological evolution created opportunities for new entrants to disrupt established players through superior technology and execution.

The investment structure Rock negotiated for Intel reflected the evolution of venture capital deal-making since his pioneering work with Fairchild. Rather than selling the company to a corporate parent, Intel was structured as an independent company with professional venture capital backing. Rock's firm, Davis & Rock, led a $2.5 million funding round that included participation from other prominent venture investors. This funding level was substantial for its time, reflecting both the ambitious scope of Intel's plans and the investors' confidence in the founding team's ability to execute.

Rock's involvement with Intel extended far beyond providing capital. He became Intel's chairman and played a crucial role in recruiting additional management talent, particularly Andy Grove, who would become one of the most celebrated CEOs in American business history. Rock also provided strategic guidance on product development, market positioning, and corporate development decisions that proved crucial to Intel's success.

The venture capital investment in Intel also reflected important lessons from earlier semiconductor investments. Rock and his co-investors structured the deal to give the founders substantial equity stakes while ensuring that the company had sufficient capital to fund product development and manufacturing scale-up. They also negotiated governance rights that allowed investors to monitor the company's progress and provide input on major strategic decisions without micromanaging day-to-day operations.

The Microprocessor Revolution

Intel's early success came from memory products, particularly dynamic random-access memory (DRAM) chips that revolutionized computer design by providing fast, reliable, and increasingly affordable data storage. The company's 1103 DRAM, introduced in 1970, became the world's best-selling semiconductor memory chip and established Intel as a major force in the industry. However, Intel's most significant contribution to the technology revolution came from what was initially conceived as a side project: the development of the microprocessor.

In 1969, a Japanese calculator company called Busicom approached Intel to develop a set of custom chips for a new line of calculators. The conventional approach would have been to design separate chips for different calculator functions, but Intel engineer Ted Hoff proposed a revolutionary alternative: a single general-purpose chip that could be programmed to perform different functions. This programmable chip, which Intel designated the 4004, became the world's first commercial microprocessor.

The significance of the microprocessor invention can hardly be overstated. For the first time, the power of a computer's central processing unit could be contained on a single silicon chip, making it possible to build computers that were smaller, less expensive, and more reliable than anything previously imagined. The microprocessor would eventually enable the personal computer revolution, transform countless industries, and create entirely new categories of products and services.

Initially, however, Intel's management didn't fully grasp the revolutionary potential of their invention. The microprocessor was developed primarily to fulfill the Busicom contract, and Intel viewed it as a specialized product for calculator and simple computer applications. It was only through the strategic insight of Andy Grove and other Intel executives that the company began to understand the microprocessor's broader potential and the need to develop it as a standalone product rather than merely a component for other manufacturers.

The development of the microprocessor also illustrated the crucial role that venture capital played in funding long-term research and development. Unlike public companies, which faced pressure to generate quarterly earnings growth, venture-backed Intel could invest heavily in developing new technologies with uncertain market potential. The patient capital provided by venture investors allowed Intel to pursue ambitious research projects and make the substantial investments in manufacturing capability needed to produce complex semiconductor devices.

Arthur Rock and Intel's other venture investors understood that breakthrough technologies often required years of development before generating significant revenues. They were willing to provide multiple rounds of financing as Intel expanded its operations and invested in new product development. This long-term perspective proved crucial to Intel's success, as the company's most important innovations often required sustained investment before achieving commercial success.

Andy Grove and Operational Excellence

While Noyce and Moore provided Intel's technical vision and entrepreneurial drive, the company's transformation into a global technology leader required exceptional operational management. Andy Grove, recruited in 1968 as Intel's third employee, brought the discipline, strategic thinking, and management expertise that would make Intel one of the most successful and influential companies of the late 20th century.

Grove's background was uniquely suited to Intel's needs. As a Hungarian immigrant who had fled the Soviet invasion of his homeland, he brought both intellectual intensity and personal determination to his work. His doctoral training in chemical engineering provided technical credibility with Intel's engineer-heavy workforce, while his experience in semiconductor manufacturing at Fairchild had taught him the importance of operational excellence in a rapidly evolving industry.

Under Grove's leadership, Intel developed a corporate culture that became legendary for its combination of technical excellence, competitive intensity, and operational discipline. Grove instituted management practices that emphasized measurable objectives, rigorous performance evaluation, and continuous improvement. His philosophy of "constructive confrontation" encouraged employees to challenge ideas and assumptions in pursuit of better solutions, while his focus on "output-oriented management" ensured that the company remained focused on delivering results rather than just developing impressive technologies.

Grove's management approach proved particularly valuable as Intel navigated the challenges of rapid growth and intense competition. The semiconductor industry's fast-paced technological evolution meant that companies needed to continuously innovate while simultaneously scaling manufacturing operations and entering new markets. Grove's systematic approach to management helped Intel maintain its technical edge while building the organizational capabilities needed to compete effectively in global markets.

The venture capital investors who backed Intel recognized Grove's exceptional capabilities and supported his rise to leadership roles within the company. Arthur Rock, in particular, understood that successful technology companies required not just visionary founders but also world-class operational management. Rock's willingness to recruit Grove and support his increasing responsibilities reflected the sophisticated understanding of team building that distinguished the best venture capital investors.

Grove's leadership also demonstrated the importance of management succession planning in venture-backed companies. While Noyce remained Intel's public face and Moore continued to provide technical direction, Grove increasingly took responsibility for day-to-day operations and strategic execution. This transition allowed Intel's founders to focus on their areas of greatest strength while ensuring that the company had the management expertise needed for sustained growth.

Market Creation and Competitive Dynamics

Intel's success in the microprocessor market illustrates one of venture capital's most important functions: supporting entrepreneurs who create entirely new markets rather than simply competing in existing ones. When Intel introduced the 4004 microprocessor in 1971, there was no established market for general-purpose programmable processors. The company had to simultaneously develop the technology, create customer demand, and build the manufacturing capability needed to serve that demand.

This market creation process required the kind of patient capital and strategic support that venture investors were uniquely positioned to provide. Unlike traditional bank financing, which focused on cash flow from existing operations, venture capital could fund companies that were creating fundamentally new business models. Intel's venture investors understood that microprocessor development would require substantial upfront investment before generating significant revenues, and they were willing to provide multiple rounds of financing to support the company's growth.

The microprocessor market's development also demonstrated the network effects that could emerge from successful venture capital investments. As Intel's microprocessors became more powerful and affordable, they enabled the development of new categories of products, from personal computers to embedded systems in automotive and industrial applications. Each new application created additional demand for Intel's products while also generating opportunities for other entrepreneurs and companies.

Intel's competitive strategy reflected lessons learned from earlier semiconductor industry battles. Rather than competing primarily on cost, Intel focused on performance and innovation, continually developing more advanced processors that offered superior capabilities. This approach allowed the company to maintain premium pricing while building strong relationships with customers who valued technological leadership.

The company's "Intel Inside" marketing campaign, launched in the 1990s, represented a sophisticated understanding of brand building in technology markets. By creating consumer awareness of Intel's processors, the company was able to influence purchasing decisions even for complex products like personal computers where consumers had previously focused mainly on the computer manufacturer's brand. This marketing innovation helped Intel maintain its leadership position even as competition in the processor market intensified.

Grove's strategic insight that Intel should focus on microprocessors rather than memory products proved crucial to the company's long-term success. By the 1980s, Japanese manufacturers had gained significant advantages in memory production through superior manufacturing processes and lower costs. Rather than continuing to compete in a market where Intel was losing its competitive advantages, Grove led the company's strategic pivot toward microprocessors, where Intel's design capabilities and technological leadership provided more sustainable competitive advantages.

Venture Capital's Value Creation

Intel's success demonstrates several ways that venture capital creates value beyond simply providing funding. Arthur Rock and his co-investors contributed strategic guidance, management recruitment, industry connections, and credibility that proved as valuable as their financial investment. Their involvement helped Intel make better strategic decisions, attract talented employees, and build relationships with customers and partners.

Rock's role in recruiting Andy Grove illustrates venture capital's talent acquisition function. Grove's exceptional management capabilities were crucial to Intel's success, but identifying and attracting him required the kind of industry knowledge and professional networks that characterized the best venture investors. Rock's ability to recognize Grove's potential and convince him to join Intel represented a form of value creation that purely financial investors couldn't provide.

The venture investors' long-term perspective also proved crucial to Intel's development. Unlike public market investors who might have pressured the company to focus on short-term earnings, Intel's venture backers supported investments in research and development that wouldn't pay off for years. This patient capital allowed Intel to pursue the kind of ambitious innovation that created new markets and sustained competitive advantages.

Intel's eventual initial public offering in 1971 provided spectacular returns for its venture investors while also demonstrating venture capital's role in creating public market value. The IPO raised additional capital for Intel's continued growth while providing liquidity for early investors and employees. More importantly, it established Intel as a public company with access to capital markets for future expansion and acquisition opportunities.

The success of Intel's IPO also contributed to venture capital's growing reputation as a mechanism for generating superior investment returns. The substantial gains realized by Intel's venture investors attracted additional capital to the venture industry while also encouraging other entrepreneurs to pursue venture funding for their own ambitious ventures.

Technological Impact and Legacy

Intel's innovations, particularly the microprocessor, fundamentally reshaped the global economy in ways that extended far beyond the semiconductor industry. The availability of powerful, affordable processors enabled the personal computer revolution of the 1980s and 1990s, the internet boom of the late 1990s and early 2000s, and the mobile computing revolution that continues today. Each of these technological waves created enormous value for entrepreneurs, investors, and society as a whole.

The microprocessor's impact on other industries was equally profound. Automotive manufacturers began incorporating Intel processors into engine management systems, anti-lock brakes, and entertainment systems. Industrial companies used microprocessors to create more sophisticated manufacturing equipment and process control systems. Consumer electronics manufacturers built Intel processors into everything from gaming systems to household appliances.

This broad-based technological impact demonstrates venture capital's potential to generate returns that extend far beyond direct investment gains. While Intel's venture investors certainly earned substantial financial returns, the broader economic value created by Intel's innovations was many times larger than their initial investment. The company's products enabled countless other innovations and business opportunities that collectively generated trillions of dollars in economic value.

Intel's success also established important precedents for venture capital investing in technology companies. The company's focus on continuous innovation, substantial R&D investment, and long-term competitive positioning became a model for other venture-backed technology companies. Intel's management practices, particularly under Andy Grove's leadership, influenced a generation of technology executives and entrepreneurs who applied similar approaches in their own companies.

The Intel story also demonstrates the importance of timing in venture capital investing. Arthur Rock's investment came at a crucial moment when semiconductor technology was becoming commercially viable, computer markets were expanding rapidly, and venture capital had developed the institutional capabilities needed to support ambitious technology ventures. This convergence of technological opportunity, market demand, and financial capability created the conditions for Intel's extraordinary success.

Lessons for Entrepreneurs and Investors

Intel's development offers numerous lessons for both entrepreneurs seeking venture capital funding and investors evaluating technology opportunities. For entrepreneurs, Intel demonstrates the importance of assembling world-class teams that combine technical expertise with operational excellence and strategic vision. Noyce's entrepreneurial leadership, Moore's technical insights, and Grove's operational management created a combination of capabilities that no single individual could have provided.

The Intel story also illustrates the value of focusing on large, growing markets with the potential for disruption through superior technology. Rather than competing in mature markets with established players, Intel created entirely new market categories where its technological advantages could translate into sustainable competitive positions. This market creation approach required substantial risk-taking and long-term investment, but it also generated extraordinary returns.

For venture investors, Intel demonstrates the importance of backing exceptional teams working on transformative technologies in large markets. Arthur Rock's investment decision was based primarily on his assessment of Noyce and Moore's capabilities rather than detailed financial projections or market studies. This focus on team quality proved more valuable than traditional business plan analysis in evaluating a venture that was creating an entirely new market.

Intel's success also shows how venture investors can add value through active involvement in portfolio companies. Rock's contributions to strategic planning, management recruitment, and corporate governance helped Intel make better decisions and avoid common startup pitfalls. This hands-on approach required substantial time and expertise from the venture investors, but it significantly increased the probability of success.

The long-term nature of Intel's development underscores the importance of patient capital in venture investing. The company's most significant innovations required years of development and substantial investment before generating commercial returns. Venture investors who expected quick returns would have been disappointed, but those who understood the long-term potential of semiconductor technology were richly rewarded.

Conclusion: The Foundation of Modern Technology

Intel's story represents venture capital at its most transformative. The company's success demonstrates how patient capital, visionary entrepreneurs, and exceptional management can combine to create technologies that reshape entire industries and generate enormous value for investors and society alike. From its origins as a memory company founded by two Fairchild refugees to its emergence as the dominant microprocessor manufacturer, Intel embodied the potential of venture capital to fund and support the most ambitious technological ventures.

The microprocessor revolution that Intel initiated continues to drive innovation and economic growth decades after the company's founding. Every smartphone, laptop, and server contains descendants of Intel's original 4004 processor, while the company's continued innovation in processor technology enables new applications in artificial intelligence, autonomous vehicles, and internet-of-things devices. This sustained technological impact demonstrates venture capital's potential to generate returns that compound over decades rather than years.

Intel's success also established crucial precedents for the venture capital industry. The company's development showed that venture investors could successfully back companies creating entirely new markets, that patient capital could support long-term innovation, and that active investor involvement could significantly increase the probability of success. These lessons would prove invaluable as venture capital evolved to support subsequent waves of technological innovation, from personal computers and biotechnology to internet services and mobile computing.

As Intel continued to grow and dominate the microprocessor market, its success inspired countless entrepreneurs and attracted enormous amounts of capital to venture investing. The company's extraordinary returns demonstrated venture capital's potential to generate superior investment performance while funding the technologies that would define the future of human civilization. In this sense, Intel represented not just a successful investment but a proof of concept for venture capital's most ambitious aspirations.

Chapter 5

The Apple Phenomenon

The mythology surrounding Apple Computer's founding has become so deeply embedded in American entrepreneurial folklore that separating fact from fiction requires careful archaeological work. The image of two college dropouts tinkering in a suburban garage, armed with little more than technical brilliance and revolutionary vision, has inspired countless would-be entrepreneurs. Yet this romantic narrative obscures a more complex and instructive reality: Apple's transformation from garage startup to industry giant was fundamentally enabled by sophisticated venture capital intervention at precisely the right moment.

Beyond the Garage: The Real Origins

In the spring of 1976, Steve Jobs and Steve Wozniak were indeed working out of the Jobs family garage in Los Altos, California. Wozniak, the technical genius, had created what would become the Apple I, a revolutionary personal computer that existed primarily as a bare circuit board requiring users to add their own keyboard, monitor, and power supply. Jobs, recognizing the commercial potential that his more introverted partner couldn't see, pushed for commercialization.

The garage phase, while real, was brief and limited. The two Steves managed to scrape together $1,300 in initial capital, Jobs sold his Volkswagen van, and Wozniak parted with his HP calculator. This modest sum allowed them to order the first batch of components and officially incorporate Apple Computer Company on April 1, 1976. They filled their initial orders for fifty Apple I computers to the Byte Shop, a local computer retailer, earning enough to keep the operation alive but hardly enough to scale a business.

The Apple I, priced at $666.66, was primarily purchased by electronics hobbyists who appreciated Wozniak's elegant engineering. But Jobs harbored grander ambitions. He envisioned a computer that ordinary consumers could use, a machine that would democratize computing power and bring technology to the masses. This vision would require the Apple

II, a far more sophisticated and user-friendly machine that Wozniak was already developing.

The Capital Constraint

By late 1976, the fundamental constraints of bootstrap financing had become painfully clear. Building the Apple II required significant upfront investment in tooling, inventory, and manufacturing capacity. The sleek plastic case alone would cost hundreds of thousands of dollars to design and produce. More importantly, scaling production to meet anticipated demand would require working capital that far exceeded what the founders could generate from Apple I sales.

Jobs understood that transforming Apple from a garage workshop into a real company would require professional investment. He began reaching out through his limited network, seeking introductions to potential investors. The consumer electronics industry was notoriously capital-intensive, and personal computers represented an entirely unproven market category. Most traditional lenders and investors couldn't comprehend the opportunity.

This is where the popular narrative often jumps directly to venture capital success, but the reality included several false starts and near-misses. Jobs initially approached Nolan Bushnell, founder of Atari and Jobs' former employer, seeking a $50,000 investment. Bushnell declined but provided something more valuable: an introduction to Don Valentine, founding partner of Sequoia Capital.

Enter Don Valentine: The Venture Capitalist's Perspective

Don Valentine's first encounter with the young Apple founders has become venture capital legend. Valentine later recalled his initial impression: "Why did you send me these renegades from the human race?" The long-haired, sandal-wearing Jobs seemed to embody the 1970s counterculture that mainstream business found alienating. Yet Valentine, despite his conservative appearance and traditional business background, possessed the pattern recognition skills that defined great venture investors.

Valentine saw past the superficial presentation to identify several compelling factors. First, the technical product was genuinely innovative, Wozniak's engineering represented a significant advance in price-performance for personal computers. Second, the market timing appeared favorable, with computing costs declining and consumer interest growing. Third, and perhaps most importantly, Jobs demonstrated the rare combination of technical understanding and commercial intuition that Valentine recognized as essential for technology entrepreneurship.

However, Valentine also identified critical gaps in the founding team. Neither Jobs nor Wozniak possessed meaningful business experience. They lacked the operational expertise necessary to scale manufacturing, build distribution channels, and manage rapid growth. Valentine concluded that Apple needed seasoned business leadership before institutional investment would be appropriate.

The Mike Markkula Solution

Rather than investing directly, Valentine introduced the founders to Mike Markkula, a recently retired Intel executive who had accumulated substantial wealth from his equity stakes in Fairchild Semiconductor and Intel. At thirty-four, Markkula represented a new breed of technology investor, someone who combined deep industry expertise with personal capital and operational experience.

Markkula's background was precisely what Apple needed. During his tenure at Intel, he had witnessed the explosive growth potential of semiconductor businesses and understood the manufacturing and marketing challenges that high-tech companies faced during rapid scaling. He had also observed how early-stage technology companies could create enormous value through successful product launches and market development.

When Markkula first encountered the Apple II prototype in late 1976, he immediately grasped its significance. Unlike the Apple I, which required technical expertise to assemble and operate, the Apple II was designed as a complete system. Wozniak had integrated color graphics, sound capabilities, and expandable memory into an elegant package that could appeal to non-technical users. The machine represented a fundamental shift from computers as hobbyist tools to computers as consumer appliances.

The Investment Decision: Beyond Capital

Markkula's decision to invest in Apple reflected sophisticated risk assessment and strategic thinking. He committed $92,000 of his own money for a one-third equity stake and guaranteed a $250,000 line of credit. But more importantly, he provided the business framework that would enable Apple to scale successfully.

Markkula insisted on incorporating as Apple Computer Inc., establishing professional corporate governance structures that would support future investment rounds. He developed Apple's first comprehensive business plan, projecting revenues of $500 million within two years, a forecast that seemed wildly optimistic but proved remarkably accurate. He also articulated Apple's core philosophy in three principles that would guide the company's development: empathy (understanding customer needs), focus (eliminating unnecessary complexity), and impute (ensuring that product design communicated quality and value).

Perhaps most crucially, Markkula agreed to serve as interim CEO while the company searched for permanent professional management. This hands-on involvement distinguished his investment from typical angel funding.

Markkula wasn't simply providing capital; he was contributing his time, expertise, and reputation to Apple's success.

Sequoia Capital's Strategic Investment

With Markkula's involvement legitimizing the opportunity, Don Valentine and Sequoia Capital made their formal investment in January 1977. Sequoia invested $150,000 for approximately 10% of the company, valuing Apple at roughly $1.5 million. This relatively modest investment reflected both the early stage of the company and the unproven nature of the personal computer market.

Valentine's decision to invest represented classic venture capital pattern recognition. He had previously invested in semiconductor companies and understood the potential for electronics miniaturization to create new market categories. He recognized that declining component costs would eventually make personal computers affordable for mainstream consumers. Most importantly, he believed that Apple's combination of technical innovation and design sensibility could create a sustainable competitive advantage.

Sequoia's investment terms included typical venture capital provisions: anti-dilution protection, board representation, and liquidation preferences. But Valentine also insisted on recruiting professional management to complement the founding team. This led to the hiring of Mike Scott as CEO in May 1977, allowing Markkula to focus on strategic planning and marketing while Jobs concentrated on product development.

The Apple II Launch: Venture-Backed Innovation

The Apple II's launch at the West Coast Computer Faire in April 1977 demonstrated how venture capital could accelerate product development and market entry. The investment had funded critical improvements in product design, manufacturing setup, and marketing presentation. Apple's booth featured a professionally designed display, polished marketing materials, and working demonstration units that showcased the computer's capabilities.

The venture backing also enabled Apple to implement an aggressive pricing strategy. At $1,298 for the base model, the Apple II was positioned as a premium product that delivered superior value rather than competing solely on price. This strategy reflected Markkula's marketing expertise and Valentine's understanding of technology adoption patterns.

The market response exceeded all projections. Apple received hundreds of orders at the computer fair and quickly established relationships with retail partners nationwide. The company's revenues grew from $7.8 million in 1978 to $47.9 million in 1979, validating the venture investors' confidence in the market opportunity.

Building the Ecosystem: Software and Distribution

Venture capital support enabled Apple to think systematically about market development rather than simply selling hardware. Markkula recognized that the personal computer industry would succeed only if customers could access useful software applications. He encouraged third-party software development while investing in Apple's own programming capabilities.

The introduction of VisiCalc, the first electronic spreadsheet program, exclusively for the Apple II platform created a "killer application" that drove hardware adoption among business users. This software exclusivity was partly the result of strategic relationships that venture-backed Apple could pursue more effectively than bootstrapped competitors.

Similarly, Apple invested heavily in distribution channel development. The company established a network of authorized dealers, provided comprehensive training and support, and maintained strict quality standards. This retail strategy required significant upfront investment but created sustainable competitive advantages that pure technology innovation alone couldn't provide.

The IPO: Venture Capital's Ultimate Validation

Apple Computer's initial public offering on December 12, 1980, represented one of venture capital's most spectacular early successes. The offering raised $96.8 million for the company while creating paper wealth of over $1.2 billion for existing shareholders. At the time, it was the largest IPO since Ford Motor Company went public in 1956.

The IPO's success validated both the personal computer market and the venture capital model. Markkula's initial investment of $92,000 was worth approximately $203 million at the IPO price. Sequoia Capital's $150,000 investment had grown to roughly $58 million. These returns demonstrated venture capital's potential to generate extraordinary profits by identifying and nurturing breakthrough technologies.

More importantly, the IPO established personal computers as a legitimate industry worthy of serious investment. It attracted attention from institutional investors, strategic partners, and entrepreneurs who might otherwise have ignored the sector. The wealth created by Apple's public offering would fund subsequent generations of technology startups and venture funds.

Lessons in Venture Capital Value Creation

Apple's transformation from garage startup to public company illuminated several key principles of venture capital value creation. First, timing proved crucial, the investment coincided with declining component costs, improving technology, and growing consumer interest in personal computers. Second, the combination of technical innovation and business expertise was essential; neither founding vision nor professional management alone would have sufficed.

Third, venture capital's value extended far beyond financial investment. Markkula's operational involvement and Valentine's strategic guidance were arguably more important than their capital contributions. The investors provided credibility, industry connections, and business frameworks that enabled rapid scaling.

Finally, Apple demonstrated how venture capital could help create entirely new market categories rather than simply funding incremental improvements. The personal computer industry didn't exist in meaningful form before companies like Apple established it. Venture investment enabled entrepreneurs to pursue transformational opportunities that traditional financing couldn't support.

The Competitive Response: An Industry Transformed

Apple's success triggered an immediate competitive response that validated the market opportunity while creating new challenges. IBM's entry into personal computers in 1981, along with numerous clone manufacturers, intensified competition and compressed profit margins. But this competition also expanded the overall market, creating opportunities for component suppliers, software developers, and service providers.

The venture capital industry took note of Apple's success and began investing more aggressively in personal computer companies. Commodore, Tandy, and dozens of smaller firms received venture funding to pursue various market niches. While most of these companies failed to achieve Apple's success, their collective efforts accelerated technological development and market adoption.

Conclusion: Mythology and Reality

The Apple phenomenon represents venture capital's capacity to transform innovative ideas into market-leading companies. While the garage mythology captures important truths about entrepreneurial vision and technical innovation, the complete story reveals venture capital's crucial role in providing the resources, expertise, and strategic framework necessary for rapid scaling.

Mike Markkula's investment and operational involvement, combined with Sequoia Capital's financial backing and strategic guidance, enabled Apple to execute a vision that might otherwise have remained a hobbyist curiosity. The partnership between entrepreneurs and investors created value that neither could have achieved independently.

This model, combining entrepreneurial innovation with venture capital resources and expertise would be replicated countless times throughout Silicon Valley's development. Apple's success established the template for technology venture investing and demonstrated how patient capital could generate extraordinary returns while building transformational companies.

The Apple phenomenon proved that venture capital could do more than simply finance existing businesses; it could help create entirely new industries. This lesson would inspire generations of entrepreneurs and investors to pursue increasingly ambitious visions, fundamentally reshaping the global economy through technology-driven innovation.

Chapter 6

Biotech's Brave New World

The birth of biotechnology as a venture-capital-backed industry represented perhaps the most audacious leap of faith in the history of American investing. Unlike semiconductors or personal computers, which built upon decades of established engineering principles, biotechnology required venture capitalists to bet on an entirely theoretical possibility: that the fundamental processes of life could be harnessed, manipulated, and commercialized. When Kleiner Perkins Caufield & Byers decided to fund a small South San Francisco company called Genentech in 1976, they were essentially wagering that science fiction could become science fact and profitable business reality.

This leap into the biological sciences marked a pivotal moment not just for venture capital, but for the entire trajectory of modern medicine and commerce. The biotech revolution would ultimately spawn trillion-dollar markets, transform the pharmaceutical industry, and fundamentally alter humanity's relationship with disease, aging, and the basic building blocks of life itself. Yet this transformation began with a handful of scientists, entrepreneurs, and investors willing to navigate uncharted territory where the rules of traditional business barely applied.

The Scientific Foundation: Recombinant DNA's Promise

The story of biotechnology venture capital begins in the laboratories of Stanford University and the University of California, San Francisco, where researchers in the early 1970s were developing the techniques that would make genetic engineering possible. The breakthrough discovery of restriction enzymes, molecular scissors that could cut DNA at specific sequences combined with DNA ligases that could rejoin genetic material, created the theoretical foundation for recombinant DNA technology.

Stanley Cohen at Stanford and Herbert Boyer at UCSF had demonstrated that genes from one organism could be inserted into another, effectively allowing scientists to reprogram living cells to produce desired proteins. The implications were staggering: bacteria could potentially be engineered to manufacture human insulin, growth hormone, or any other protein whose genetic code could be identified and isolated. This represented not merely an incremental advance in pharmaceutical manufacturing, but a fundamental shift from chemistry-based drug discovery to biology-based therapeutics.

However, the gap between laboratory demonstration and commercial application remained enormous. The techniques were complex, unreliable, and required expertise that existed only in a handful of academic laboratories. The regulatory pathway for genetically engineered medicines was entirely undefined. The capital requirements for scaling biotechnology production were largely unknown. Most daunting of all, the timeline from concept to approved product was expected to span decades, not years.

Traditional pharmaceutical companies, with their focus on chemical compound development and established manufacturing processes, were initially skeptical of biotechnology's commercial potential. The major drug manufacturers had invested billions in chemistry-based research and development infrastructure. They possessed deep expertise in chemical synthesis, traditional fermentation, and small-molecule drug development, but virtually no knowledge of genetic engineering or protein manufacturing.

This created an opportunity for entrepreneurial ventures willing to pioneer entirely new approaches to drug development. Yet pursuing such opportunities would require investors comfortable with extraordinary scientific risk, regulatory uncertainty, and development timelines that dwarfed even the longest semiconductor product cycles.

Enter Robert Swanson: The Venture Catalyst

The transformation of academic research into commercial enterprise required a unique catalyst: someone who could bridge the worlds of science and business while possessing the vision and persistence necessary to navigate uncharted territory. Robert Swanson, a young associate at Kleiner Perkins, emerged as precisely such a figure, though his background seemed unlikely preparation for biotechnology entrepreneurship.

Swanson had joined Kleiner Perkins in 1970 straight from MIT's Sloan School of Management, where he had focused on traditional industrial financing rather than life sciences. His early work at the venture firm involved investments in conventional manufacturing and technology companies. However, Swanson possessed an unusual combination of analytical rigor and entrepreneurial intuition that enabled him to recognize paradigm-shifting opportunities even outside his immediate area of expertise.

In 1975, while researching potential investment opportunities in genetic engineering, Swanson encountered Herbert Boyer's research on recombinant DNA technology. Boyer had co-authored several of the foundational papers on genetic engineering and possessed deep technical knowledge of the emerging field. However, like most academic researchers, he had little understanding of commercial applications or business development.

Swanson's crucial insight was recognizing that the gap between academic research and commercial application represented an entrepreneurial opportunity rather than merely a technical challenge. He understood that venture capital could provide not only funding but also the business expertise, strategic planning, and operational support necessary to transform laboratory techniques into scalable commercial processes.

The meeting between Swanson and Boyer in early 1976 has become a biotechnology legend. Swanson cold-called Boyer requesting a brief meeting to discuss commercial applications of recombinant DNA technology. Boyer, initially skeptical of business involvement in academic research, agreed to a short conversation that ultimately extended for several hours as both men recognized the potential for collaboration.

Genentech's Formation: Science Meets Capital

The founding of Genentech in April 1976 represented a novel experiment in venture capital investing. Unlike previous high-technology investments, which typically involved entrepreneurs with industry experience developing incremental improvements to existing products, Genentech was attempting to create an entirely new industry based on unproven scientific techniques.

Swanson and Boyer's initial partnership reflected the unique challenges of biotechnology entrepreneurship. Boyer contributed scientific expertise and access to cutting-edge research, while Swanson provided business development skills and connections to venture capital funding. Their collaboration established a template that would be replicated throughout the biotech industry: the scientist-entrepreneur partnership backed by specialized venture capital.

Kleiner Perkins' decision to fund Genentech required extraordinary confidence in both the scientific opportunity and the entrepreneurial team. The firm's partners, led by Eugene Kleiner and Tom Perkins, had built their reputation on semiconductor and computer investments where technological risks were substantial but market applications were relatively clear. Biotechnology presented even greater technical uncertainty combined with regulatory complexity that had no precedent in their previous investments.

The initial funding round of $100,000 was modest even by 1976 standards, reflecting both the early stage of the company and the experimental nature of the investment. This seed funding supported basic research aimed at demonstrating the commercial feasibility of recombinant DNA techniques. The investors understood that years of additional development would be required before any products could reach market, making Genentech fundamentally different from the rapid commercialization cycles typical of electronics investments.

Technical Milestones and Proof of Concept

Genentech's early technical achievements demonstrated both the promise and challenges of biotechnology entrepreneurship. The company's first major milestone came in August 1977 when its scientists successfully produced human somatostatin, a human hormone using genetically engineered bacteria. While somatostatin itself had limited commercial applications, the achievement proved that human proteins could be manufactured using recombinant DNA techniques.

This technical success was crucial for attracting additional venture capital funding. The ability to produce any human protein using bacterial manufacturing opened possibilities for treating diseases that had previously been intractable. Diabetes, growth hormone deficiency, hemophilia, and numerous other conditions caused by protein deficiencies could potentially be addressed through biotechnology rather than traditional pharmaceutical approaches.

However, the somatostatin achievement also highlighted the enormous challenges ahead. The quantities produced were minuscule, the manufacturing process was unreliable, and the protein's biological activity was inconsistent. Scaling laboratory techniques to industrial production would require solving thousands of technical problems while meeting regulatory standards that were still being developed.

The regulatory environment presented particularly complex challenges. The Food and Drug Administration had no established procedures for evaluating genetically engineered medicines. Environmental safety concerns about recombinant DNA research had prompted heated public debates and congressional hearings. The National Institutes of Health had implemented strict guidelines governing genetic engineering research that complicated commercial development.

Human Insulin: The First Commercial Breakthrough

Genentech's development of human insulin represented biotechnology's first major commercial validation and established many of the investment patterns that would characterize the industry. The insulin project began in 1978 with funding from a partnership with Eli Lilly and Company, marking the first collaboration between a biotech startup and an established pharmaceutical company.

The choice of insulin as a target product reflected sophisticated strategic thinking about biotechnology commercialization. Insulin was an established medicine with a large existing market, eliminating the need to educate physicians or patients about therapeutic benefits. The existing insulin supply, derived from animal pancreases, had known limitations including allergic reactions and supply constraints. Human insulin produced through genetic engineering promised to address these problems while providing a superior therapeutic profile.

From a venture capital perspective, the insulin project offered several attractive characteristics. The market opportunity was substantial and well-defined. The regulatory pathway, while complex, was more predictable than for entirely novel therapeutics. The partnership with Eli Lilly provided both validation and access to manufacturing, distribution, and regulatory expertise that Genentech lacked.

The technical challenges, however, remained formidable. Producing insulin required expressing two separate protein chains in bacteria, purifying the proteins, and correctly folding them into biologically active hormones. Each step presented manufacturing difficulties that had no precedent in traditional pharmaceutical production. The purification processes alone required developing entirely new separation techniques and quality control methods.

Venture investors followed the insulin development program with intense interest, recognizing that success would validate the entire biotechnology investment thesis while failure would severely damage the industry's credibility. Kleiner Perkins provided additional funding rounds, but also began seeking co-investors to share both the risks and potential rewards.

The Investment Syndicate: Spreading Risk and Expertise

As Genentech's capital requirements grew, Kleiner Perkins assembled an investment syndicate that reflected the unique challenges of biotechnology venture capital. The syndicate included traditional venture firms like Mayfield Fund and Institutional Venture Associates, but also attracted investors with pharmaceutical industry experience and scientific expertise.

This diversified investor base provided more than just capital. Pharmaceutical industry veterans contributed regulatory knowledge and market insights that pure technology investors lacked. Academic connections helped attract scientific talent and maintained relationships with university research programs. International investors brought perspectives on global markets and regulatory environments.

The syndication approach also helped establish biotechnology as a legitimate venture capital category. By involving multiple respected venture firms, Kleiner Perkins reduced the perception that biotechnology was merely a speculative experiment by a single investment group. The broader venture capital community began developing expertise and investment criteria specifically for life sciences opportunities.

However, syndicated investing in biotechnology also revealed unique challenges compared to traditional venture investments. The long development timelines required sustained commitment over many years, testing investor patience and fund structures designed for shorter investment cycles. The regulatory complexity demanded specialized expertise that few venture firms possessed. The capital intensity often exceeded what individual venture funds could comfortably support.

Regulatory Navigation: FDA and the New Paradigm

The development of regulatory frameworks for biotechnology products represented a parallel innovation process that was just as crucial as the scientific and business developments. When Genentech began developing human insulin, no established procedures existed for evaluating genetically engineered medicines. The FDA faced the unprecedented challenge of assessing both the safety and efficacy of products created through entirely novel manufacturing processes.

The regulatory uncertainty created significant risks for biotechnology investors. Traditional pharmaceutical development followed well-established pathways where regulatory requirements, while demanding, were predictable. Biotechnology companies faced the possibility that regulatory agencies might require entirely new types of safety data or impose manufacturing standards that could make commercial production economically unfeasible.

Genentech's approach to regulatory strategy became a model for the industry. Rather than waiting for clear guidance, the company proactively engaged with FDA officials to discuss their development programs and seek preliminary feedback on regulatory requirements. This collaborative approach helped establish precedents while building relationships with regulatory personnel who were simultaneously learning about biotechnology applications.

The FDA's eventual approval of human insulin in 1982 represented a watershed moment for both biotechnology and venture capital. The approval validated the regulatory pathway for genetically engineered medicines while demonstrating that biotechnology products could meet the same safety and efficacy standards required of traditional pharmaceuticals. This regulatory success attracted additional venture capital investment while encouraging pharmaceutical companies to develop internal biotechnology capabilities.

The IPO Revolution: Public Markets Embrace Biotechnology

Genentech's initial public offering on October 14, 1980, created one of the most spectacular debut performances in stock market history. The stock opened at $35 per share and closed at $89, providing investors with immediate returns that exceeded most venture capital investments over their entire holding periods. The IPO raised $35 million for the company while creating paper profits of over $200 million for existing shareholders.

The public market reception of Genentech's IPO reflected investor enthusiasm for biotechnology's commercial potential, but also revealed the speculative nature of early biotech investing. At the time of the IPO, Genentech had no approved products, minimal revenues, and faced years of additional development before any therapeutic could reach market. The valuation was based entirely on future potential rather than current financial performance.

From a venture capital perspective, the IPO provided crucial validation and liquidity. Kleiner Perkins' initial investment of $100,000 was worth approximately $8 million at the IPO price, representing an extraordinary return that attracted attention throughout the venture capital industry. The success also established biotechnology as a category capable of generating the type of outsized returns that venture investors required.

However, the IPO also created new challenges for biotechnology venture capital. Public market investors demanded regular progress updates and quarterly earnings growth that were incompatible with biotechnology's long development cycles. The pressure for short-term results could distort company priorities and encourage premature product launches or unrealistic timeline commitments.

Kleiner Perkins' Life Sciences Evolution

Genentech's success transformed Kleiner Perkins from a traditional technology venture firm into one of the world's leading life sciences investors. The firm's partners recognized that biotechnology represented a fundamental shift in innovation potential that warranted sustained investment focus rather than occasional opportunistic investments.

This strategic evolution required developing new expertise and investment criteria specifically adapted to life sciences opportunities. Traditional venture capital due diligence focused on market size, competitive dynamics, and management team experience, factors that were often impossible to evaluate meaningfully in biotechnology's early stages. Life sciences investing demanded deeper scientific understanding, regulatory knowledge, and patience for development timelines that could span decades.

Kleiner Perkins began recruiting partners with pharmaceutical industry experience and scientific backgrounds. The firm established relationships with academic medical centers and research institutions to identify promising technologies before they became widely known. They developed specialized approaches to evaluating scientific risk, regulatory pathways, and market potential for therapeutic applications.

The firm's life sciences investment thesis extended beyond therapeutics to include medical devices, diagnostics, and research tools. This broader approach recognized that biotechnology was creating opportunities throughout the healthcare value chain, not just in drug development. Companies developing DNA sequencing equipment, laboratory automation systems, and diagnostic tests could achieve commercial success with shorter development timelines and lower regulatory requirements than therapeutic companies.

Industry-Wide Impact: The Biotech Investment Wave

Genentech's success triggered a wave of biotechnology investment that fundamentally reshaped both venture capital and the pharmaceutical industry. Between 1980 and 1985, venture firms invested over $1 billion in biotechnology companies, creating hundreds of startups pursuing various therapeutic and diagnostic opportunities.

This investment surge created a new ecosystem of biotechnology entrepreneurship. Scientists with promising research began leaving academic positions to found companies. Pharmaceutical industry veterans joined startups as executives and advisors. Specialized service providers emerged to support biotechnology development, from contract research organizations to specialized legal and consulting firms.

The venture capital industry itself evolved to accommodate biotechnology investing. Firms began raising larger funds with longer investment horizons to match biotech development cycles. New venture partnerships emerged focused exclusively on life sciences opportunities. Corporate venture capital programs were established by pharmaceutical companies seeking access to biotechnology innovations.

However, the biotechnology investment wave also revealed the risks inherent in frontier technology investing. Many biotechnology startups founded in the early 1980s failed to develop viable products, burned through their venture funding, and never achieved commercial success. The high failure rates tested investor patience and highlighted the challenges of evaluating scientific risk in venture capital contexts.

Long-Term Development Cycles: Patient Capital Requirements

Biotechnology's extended development timelines created unique challenges for venture capital fund structures and investor expectations. Traditional venture capital funds operated on seven-to-ten-year cycles, expecting portfolio companies to achieve liquidity through acquisitions or IPOs within that timeframe. Biotechnology companies often required fifteen to twenty years to develop products from initial research through regulatory approval and market launch.

This timing mismatch forced venture investors to develop new approaches to biotechnology funding. Some firms established evergreen funds that could hold investments indefinitely rather than forcing premature exits to meet fund liquidation deadlines. Others structured biotechnology investments through multiple funds, transferring companies from early-stage funds to later-stage vehicles as development progressed.

The patient capital requirements also attracted new categories of investors to biotechnology venture capital. Pension funds, university endowments, and family offices with longer investment horizons became increasingly important sources of biotechnology venture funding. These institutional investors were better positioned to tolerate the extended development cycles that biotechnology demanded.

Corporate strategic investors also played crucial roles in biotechnology development. Pharmaceutical companies established venture capital arms specifically to invest in biotechnology startups, providing both capital and industry expertise. These corporate investors often had strategic rather than purely financial motivations, seeking access to promising technologies that could complement their internal development programs.

Risk-Return Profiles: The Life Sciences Premium

The unique characteristics of biotechnology investing created distinctive risk-return profiles that differed significantly from traditional venture capital categories. Biotechnology investments typically required larger capital commitments over longer periods, with binary outcomes determined by regulatory approvals rather than market adoption curves.

Successful biotechnology investments could generate extraordinary returns when breakthrough therapeutics achieved market success. Companies developing treatments for previously incurable diseases could capture market values in the tens of billions of dollars. However, the vast majority of biotechnology investments resulted in total losses when clinical trials failed or regulatory approvals were denied.

This risk profile attracted venture investors comfortable with high-stakes, high-reward opportunities, but deterred those seeking more predictable returns. Biotechnology venture capital became increasingly specialized, with dedicated funds and investment professionals focused exclusively on life sciences opportunities.

The binary nature of biotechnology outcomes also influenced investment strategies and portfolio construction. Successful biotechnology venture funds typically made larger numbers of smaller initial investments, recognizing that most would fail completely while a few might generate fund-returning profits. This approach required different capital allocation and risk management techniques compared to traditional technology venture investing.

Conclusion: Pioneering a New Investment Frontier

The emergence of biotechnology as a venture capital category represented one of the most ambitious expansions of risk capital into uncharted territory. The decision by firms like Kleiner Perkins to back Genentech required extraordinary confidence in scientific progress and commercial potential that existed only in theoretical form.

The success of early biotechnology investments validated venture capital's ability to fund paradigm-shifting innovations that traditional financing sources couldn't support. The patient capital, business expertise, and strategic guidance provided by venture investors proved crucial in transforming academic research into commercial enterprises capable of addressing humanity's most challenging diseases.

However, biotechnology venture capital also revealed the limits and challenges of funding frontier science. The extended development timelines, regulatory complexity, and binary risk profiles demanded new approaches to investment evaluation, portfolio management, and fund structure. The industry's evolution continues today as venture capitalists grapple with even more ambitious opportunities in areas like gene therapy, regenerative medicine, and synthetic biology.

The biotechnology revolution initiated by Genentech and its venture capital backers ultimately transformed medicine, created trillions of dollars in economic value, and established life sciences as one of venture capital's most important investment categories. This transformation began with a willingness to venture into biology's brave new world, armed with little more than scientific curiosity and entrepreneurial ambition.

Part III: The Scaling Era (1980s-1990s)

Chapter 7

Cisco and the Network Effect

In the annals of venture capital history, few investments have demonstrated the transformative power of network effects quite like Cisco Systems. What began as a husband-and-wife team's frustration with connecting incompatible computer networks at Stanford University would evolve into one of the most valuable companies in the world, fundamentally reshaping how information flows across the globe. The story of Cisco's venture-backed journey from garage startup to networking giant illustrates how patient capital, strategic vision, and aggressive execution can create entirely new industries while generating extraordinary returns for investors willing to bet on infrastructure technologies that others couldn't yet imagine needing.

The Cisco phenomenon represents a masterclass in recognizing and capitalizing on network effects, the economic principle that a product or service becomes more valuable as more people use it. Unlike traditional businesses where competition typically reduces profitability, networking companies benefit from widespread adoption of their standards and protocols. Cisco's venture capitalists understood this dynamic earlier and more completely than most, enabling them to support business strategies that seemed counterintuitive but ultimately created sustainable competitive advantages and massive market value.

The Stanford Genesis: Academic Frustration Meets Entrepreneurial Opportunity

The origins of Cisco Systems trace back to Stanford University's computer science department in the early 1980s, where Leonard Bosack managed computer systems and Sandy Lerner oversaw networks at the Graduate School of Business. Both institutions operated sophisticated computer networks, but the incompatible protocols and hardware made communication between buildings virtually impossible. Academic researchers working on collaborative projects found themselves physically carrying floppy disks between departments, a primitive solution that highlighted the pressing need for internetworking technology.

Bosack and Lerner's personal relationship complicated their professional collaboration, but their technical partnership proved extraordinarily productive. Bosack possessed deep expertise in networking protocols and hardware design, while Lerner understood the practical challenges of managing complex computer systems in institutional environments. Their combined knowledge positioned them to recognize both the technical feasibility and commercial potential of universal networking solutions.

The specific technical challenge they faced involved connecting different types of computer networks using incompatible communication protocols. Local area networks (LANs) had proliferated throughout corporate and academic environments, but each typically used proprietary protocols that couldn't communicate with other networks. The emerging TCP/IP protocol suite promised universal connectivity, but implementing these standards required sophisticated hardware and software that didn't yet exist in commercial form.

Working nights and weekends, Bosack and Lerner developed a device they called a "router", essentially a specialized computer that could translate between different networking protocols while forwarding data packets toward their intended destinations. The router concept wasn't entirely original; similar devices existed in research laboratories and specialized military applications. However, Bosack and Lerner's implementation offered superior performance, reliability, and ease of use compared to existing alternatives.

Their initial router design solved Stanford's internal networking problems while demonstrating the broader market potential for internetworking equipment. As word spread throughout Silicon Valley's tight-knit technical community, other organizations began requesting similar devices. Bosack and Lerner found themselves inadvertently operating a small business from their home, assembling routers by hand and providing technical support to early customers.

Bootstrap Beginnings: The Challenges of Hardware Entrepreneurship

The transition from academic side project to commercial enterprise proved more challenging than Bosack and Lerner had anticipated. Unlike software development, which required minimal upfront investment, hardware manufacturing demanded significant capital for components, testing equipment, and inventory. Each router required expensive microprocessors, memory chips, and networking interfaces that had to be purchased before products could be assembled and sold.

The founders initially attempted to bootstrap their operations through customer prepayments and personal savings. They incorporated Cisco Systems in December 1984, working from their home in Menlo Park while maintaining their Stanford positions. The company name derived from "San Francisco," reflecting their geographic roots, though the lowercase "cisco" styling wouldn't emerge until years later during a corporate rebranding effort.

Early customer relationships developed through personal networks and word-of-mouth referrals rather than formal marketing efforts. Stanford's academic connections proved invaluable, as university researchers and computer center managers throughout California needed similar internetworking solutions. Government laboratories and defense contractors represented another important customer segment, given their extensive computer networks and generous technology budgets.

However, bootstrap financing severely constrained Cisco's growth potential. Manufacturing capacity remained limited by working capital constraints, forcing the company to maintain extensive customer waiting lists. Quality control suffered as production scaled beyond what two people could personally manage. Most critically, competitors with superior financial resources were beginning to recognize the router market's potential, threatening to overwhelm Cisco through aggressive pricing and faster product development.

The technical demands of router development also exceeded what bootstrap resources could support. Next-generation networking protocols required more sophisticated hardware and software than Bosack and Lerner could develop without additional engineering talent. International markets demanded regulatory approvals and local support capabilities that small companies struggled to provide. Enterprise customers increasingly requested product features and reliability guarantees that required substantial engineering investments.

Sequoia Capital: Pattern Recognition and Strategic Vision

Don Valentine's decision to investigate Cisco Systems reflected Sequoia Capital's systematic approach to identifying emerging technology markets. By 1987, Valentine had observed the explosive growth of personal computers and recognized that widespread computer adoption would inevitably create demand for networking infrastructure. The venture capital industry's success with semiconductor and computer companies had demonstrated the enormous value creation potential in fundamental technology markets.

Valentine's initial assessment of Cisco focused on market timing and competitive positioning rather than immediate financial performance. The company's revenues were growing rapidly but remained modest by venture capital standards. More importantly, Cisco controlled critical intellectual property in router technology while serving customers whose networking requirements were expanding exponentially.

The investment thesis rested on several key insights about technology infrastructure markets. First, networking represented a natural monopoly where standardization benefits encouraged market concentration around dominant platforms. Second, the shift toward distributed computing would create sustained demand for internetworking equipment regardless of specific computer technologies. Third, early market leadership in infrastructure categories often translated into sustainable competitive advantages that persisted for decades.

Valentine also recognized that Cisco's technical founders lacked the business experience necessary to scale a hardware manufacturing company. While Bosack and Lerner possessed exceptional engineering skills, they had limited knowledge of finance, marketing, operations, or strategic planning. Venture capital could provide both the financial resources and management expertise necessary to transform Cisco from a successful garage operation into an industry-leading enterprise.

The due diligence process revealed both Cisco's potential and its limitations. The company's router technology was genuinely superior to existing alternatives, offering better performance and reliability at competitive prices. Customer loyalty was extraordinarily high, with organizations typically purchasing additional Cisco equipment rather than switching to alternative vendors. However, the founders' management approach remained informal and reactive, lacking the systematic planning necessary for rapid scaling.

The $2.5 Million Bet: Venture Capital Transforms Cisco

Sequoia Capital's investment in Cisco Systems in December 1987 provided $2.5 million in exchange for approximately 30% of the company. The funding round valued Cisco at roughly $8 million, reflecting both the company's impressive growth trajectory and the substantial risks inherent in hardware entrepreneurship. The investment terms included typical venture capital provisions such as board representation, anti-dilution protection, and liquidation preferences.

More important than the financial terms was Sequoia's strategic involvement in Cisco's transformation from entrepreneurial startup to professional organization. Valentine insisted on recruiting experienced management to complement the founding team's technical expertise. This led to the hiring of John Morgridge as CEO in 1988, bringing decades of experience in technology marketing and operations management.

Morgridge's appointment reflected Sequoia's sophisticated understanding of scaling challenges in hardware businesses. Unlike software companies, which could often grow rapidly with minimal additional investment, router manufacturing required careful coordination of engineering, procurement, manufacturing, and quality control processes. International expansion demanded local partnerships and regulatory compliance capabilities that exceeded what startup teams typically possessed.

The venture capital funding enabled Cisco to address several critical constraints simultaneously. Engineering headcount expanded dramatically, allowing the development of next-generation router products while maintaining existing product lines. Manufacturing operations were professionalized with dedicated facilities, automated testing equipment, and formal quality control procedures. International sales and support capabilities were established to serve the growing global market for networking equipment.

Perhaps most importantly, the investment provided strategic flexibility during a period of rapid technological change. The networking industry was evolving quickly as new protocols emerged and performance requirements increased. Well-funded competitors like 3Com, Bridge Communications, and Wellfleet were investing heavily in alternative approaches to internetworking. Cisco's venture backing enabled aggressive research and development investments while maintaining competitive pricing.

John Morgridge: Professional Management and Strategic Focus

The recruitment of John Morgridge as Cisco's CEO represented a crucial inflection point in the company's development from technical innovation to market leadership. Morgridge brought extensive experience from Honeywell and other technology companies, understanding both the operational challenges of hardware manufacturing and the strategic dynamics of infrastructure markets.

Morgridge's management philosophy emphasized systematic planning, disciplined execution, and customer-focused product development. He established formal processes for engineering project management, manufacturing quality control, and sales channel development. These operational improvements enabled Cisco to scale production while maintaining the product reliability that had established the company's reputation.

More strategically, Morgridge recognized that Cisco's long-term success depended on establishing the company's router architecture as an industry standard. This required balancing proprietary technology development with open protocol support, ensuring that Cisco's products could integrate seamlessly with competitors' equipment while maintaining performance advantages that encouraged customer loyalty.

The standardization strategy proved crucial as the internetworking market evolved from specialized niche to mainstream requirement. Organizations implementing computer networks increasingly demanded equipment that supported multiple protocols and could interoperate with existing infrastructure. Cisco's commitment to protocol compatibility positioned the company as the safe choice for risk-averse enterprise customers.

Morgridge also implemented aggressive international expansion plans that positioned Cisco as a global networking supplier before most competitors recognized international opportunities. European and Asian markets for networking equipment were developing rapidly as organizations worldwide adopted distributed computing architectures. Early international presence enabled Cisco to establish customer relationships and local partnerships that would prove invaluable as these markets matured.

The Internet Infrastructure Buildout: Perfect Market Timing

Cisco's venture-backed expansion coincided with the explosive growth of Internet infrastructure that would define the 1990s technology boom. The National Science Foundation's decision to commercialize Internet access in 1991 created enormous demand for routers, switches, and other networking equipment. Organizations that had previously relied on proprietary networking solutions began migrating toward TCP/IP-based architectures that required exactly the types of products Cisco manufactured.

The timing proved extraordinary for venture capital returns. Internet service providers needed sophisticated routing equipment to manage traffic between networks. Corporations implementing wide-area networks required routers that could handle multiple protocols and provide reliable connectivity. Universities and government agencies upgrading their networking infrastructure represented additional market segments with substantial budgets and demanding performance requirements.

Cisco's product portfolio positioned the company perfectly for this infrastructure buildout. The company's routers handled Internet traffic routing more efficiently than alternatives, making them essential components for organizations building large-scale networks. Advanced features like dynamic routing protocols and redundant connectivity options provided the reliability that mission-critical applications demanded.

The market expansion also validated Sequoia Capital's investment thesis about network effects in infrastructure markets. As more organizations adopted Cisco's routing equipment, network administrators became familiar with the company's configuration interfaces and management tools. This installed base knowledge created switching costs that encouraged additional Cisco purchases, even when competitors offered lower prices or superior features.

Strategic Acquisitions: Growth Through Market Consolidation

Under Morgridge's leadership and with Sequoia's strategic guidance, Cisco pioneered the use of acquisitions as a core growth strategy in technology markets. Rather than attempting to develop all necessary technologies internally, Cisco systematically acquired companies with complementary products, innovative technologies, or access to new market segments.

This acquisition strategy reflected sophisticated thinking about technology market dynamics and product development efficiency. Networking technology was evolving rapidly across multiple dimensions simultaneously, routing protocols, switching architectures, network management systems, and security features all required substantial engineering investments. Internal development of all necessary technologies would have required enormous engineering resources and extended time-to-market cycles.

Acquisitions enabled Cisco to accelerate product development while eliminating potential competitors. The company typically acquired smaller firms with innovative technologies or specialized expertise, integrating their products into Cisco's broader networking portfolio. This approach provided immediate access to new technical capabilities while removing competitive threats that might otherwise have challenged Cisco's market position.

The financial structure of Cisco's acquisitions also demonstrated venture capital's influence on strategic thinking. Many target companies were themselves venture-backed startups seeking liquidity for their investors. Cisco's acquisition offers often provided attractive returns for venture capitalists while giving acquired companies access to the resources necessary for global market expansion.

Successful integration of acquired companies required sophisticated organizational capabilities that Morgridge developed with Sequoia's guidance. Cisco established systematic processes for evaluating acquisition targets, conducting due diligence, and integrating new technologies and personnel. These capabilities became competitive advantages that enabled Cisco to pursue acquisitions more effectively than competitors.

The Public Offering: Venture Capital's Ultimate Validation

Cisco Systems' initial public offering in February 1990 represented one of venture capital's most successful early exits, generating extraordinary returns while positioning the company for continued growth. The offering raised $224 million at a share price of $18, valuing the company at approximately $224 million and providing existing shareholders with immediate liquidity.

Sequoia Capital's investment returns exemplified venture capital's potential for creating substantial wealth through patient capital and strategic guidance. The firm's initial $2.5 million investment was worth approximately $170 million at the IPO price, representing a return multiple of nearly 70x over slightly more than two years. These returns validated both the investment thesis about networking infrastructure and the execution capabilities that Sequoia had helped develop.

The public offering also provided Cisco with permanent capital for continued expansion and acquisition activity. Unlike debt financing or additional venture capital rounds, the IPO proceeds didn't require periodic repayment or surrender of additional equity. This financial flexibility proved crucial as Cisco pursued aggressive growth strategies during the subsequent Internet boom.

Public market investors' enthusiastic reception of Cisco's IPO reflected broader recognition of networking infrastructure's strategic importance. The stock price increased substantially following the offering as institutional investors recognized the company's position in a rapidly expanding market. This market validation attracted additional customer attention while providing acquisition currency for future growth initiatives.

Network Effects: The Economics of Infrastructure Dominance

Cisco's post-IPO evolution illustrated the powerful economics of network effects in infrastructure markets. As more organizations adopted Cisco's networking equipment, the company's products became increasingly valuable to existing and prospective customers. Network administrators trained on Cisco equipment preferred purchasing additional Cisco products to minimize learning costs and ensure compatibility.

These network effects created sustainable competitive advantages that traditional manufacturing businesses rarely achieved. Competitors could develop superior technology or offer lower prices, but overcoming Cisco's installed base advantages required customers to abandon existing investments and retrain technical personnel. The switching costs associated with changing networking vendors often exceeded the potential benefits of alternative products.

The network effects also extended to Cisco's ecosystem of partners, resellers, and service providers. Companies that developed expertise in installing and maintaining Cisco equipment had strong incentives to recommend Cisco products to their customers. Training programs and certification processes further reinforced these relationships while creating barriers to competitive entry.

Venture capital's patient approach to building these network effects proved crucial for long-term value creation. Rather than optimizing for immediate profitability, Cisco invested heavily in market share expansion, customer service, and ecosystem development. These investments reduced short-term financial performance but created the foundation for sustained competitive advantages.

Global Expansion and Market Leadership

Cisco's venture-backed international expansion established the company as the dominant global supplier of networking equipment before most competitors recognized international opportunities. Morgridge's systematic approach to entering new markets combined local partnerships with direct sales capabilities, ensuring that Cisco could serve customers' needs while maintaining control over strategic relationships.

The international expansion strategy reflected lessons learned from previous venture capital investments in technology infrastructure. Companies that established early leadership in global markets often maintained those positions for decades, as switching costs and network effects reinforced their competitive advantages. Cisco's early international presence positioned the company to benefit from worldwide Internet adoption.

European and Asian markets for networking equipment developed differently than North American markets, requiring customized products and localized support capabilities. Cisco's venture-backed financial resources enabled the company to make necessary investments in regional customization while maintaining product compatibility and performance standards.

The global expansion also provided geographic diversification that reduced Cisco's dependence on any single market or customer segment. This diversification proved valuable during economic downturns or regional technology spending cycles, as strong performance in some markets could offset weakness in others.

Competitive Dynamics: Defending Network Leadership

Cisco's market leadership attracted aggressive competitive challenges from both established technology companies and venture-backed startups. Companies like 3Com, Bay Networks, and Cabletron invested heavily in developing alternative networking technologies while attempting to displace Cisco's dominant market position.

The competitive dynamics illustrated both the advantages and vulnerabilities of network effects-based business models. Cisco's installed base and ecosystem relationships provided substantial defensive advantages, but technological shifts or changes in customer requirements could potentially undermine these positions. Maintaining leadership required continuous innovation and aggressive response to competitive threats.

Cisco's acquisition strategy proved particularly effective for neutralizing competitive challenges. Rather than engaging in prolonged technology battles with innovative startups, Cisco often acquired promising competitors before they could establish independent market positions. This approach eliminated threats while incorporating innovative technologies into Cisco's product portfolio.

The venture capital community's involvement in competitive dynamics added additional complexity to market competition. Many of Cisco's competitors were themselves venture-backed companies pursuing alternative approaches to networking technology. The success or failure of these competitive investments would influence venture capital's continued support for networking innovation.

Conclusion: Infrastructure, Network Effects, and Venture Capital

Cisco Systems' transformation from Stanford garage project to global networking leader demonstrated venture capital's unique ability to identify and develop infrastructure opportunities with powerful network effects. Sequoia Capital's investment enabled Cisco to scale beyond bootstrap constraints while providing the strategic guidance necessary for market leadership.

The Cisco phenomenon illustrated several crucial principles for venture capital investing in infrastructure markets. First, timing proved essential, the investment coincided with explosive demand for internetworking equipment that would reshape global communications. Second, network effects created sustainable competitive advantages that justified patient capital and market share investments over immediate profitability.

Third, professional management expertise was crucial for scaling hardware manufacturing businesses beyond entrepreneurial origins. Morgridge's operational capabilities and strategic vision, combined with Sequoia's guidance, transformed Cisco from technical innovation into market-leading enterprise.

Finally, Cisco's success validated venture capital's role in creating entirely new technology markets rather than simply funding incremental innovations. The internetworking industry that Cisco helped establish would eventually support trillions of dollars in global communications and commerce, demonstrating infrastructure investment's potential for broad economic impact.

The network effects that drove Cisco's success would become increasingly important as technology markets evolved toward platform-based business models. Cisco's venture-backed journey provided a template for identifying and developing companies that could benefit from positive feedback loops between user adoption and value creation, a model that would prove essential for understanding and investing in the Internet economy's continued evolution.

Chapter 8

The Software Transformation

The emergence of software as a dominant force in venture capital investing represented one of the most profound shifts in the industry's history. Unlike the hardware-centric investments that had defined Silicon Valley's early decades, software companies promised revolutionary economics: products that could be replicated infinitely at near-zero marginal cost, business models that generated recurring revenue streams, and scalability that defied traditional manufacturing constraints. The transformation from hardware to software investing would fundamentally reshape venture capital's approach to due diligence, valuation, and portfolio construction while creating some of the most valuable companies in business history.

This shift wasn't merely technological, it represented a complete reimagining of how technology companies could create and capture value. Software companies like Oracle, Microsoft, and later enterprise software pioneers demonstrated that intellectual property embedded in code could generate more sustainable competitive advantages and higher returns than physical products requiring continuous manufacturing investment. Venture capitalists who recognized this transformation early positioned themselves to benefit from one of the greatest wealth creation periods in modern economic history.

The Hardware Legacy: Understanding the Transition

To appreciate the magnitude of software's impact on venture capital, it's essential to understand the hardware-dominated landscape that preceded it. Throughout the 1960s and 1970s, technology venture investing focused primarily on semiconductor companies, computer manufacturers, and telecommunications equipment providers. These businesses required substantial capital investments in manufacturing facilities, inventory management, and physical distribution networks.

Hardware companies faced predictable economic constraints that limited their scalability and profitability. Each additional unit sold required corresponding investments in raw materials, manufacturing capacity, and logistics. Competition typically centered on performance improvements and cost reduction, creating relentless pressure on profit margins. Success demanded excellence in engineering, manufacturing, and supply chain management, disciplines that required deep expertise but offered limited opportunities for exponential growth.

The venture capital industry had adapted its investment strategies to accommodate hardware economics. Due diligence processes emphasized manufacturing capabilities, component sourcing, and production scalability. Valuation models reflected the capital-intensive nature of hardware businesses and their typically linear growth trajectories. Portfolio construction balanced the substantial capital requirements of hardware companies against the extended timelines required to achieve meaningful scale.

However, by the early 1980s, several trends were converging to create new opportunities beyond traditional hardware investing. The proliferation of standardized computer platforms was reducing the need for custom hardware solutions while creating demand for software applications that could run across multiple systems. The declining cost of computing power was making software-intensive solutions economically viable for a broader range of business applications. Most importantly, the emergence of personal computers was creating mass markets for software products that could be distributed without requiring dedicated hardware platforms.

Oracle's Database Revolution: Larry Ellison and the Enterprise Opportunity

The story of Oracle Corporation exemplifies how visionary entrepreneurs and prescient venture capitalists could recognize software's transformative potential before it became obvious to mainstream investors. Larry Ellison's journey from ambitious programmer to database software pioneer illustrated both the opportunities and challenges of building enterprise software companies in an era when most technology investment focused on hardware solutions.

Ellison's insight centered on recognizing that businesses would increasingly need sophisticated database management systems as they computerized their operations. Traditional data storage approaches, which relied on hierarchical or network database models, were complex to implement and difficult to maintain. The relational database concept, pioneered by IBM researcher Edgar Codd, promised to simplify data management while providing more flexible query capabilities.

However, IBM's commercial implementation of relational database technology was progressing slowly, constrained by the company's commitment to existing mainframe software architectures and concern about cannibalizing established product lines. This created an entrepreneurial opportunity for smaller companies willing to bet entirely on the relational database approach without worrying about compatibility with legacy systems.

Ellison founded Software Development Laboratories (later renamed Oracle) in 1977 with co-founders Bob Miner and Ed Oates. The company's initial focus was developing a relational database management system that could run on minicomputers rather than requiring expensive mainframe hardware. This positioning reflected sophisticated strategic thinking about technology adoption patterns and customer economics.

The decision to target minicomputers rather than mainframes was crucial for several reasons. Minicomputer customers typically had smaller budgets and less sophisticated technical requirements than mainframe users, making them more willing to experiment with unproven software from startup companies. The minicomputer market was also growing rapidly as organizations sought alternatives to expensive mainframe solutions. Most importantly, success in the minicomputer market could provide the foundation for eventually competing with IBM in the more lucrative mainframe segment.

Venture Capital's Database Bet: Recognizing Software Economics

Oracle's early venture capital funding came from Sequoia Capital, demonstrating Don Valentine's continued ability to identify paradigm-shifting opportunities before they became widely recognized. The decision to invest in database software required understanding both the technical merits of relational database technology and the business model advantages that software companies could achieve.

From a technical perspective, Valentine and his partners recognized that relational databases represented a fundamental improvement over existing data management approaches. The ability to query databases using standard SQL commands would dramatically reduce the programming expertise required to develop business applications. This standardization would accelerate software development while reducing the costs associated with maintaining custom database systems.

More importantly from a venture capital perspective, database software demonstrated the economic characteristics that would make software investing attractive. Once developed, database software could be replicated and distributed at minimal marginal cost. Customer switching costs were substantial, as organizations would need to convert existing data and retrain personnel to adopt alternative database systems. Successful database companies could therefore generate recurring revenue streams with high profit margins and predictable cash flows.

Oracle's business model also illustrated software's scalability advantages. Unlike hardware companies that required proportional increases in manufacturing capacity to serve additional customers, Oracle could serve dramatically more customers with relatively modest increases in engineering and support personnel. This scalability meant that successful software companies could achieve much higher returns on invested capital than comparable hardware businesses.

The venture capital due diligence process for Oracle required developing new frameworks for evaluating software companies. Traditional metrics like manufacturing efficiency and inventory management were irrelevant for software businesses. Instead, investors needed to assess software functionality, development team capabilities, market timing, and competitive positioning factors that hadn't been central to hardware investing.

Microsoft's Platform Strategy: Bill Gates and the Personal Computer Revolution

While Oracle was pioneering enterprise database software, Microsoft was demonstrating software's potential in personal computer markets. Bill Gates' strategic vision of software platforms that could generate ecosystem effects represented another crucial development in software's emergence as a dominant technology category.

Microsoft's success illustrated how software companies could create value through network effects and platform dynamics rather than simply superior product functionality. The MS-DOS operating system became valuable not just because of its technical capabilities, but because widespread adoption encouraged software developers to create applications for the platform. This created positive feedback loops where platform adoption encouraged application development, which in turn drove additional platform adoption.

The platform strategy also demonstrated software's potential for creating sustainable competitive advantages. Once developers had invested in learning Microsoft's programming interfaces and customers had purchased applications designed for MS-DOS, switching to alternative operating systems became increasingly expensive and disruptive. These switching costs provided Microsoft with pricing power and market stability that hardware companies rarely achieved.

From a venture capital perspective, Microsoft's evolution (though the company didn't accept venture funding) illustrated the enormous value creation potential in software platform businesses. The combination of network effects, switching costs, and scalable economics could generate market valuations that dwarfed comparable hardware companies. This recognition encouraged venture investors to seek similar platform opportunities in other software categories.

The Enterprise Software Emergence: Beyond Databases and Operating Systems

The success of Oracle and Microsoft encouraged entrepreneurs and venture capitalists to explore software opportunities throughout the enterprise technology landscape. Companies like Lotus Development (spreadsheet software), WordPerfect (word processing), and Ashton-Tate (database applications) demonstrated that software could address virtually any business function that involved information processing.

Enterprise software companies offered particularly attractive investment characteristics. Business customers typically had larger budgets than individual consumers and were willing to pay premium prices for software that could improve productivity or reduce operational costs. Enterprise software also generated more predictable revenue streams, as businesses rarely abandoned software applications that had become integral to their operations.

The sales cycles for enterprise software were longer than consumer software, but the resulting customer relationships were typically more stable and profitable. Enterprise customers often purchased software maintenance contracts, training services, and customization consulting that generated recurring revenue streams beyond initial license fees. These service revenues often carried higher profit margins than software licenses while creating additional barriers to customer switching.

Venture capitalists began developing specialized expertise in enterprise software markets, learning to evaluate factors like customer acquisition costs, sales cycle lengths, and customer lifetime values that were specific to software business models. The due diligence process evolved to emphasize software functionality, competitive differentiation, and go-to-market strategies rather than the manufacturing and distribution capabilities that hardware investing required.

Software Development Economics: The Venture Capital Advantage

The economics of software development created unique advantages for venture capital-backed companies compared to established technology firms. Large corporations with existing hardware revenues often struggled to justify significant investments in software development, particularly when software products might cannibalize profitable hardware sales or require developing entirely new sales and marketing capabilities.

Venture-backed software startups faced no such constraints. They could focus entirely on software opportunities without worrying about protecting existing revenue streams or adapting established organizational structures. This enabled more aggressive innovation and faster response to changing market requirements.

The capital requirements for software development were also more compatible with venture capital fund structures than hardware businesses. Software companies typically required smaller initial investments and could achieve positive cash flows more quickly than hardware manufacturers. This reduced the total capital requirements while shortening the time to potential exits through acquisitions or public offerings.

Software development also offered more predictable project management characteristics than hardware engineering. While software projects could certainly experience delays and technical challenges, they weren't subject to the component shortages, manufacturing defects, or supply chain disruptions that could devastate hardware company schedules. This predictability made venture capital planning and portfolio management more straightforward.

Recurring Revenue Models: The SaaS Revolution's Precursors

While the Software-as-a-Service (SaaS) model wouldn't fully emerge until the Internet era, early enterprise software companies were already experimenting with recurring revenue approaches that would later become standard practice. Software maintenance contracts, training services, and customization consulting provided ongoing revenue streams that reduced dependence on new license sales.

These recurring revenue components were particularly attractive to venture investors because they created more predictable cash flows and higher customer lifetime values. Companies that could generate 40-50% of their revenue from maintenance and services enjoyed more stable financial performance and were less vulnerable to economic downturns or competitive pressures.

The recurring revenue models also demonstrated software's potential for creating customer dependency relationships that were more valuable than traditional product sales. Customers who relied on software applications for critical business processes had strong incentives to maintain their vendor relationships even when alternative products might offer superior features or lower initial costs.

Venture capitalists began incorporating recurring revenue metrics into their evaluation processes, recognizing that companies with higher percentages of predictable revenue commanded premium valuations and generated more consistent returns. This focus on recurring revenue would become increasingly important as software business models continued evolving toward subscription-based approaches.

International Software Markets: Global Scaling Opportunities

Software's digital nature created unprecedented opportunities for international expansion that hardware companies couldn't easily match. While hardware manufacturers needed to establish local distribution networks, inventory management systems, and service capabilities, software companies could potentially serve global markets from centralized development centers.

However, international software expansion also presented unique challenges that venture capitalists needed to understand and address. Language localization required significant development investments, particularly for complex enterprise applications with extensive user interfaces. Cultural differences in business processes meant that software designed for American markets might not address the requirements of international customers.

Regulatory requirements also varied significantly across international markets, particularly for financial and healthcare software applications. Companies seeking global expansion needed to invest in compliance capabilities and legal expertise that domestic-focused businesses could avoid.

Despite these challenges, successful international expansion could dramatically increase software companies' addressable markets while providing geographic diversification that reduced dependence on any single economy. Venture capitalists who understood international software markets could help their portfolio companies capture these opportunities while avoiding common pitfalls.

The Venture Capital Learning Curve: New Investment Frameworks

The shift toward software investing required venture capitalists to develop entirely new frameworks for evaluating companies and managing portfolios. Traditional hardware-focused due diligence processes were inadequate for assessing software companies' competitive positions, technical capabilities, and market opportunities.

Software due diligence needed to evaluate factors like code quality, development methodologies, and intellectual property protection strategies that weren't relevant for hardware companies. Understanding software functionality often required technical expertise that hardware-focused venture capitalists didn't possess, leading many firms to recruit partners with software development backgrounds.

Valuation models also needed substantial revision to accommodate software economics. Traditional approaches based on manufacturing capacity, inventory values, and physical asset utilization were meaningless for software companies. Instead, valuation required understanding customer acquisition costs, lifetime values, and scalability metrics that were specific to software business models.

Portfolio management strategies evolved to reflect software companies' different capital requirements and growth trajectories. Software companies could often achieve substantial growth with smaller capital investments than hardware businesses, but they also faced different competitive risks and market dynamics that required specialized understanding.

Competitive Dynamics: Software vs. Hardware Strategies

The emergence of software as a dominant technology category created complex competitive dynamics between new software companies and established hardware manufacturers. Many hardware companies attempted to defend their market positions by developing software capabilities, while pure software companies sought to displace hardware-centric solutions with more efficient alternatives.

These competitive battles often centered on business model differences rather than pure technical capabilities. Software companies could offer lower total cost of ownership by eliminating hardware maintenance requirements and providing more flexible deployment options. Hardware companies countered by emphasizing performance advantages and integration benefits that software-only solutions couldn't match.

Venture capitalists found themselves funding companies on both sides of these competitive battles, requiring sophisticated understanding of how software and hardware alternatives would evolve over time. The outcomes of these competitions would determine which business models and technologies would dominate future markets.

Customer Adoption Patterns: Enterprise Software Sales Cycles

Enterprise software sales required fundamentally different approaches than hardware sales, creating new challenges and opportunities for venture-backed companies. Software purchasing decisions often involved multiple stakeholders within customer organizations, including IT departments, end users, and senior executives with different priorities and evaluation criteria.

The intangible nature of software made customer evaluation processes more complex than hardware assessments. Customers couldn't physically inspect software products or easily compare performance characteristics across different vendors. This placed greater emphasis on demonstration capabilities, reference customers, and vendor credibility factors that influenced purchasing decisions.

Software companies also needed to invest more heavily in customer education and change management support than hardware vendors.

Implementing new software applications often required customers to modify existing business processes and retrain employees, creating implementation challenges that could affect customer satisfaction and future purchase decisions.

Venture capitalists learned to evaluate software companies' sales and marketing capabilities alongside their technical development capabilities, recognizing that commercial success required excellence in customer acquisition and relationship management as well as product development.

Integration Challenges: Software in Hardware-Dominant Environments

Early enterprise software companies often faced significant challenges integrating their products with existing hardware-centric IT infrastructures. Most corporate computing environments were designed around proprietary hardware platforms with limited support for third-party software applications.

These integration challenges created both obstacles and opportunities for venture-backed software companies. Companies that could solve complex integration problems often developed strong competitive advantages and customer loyalty. However, integration difficulties could also slow customer adoption and increase implementation costs that made software solutions less attractive than hardware alternatives.

Successful software companies learned to invest heavily in integration capabilities and partnership relationships with hardware vendors. These investments were often necessary for market acceptance but could consume substantial resources that might otherwise have been devoted to product development or customer acquisition.

The Platform Evolution: From Applications to Infrastructure

As software markets matured, venture capitalists began recognizing opportunities in software infrastructure and development tools that could support the growing ecosystem of application software companies. Companies developing databases, development environments, and middleware platforms could potentially serve multiple application vendors while creating platform effects similar to those achieved by operating system companies.

Infrastructure software often required larger initial investments and longer development timelines than application software, but successful platforms could generate more sustainable competitive advantages and higher long-term returns. The network effects created by developer adoption could provide natural monopoly characteristics that were particularly valuable for venture capital investment strategies.

The evolution toward software platforms also created new categories of investment opportunities in development tools, testing frameworks, and deployment systems that could improve software development productivity. These infrastructure investments often had less obvious market potential than application software but could generate substantial returns by enabling broader software industry growth.

Conclusion: The Software Imperative

The transformation from hardware to software investing represented one of venture capital's most successful adaptations to changing technology landscapes. Venture capitalists who recognized software's superior economics, scalability, recurring revenue potential, and network effects positioned themselves to benefit from decades of extraordinary value creation.

The software transformation also demonstrated venture capital's role in accelerating paradigm shifts within technology markets. By providing early-stage funding and strategic guidance to software pioneers like Oracle, venture investors helped establish entirely new categories of technology companies that would eventually dominate global markets.

The lessons learned during software's emergence would prove crucial for understanding subsequent technology shifts toward Internet-based services, mobile applications, and cloud computing platforms. The emphasis on scalability, network effects, and recurring revenue models that characterized successful software investing became fundamental principles for evaluating technology investment opportunities.

Most importantly, the software transformation established the template for how venture capital could identify and develop companies that leveraged intellectual property and network effects rather than physical assets and manufacturing capabilities. This approach would become increasingly important as technology markets continued evolving toward digital platforms and service-based business models that could achieve unprecedented scale and profitability.

Chapter 9

Going Global

The globalization of venture capital represented a fundamental shift from Silicon Valley's insular origins to a worldwide network of innovation and investment that would reshape the global economy. What began as a uniquely American phenomenon, the marriage of entrepreneurial ambition with patient capital gradually evolved into an international movement that transcended borders, cultures, and economic systems. This transformation wasn't merely about American venture capitalists investing overseas or foreign entrepreneurs seeking Silicon Valley funding; it represented the emergence of indigenous venture capital ecosystems worldwide, each adapted to local conditions while drawing inspiration from the American model.

The journey from domestic to global venture capital involved navigating complex challenges that extended far beyond traditional investment considerations. Cultural differences in business practices, regulatory environments, and entrepreneurial attitudes created obstacles that purely financial analysis couldn't address. Yet the potential rewards, access to untapped talent pools, emerging markets with explosive growth potential, and diversification benefits drove venture capitalists to persist through these complications. The resulting global venture capital network would become one of the most powerful forces for international economic development and technological advancement in modern history.

The Domestic Foundation: Silicon Valley's Unique Ecosystem

Understanding venture capital's global expansion requires appreciating the unique conditions that enabled its initial success in Silicon Valley. The region's concentration of world-class universities, particularly Stanford and UC Berkeley, provided a continuous stream of technically trained entrepreneurs and cutting-edge research. The presence of established technology companies like Hewlett-Packard, Fairchild Semiconductor, and later Intel created a pool of experienced executives and engineers comfortable with technology risk-taking.

Perhaps most importantly, Silicon Valley developed a cultural acceptance of failure that was unusual in American business and virtually unknown in most international markets. Entrepreneurs who had failed in previous ventures weren't stigmatized but were often viewed as more experienced and potentially valuable partners for future opportunities. This failure tolerance was essential for venture capital success, as the asset class depends on making numerous high-risk investments with the expectation that most will fail while a few generate extraordinary returns.

The legal and regulatory environment in California and the United States also provided crucial support for venture capital development. Securities regulations permitted accredited investors to participate in high-risk private investments. Tax policies favored long-term capital gains and provided incentives for entrepreneurial activity. Bankruptcy laws allowed failed entrepreneurs to recover relatively quickly rather than bearing personal liability indefinitely.

The network effects within Silicon Valley created self-reinforcing advantages that would be difficult to replicate elsewhere. Successful entrepreneurs often became angel investors or venture capital partners, recycling their knowledge and capital into new ventures. Law firms, accounting practices, and consulting companies developed specialized expertise in serving venture-backed companies. The concentration of activity created informal information networks that facilitated deal flow, due diligence, and strategic partnerships.

These favorable conditions weren't accidents of geography but rather the result of deliberate policy choices and cultural evolution over several decades. Replicating venture capital's success in other regions would require understanding these underlying factors and adapting them to different cultural and regulatory contexts.

Early International Forays: Learning Through Experience

The first significant attempts at international venture capital expansion emerged in the late 1970s and early 1980s as successful American venture capitalists sought to leverage their expertise in new markets. These early efforts were often extensions of existing portfolio companies' international expansion strategies rather than independent investment initiatives.

European markets represented the most natural starting point for international expansion, given their developed economies, established financial markets, and relatively familiar regulatory environments. However, even these apparently similar markets presented unexpected challenges that required substantial learning and adaptation.

The United Kingdom offered perhaps the most accessible international opportunity, sharing language and legal traditions with the United States while possessing sophisticated financial markets and a tradition of entrepreneurial activity. Early American venture investments in British companies revealed both opportunities and obstacles that would characterize international expansion more broadly.

Cultural differences in business practices proved more significant than many American investors had anticipated. British entrepreneurs and executives often approached business relationships, risk assessment, and growth strategies differently than their American counterparts. The more hierarchical nature of many European business cultures could conflict with the collaborative, informal style that characterized successful Silicon Valley companies.

Regulatory environments, even in developed markets, often lacked the frameworks that supported venture capital activity in the United States. Securities regulations might not permit certain types of private investments, or might impose disclosure requirements that compromised competitive confidentiality. Tax policies frequently penalized equity-based compensation or long-term capital gains in ways that reduced entrepreneurial incentives.

Perhaps most challenging was the absence of supporting ecosystems that made venture capital efficient in Silicon Valley. International markets often lacked the specialized service providers, experienced management talent, and informal networks that facilitated rapid company scaling in the United States.

The Technology Transfer Model: Exporting Silicon Valley Innovation

One of the earliest approaches to international venture capital involved technology transfer strategies that sought to commercialize American innovations in international markets. This model typically involved licensing established technologies to international partners or investing in overseas companies that could adapt American products for local markets.

The technology transfer approach offered several advantages for American venture capitalists. It leveraged proven technologies and business models while avoiding the risks associated with entirely novel innovations. International partners provided local market knowledge and regulatory expertise that American investors lacked. The strategies could often achieve faster time-to-market and required lower initial investments than developing new technologies independently.

However, technology transfer also presented significant limitations. The most valuable innovations were often too strategic for American companies to license internationally. Adapting technologies for local markets frequently required more extensive modifications than initially anticipated. International partners might lack the execution capabilities necessary to successfully commercialize sophisticated technologies.

The model also raised questions about long-term competitive positioning. Companies built primarily around licensed technologies might struggle to develop independent innovation capabilities that could sustain competitive advantages over time. American licensors retained control over future technology development, potentially limiting their international partners' strategic flexibility.

Despite these limitations, technology transfer provided valuable learning opportunities for both American venture capitalists and international entrepreneurs. The experience of working together revealed cultural differences, regulatory challenges, and market dynamics that would inform more sophisticated international strategies in subsequent years.

European Venture Capital Development: Indigenous Innovation

The emergence of indigenous European venture capital represented a more sustainable approach to international expansion than technology transfer or direct American investment. Rather than simply importing Silicon Valley models, European entrepreneurs and investors began developing venture capital strategies adapted to local conditions and opportunities.

The United Kingdom led European venture capital development, building on its established financial markets and entrepreneurial traditions. British venture capital firms like 3i (formerly ICFC) and Apax Partners demonstrated that venture capital could succeed within European regulatory and cultural frameworks while maintaining the patient capital and growth focus that characterized American venture investing.

Continental European markets presented greater challenges due to different legal traditions, more restrictive securities regulations, and cultural attitudes that were often skeptical of entrepreneurial risk-taking. However, government initiatives in countries like France, Germany, and the Netherlands began creating more supportive environments for venture capital development.

European venture capital also benefited from the region's strengths in certain technology areas where American dominance was less pronounced. European companies achieved early leadership in telecommunications, automotive technology, and industrial automation applications where local engineering traditions and customer relationships provided competitive advantages.

The European Union's formation created additional opportunities by reducing barriers to cross-border investment and trade. European venture capitalists could pursue investment strategies across multiple countries while benefiting from increasingly harmonized regulatory frameworks and market integration.

However, European venture capital development also revealed persistent challenges that would require decades to fully address. The fragmentation of European markets into numerous national jurisdictions complicated scaling strategies and increased regulatory compliance costs. Cultural differences within Europe were often as significant as those between Europe and the United States, making pan-European investment strategies complex to implement.

Asian Markets: The Emerging Opportunity

Asian markets represented perhaps the greatest long-term opportunity for international venture capital expansion, given their large populations, rapid economic development, and increasing technological sophistication. However, Asian markets also presented the most complex challenges due to significant cultural differences, less developed financial markets, and regulatory environments that were often hostile to foreign investment.

Japan emerged as the first major Asian market for venture capital investment, building on its established position as a global technology leader. Japanese companies had demonstrated world-class capabilities in manufacturing, electronics, and automotive technology that suggested strong potential for venture-backed innovation.

However, Japanese business culture proved particularly challenging for American venture capital approaches. The emphasis on consensus decision-making, long-term employment relationships, and risk aversion conflicted with venture capital's requirements for rapid decision-making, equity-based incentives, and acceptance of high failure rates.

Japanese financial markets also lacked many of the features that supported venture capital in the United States. Public markets were less receptive to unprofitable growth companies, making exit strategies more difficult to execute. Banking relationships often took precedence over equity financing, reducing entrepreneurs' willingness to dilute ownership through venture capital investment.

South Korea and Taiwan presented alternative approaches to Asian venture capital development. Both countries had strong engineering traditions and increasingly sophisticated technology companies, but smaller domestic markets that encouraged international expansion strategies from early company stages.

The nascent development of venture capital in China and India represented perhaps the greatest long-term opportunities, given their enormous populations and rapid economic growth. However, these markets remained largely closed to foreign investment and lacked the regulatory frameworks necessary to support substantial venture capital activity.

Cross-Border Investment Challenges: Regulatory and Cultural Barriers

International venture capital expansion revealed numerous challenges that were largely absent from domestic investing. Regulatory differences between countries often created complex compliance requirements that increased investment costs and lengthened decision-making processes.

Securities regulations varied significantly across international markets, with many countries imposing restrictions on foreign investment or requiring disclosure that could compromise competitive confidentiality. Tax treaties between countries often failed to address venture capital structures, potentially resulting in double taxation or other adverse consequences.

Currency fluctuations introduced additional risks that could significantly impact investment returns regardless of underlying company performance. Venture investments typically involved long holding periods during which exchange rates could change dramatically, potentially eliminating returns from successful investments or exacerbating losses from unsuccessful ones.

Cultural differences often proved more challenging than regulatory obstacles. Business practices, management styles, and entrepreneurial attitudes varied significantly across different countries and regions. American venture capitalists accustomed to informal, direct communication styles might struggle in cultures that emphasized hierarchy, face-saving, and indirect communication.

Legal systems based on different traditions could create unexpected complications for venture capital transactions. Civil law systems common in Continental Europe approached contract interpretation and enforcement differently than the common law systems that characterized American venture capital practice.

Exit strategies also varied significantly across international markets. Public offering processes, acquisition regulations, and market receptivity to growth companies differed substantially between countries, making exit planning more complex and uncertain.

Partnership Strategies: Local Expertise and Global Resources

Successful international venture capital expansion often required partnership strategies that combined global resources with local expertise. American venture capitalists brought capital, strategic knowledge, and access to international markets, while local partners contributed cultural understanding, regulatory expertise, and established business relationships.

These partnerships took various forms depending on specific market characteristics and investment opportunities. Joint ventures between American and international venture firms could provide balanced resource allocation while sharing both risks and returns. Strategic partnerships with established international companies offered access to distribution channels and customer relationships that could accelerate portfolio company growth.

Government partnerships became increasingly important as many countries recognized venture capital's potential for promoting economic development and technological innovation. Government-sponsored programs could provide co-investment capital, tax incentives, or regulatory flexibility that made international venture capital more attractive and successful.

However, partnerships also introduced additional complexity and potential conflicts that required careful management. Different organizational cultures, investment criteria, and strategic objectives could create disagreements about portfolio company management and exit strategies. Regulatory restrictions on foreign investment might limit partnership structures or require complex arrangements to maintain compliance.

The most successful international partnerships typically involved clear agreements about roles, responsibilities, and decision-making authority. They also required substantial cultural adaptation and learning on all sides, recognizing that effective collaboration required understanding and respecting different approaches to business and investment.

Government Initiatives: Policy Support for Innovation

Government recognition of venture capital's economic development potential led to numerous policy initiatives designed to encourage international venture capital expansion. These initiatives ranged from tax incentives and regulatory reforms to direct government investment in venture capital funds.

The United Kingdom's Enterprise Investment Scheme provided tax relief for individuals investing in qualifying venture capital funds, effectively subsidizing early-stage investment in British companies. Similar programs in other European countries offered various combinations of tax incentives, government co-investment, and regulatory flexibility.

Some governments established sovereign wealth funds or development agencies specifically focused on attracting international venture capital investment. These programs often combined capital provision with efforts to improve local entrepreneurial ecosystems through education, infrastructure development, and regulatory reform.

However, government involvement in venture capital also introduced potential complications. Political considerations might influence investment decisions in ways that compromised commercial objectives. Bureaucratic processes could slow decision-making and reduce venture capital's characteristic agility. Changes in government policy or priorities could disrupt established programs and create uncertainty for international investors.

The most successful government initiatives typically focused on removing barriers to venture capital activity rather than directly managing investment decisions. Regulatory reforms that permitted pension fund investment in venture capital, tax policies that encouraged entrepreneurial activity, and immigration policies that attracted international talent could have more sustainable impact than direct government investment programs.

Innovation Networks: Global Knowledge Transfer

The globalization of venture capital created international networks that facilitated knowledge transfer and collaboration across geographic boundaries. These networks enabled entrepreneurs and investors worldwide to benefit from best practices, lessons learned, and strategic insights developed in different markets.

Silicon Valley venture capitalists established international offices that served as bridges between American innovation and local opportunities. These offices provided intelligence about emerging technologies, market trends, and investment opportunities while offering local entrepreneurs access to Silicon Valley resources and expertise.

Academic institutions played crucial roles in international innovation networks through research collaborations, student exchange programs, and technology transfer initiatives. Universities worldwide began establishing programs specifically designed to promote entrepreneurship and venture capital activity within their regions.

Professional organizations and industry associations facilitated information sharing among international venture capital practitioners. Annual conferences, research publications, and peer networks enabled venture capitalists to learn from each other's experiences and develop more effective international strategies.

These networks also promoted talent mobility that strengthened global venture capital ecosystems. Entrepreneurs with international experience could adapt successful business models across different markets. Venture capital professionals who had worked in multiple regions developed cultural competency and market knowledge that enhanced their effectiveness as international investors.

Technology Convergence: Global Innovation Acceleration

The globalization of venture capital coincided with technological developments that were inherently international in scope. Telecommunications advances made global collaboration and market development more feasible than ever before. Standardization efforts in areas like computing and networking created international market opportunities that didn't exist in previous technology cycles.

These technological convergences created investment opportunities that required an international perspective from their inception. Companies developing global telecommunications infrastructure, international software platforms, or worldwide manufacturing systems needed capital and expertise that transcended national boundaries.

The convergence also accelerated competitive dynamics by enabling companies from any country to potentially compete in global markets. Venture capitalists who maintained purely domestic perspectives risked missing competitive threats and opportunities that could dramatically impact their portfolio companies' prospects.

Emerging Market Potential: The Next Frontier

By the 1990s, emerging markets in Asia, Latin America, and eventually Eastern Europe were beginning to develop the conditions necessary to support substantial venture capital activity. Economic liberalization, regulatory reforms, and technological infrastructure development created opportunities for international venture capital expansion into markets with enormous growth potential.

These emerging markets offered several attractive characteristics for venture capital investment. Large populations with increasing purchasing power created substantial market opportunities for successful companies. Lower labor costs could provide competitive advantages for companies requiring significant human capital. Government policies often encouraged foreign investment and technology transfer as strategies for economic development.

However, emerging markets also presented significant risks and challenges. Political instability could threaten investment security and business continuity. Regulatory environments were often unpredictable and subject to rapid change. Financial markets might lack the depth and liquidity necessary to support venture capital exit strategies.

The most successful emerging market venture capital strategies typically involved careful risk assessment, strong local partnerships, and patient capital that could weather political and economic volatility. They also required a deep understanding of local market conditions and cultural factors that influenced business success.

Conclusion: The Global Innovation Economy

The globalization of venture capital transformed both the venture capital industry and the broader global economy. What began as a uniquely American approach to funding innovation evolved into a worldwide movement that connected entrepreneurs, investors, and markets across all continents.

This transformation created unprecedented opportunities for innovation and economic development by enabling the most promising ideas to access capital regardless of their geographic origins. It also accelerated competitive dynamics by creating global markets where the best solutions could achieve worldwide impact.

The globalization process revealed that while venture capital principles could be applied internationally, successful implementation required substantial adaptation to local conditions. Cultural understanding, regulatory compliance, and partnership development became as important as traditional investment skills.

Looking forward, the global venture capital network established during this period would provide the foundation for even more ambitious international collaboration. The lessons learned from early globalization efforts would prove invaluable as venture capitalists sought to identify and develop the next generation of transformative technologies and business models on a truly worldwide scale.

The global expansion of venture capital represented more than just the international spread of a successful investment strategy, it constituted the emergence of a worldwide innovation ecosystem that would reshape economic development, technological progress, and international business relationships for decades to come.

Part IV: The Internet Revolution (1990s-2000s)

Chapter 10

Netscape and the Web

The Netscape Communications Corporation initial public offering on August 9, 1995, marked one of the most pivotal moments in venture capital history. The company's spectacular stock market debut, shares opened at $71 after being priced at $28, valuing the sixteen-month-old company at nearly $3 billion didn't merely create extraordinary returns for its venture capital backers. It announced to the world that the Internet represented a fundamental shift in computing, commerce, and human communication that would reshape virtually every aspect of modern life. More importantly for the venture capital industry, Netscape's success validated a new category of investment opportunities that would dominate the next two decades and create more wealth than any previous technology cycle.

The story of Netscape begins with Marc Andreessen, a young programmer at the University of Illinois who had helped create Mosaic, the first widely adopted web browser. When Andreessen partnered with Silicon Graphics founder Jim Clark to commercialize web browsing technology, they initiated a sequence of events that would transform the Internet from an academic research tool into the foundation of a global digital economy. The venture capitalists who recognized this transformation early, particularly John Doerr at Kleiner Perkins Caufield & Byers positioned themselves to benefit from one of the greatest wealth creation periods in business history.

The Academic Origins: From CERN to Champaign

The World Wide Web's creation at CERN by Tim Berners-Lee in 1991 provided the conceptual foundation for what would become the Internet revolution, but it was the development of user-friendly browsing software that made the web accessible to mainstream users. The National Center for Supercomputing Applications (NCSA) at the University of Illinois recognized that graphical browsing software could democratize Internet access and assigned a team of undergraduate programmers, led by Marc Andreessen, to develop what would become the Mosaic browser.

Mosaic's significance extended far beyond its technical capabilities. While earlier browsers existed, they were text-based applications that required substantial technical expertise to use effectively. Mosaic provided the first graphical interface that allowed users to navigate the web by clicking on links and viewing images embedded within text. This seemingly simple innovation transformed the web from a tool for computer scientists and researchers into a medium that virtually anyone could use.

The browser's rapid adoption demonstrated the Internet's extraordinary potential for mainstream commercialization. Within months of its release in 1993, Mosaic had been downloaded by millions of users worldwide. Universities, corporations, and government agencies began establishing web sites and exploring Internet-based applications. The web's growth trajectory suggested that Internet-related technologies might represent business opportunities comparable to the personal computer revolution.

However, NCSA's academic mission and federal funding constraints limited its ability to commercialize Mosaic directly. The center could distribute the software freely for educational and research purposes, but commercial development required different organizational structures and funding sources. This created an entrepreneurial opportunity for individuals with the vision and resources necessary to transform academic research into commercial products.

Marc Andreessen's experience developing Mosaic provided him with unique insights into both the web's commercial potential and the technical challenges involved in creating robust browsing software. His youth, he was only twenty-two when Mosaic was released, gave him a different perspective on technology adoption patterns than older software industry veterans. While established companies focused on existing markets and incremental improvements, Andreessen recognized that the web represented a paradigm shift that could create entirely new categories of software and services.

The Clark-Andreessen Partnership: Vision Meets Experience

Jim Clark's decision to recruit Marc Andreessen for a new Internet venture reflected the type of pattern recognition that distinguished successful technology entrepreneurs from those who focused on incremental improvements to existing markets. Clark had founded Silicon Graphics in 1981 and built it into a leader in high-performance computing and 3D graphics workstations. His experience scaling a hardware company from startup to industry leadership provided crucial insights into technology market development and competitive dynamics.

Clark's interest in Internet applications stemmed from his understanding that network computing would eventually challenge the desktop-centric model that had dominated personal computing since the 1980s. He believed that as Internet connectivity improved and web-based applications became more sophisticated, users would increasingly access software and data through browsers rather than installing programs locally on their computers.

This vision of network computing represented a fundamental challenge to established software companies like Microsoft, which had built their business models around selling desktop applications and operating systems. If Clark and Andreessen were correct that the web browser would become the primary interface for computer users, then Internet software companies could potentially bypass the Windows monopoly and reach users directly through web-based applications.

The partnership between Clark and Andreessen combined complementary strengths that were essential for Internet entrepreneurship. Clark contributed business experience, strategic vision, and access to capital and professional networks that startup companies required. Andreessen provided technical expertise in web technologies and deep understanding of user requirements based on his experience with Mosaic's development and adoption.

Their collaboration also reflected generational differences in approaching technology opportunities. Clark's experience with Silicon Graphics had demonstrated how hardware innovations could create new software markets, while Andreessen's work with Mosaic had shown how software innovations could create demand for new hardware capabilities. Together, they could envision Internet applications that would drive both software and hardware industry growth.

Kleiner Perkins and the Internet Bet: John Doerr's Vision

John Doerr's decision to lead Kleiner Perkins' investment in Netscape represented one of venture capital's most prescient strategic bets. Doerr had joined Kleiner Perkins in 1980 after a career at Intel, where he had witnessed the transformative impact of microprocessor technology on the computer industry. His experience with technology adoption cycles provided crucial insights into recognizing paradigm shifts before they became obvious to mainstream investors.

Doerr's investment thesis for Netscape rested on several key assumptions about Internet development and commercial potential. First, he believed that Internet usage would grow exponentially as connection speeds improved and costs declined. Second, he anticipated that businesses would increasingly use the Internet for commercial purposes as security and reliability concerns were addressed. Third, he expected that Internet-based applications would eventually challenge traditional desktop software by offering superior convenience and functionality.

The investment decision also reflected Kleiner Perkins' evolving approach to technology investing. The firm's previous successes with companies like Genentech and Sun Microsystems had demonstrated the value creation potential in funding paradigm-shifting technologies rather than incremental improvements to existing markets. Internet applications appeared to offer similar potential for creating entirely new technology categories.

However, the Internet investment also involved substantial risks that were difficult to quantify using traditional venture capital analysis. The commercial Internet was still in its infancy, with unclear regulatory frameworks, uncertain business models, and unproven revenue generation potential. Most corporations remained skeptical about Internet security and reliability for mission-critical applications.

Doerr's willingness to make a substantial investment in Netscape despite these uncertainties reflected both his confidence in the underlying technology trends and his understanding of venture capital's risk-return dynamics. If the Internet developed as rapidly as he anticipated, early investments in leading Internet companies could generate extraordinary returns that would more than compensate for the inherent risks.

The investment process also demonstrated Kleiner Perkins' operational support capabilities beyond pure financial backing. Doerr's involvement in recruiting experienced management, developing strategic partnerships, and preparing for eventual public offerings provided value that was often more important than the initial capital investment.

Building Netscape: From Concept to Commercial Product

The transformation of Netscape from entrepreneurial vision to commercial reality required solving numerous technical and business challenges that had no precedent in software industry experience. Creating a robust, commercial-grade web browser demanded more sophisticated engineering than academic software development while addressing scalability, security, and user experience requirements that Mosaic hadn't fully addressed.

The technical development process revealed both the opportunities and challenges of Internet software development. Unlike traditional software applications that ran on predictable hardware and operating system configurations, web browsers needed to function reliably across diverse computing environments while communicating with web servers using evolving and often inconsistent protocols.

Netscape's engineering team, assembled from both NCSA veterans and experienced software industry professionals, faced the challenge of reimplementing web browsing technology from scratch to avoid intellectual property conflicts with the University of Illinois. This provided an opportunity to incorporate lessons learned from Mosaic's development while designing software architecture that could support the performance and feature requirements of commercial applications.

The browser's development also required anticipating how web technologies would evolve as commercial usage expanded. Early web sites were primarily static text and images, but Netscape's engineers recognized that commercial applications would demand interactive capabilities, multimedia support, and integration with existing business systems. Building these capabilities into the browser's foundation was essential for maintaining competitive advantages as the web became more sophisticated.

The company's business model development proved as challenging as technical development. While the web browser was the initial product focus, the founding team recognized that browser software alone might not generate sufficient revenue to support a substantial business. Internet server software, development tools, and professional services represented potential additional revenue sources that could leverage Netscape's browser market position.

The Venture Capital Scaling Strategy: Beyond Traditional Software Models

Netscape's venture capital backing enabled scaling strategies that differed significantly from traditional software company approaches. The company's rapid growth trajectory and first-mover advantages in web browser technology justified aggressive expansion plans that required substantial upfront investments in engineering, marketing, and operations.

The scaling challenges also reflected unique characteristics of Internet software markets. Traditional software companies typically focused on specific customer segments or application categories, developing deep expertise and customer relationships within defined market boundaries. Internet software companies like Netscape were attempting to serve potentially unlimited user bases across all market segments simultaneously.

This universal market approach required different organizational capabilities than traditional software companies possessed. Customer support systems needed to handle enormous volumes of users with diverse technical sophistication levels. Software distribution had to accommodate millions of downloads rather than traditional retail or direct sales channels. Marketing strategies had to build brand awareness across global markets rather than targeting specific customer segments.

Venture capital's patient approach to profitability proved crucial for Netscape's scaling strategy. The company prioritized market share growth and technology leadership over immediate revenue generation, understanding that Internet markets would reward early leaders with sustainable competitive advantages. This long-term focus required investors who could tolerate substantial losses during the market development phase.

The international dimension of Internet markets also created unique opportunities and challenges for Netscape's expansion. Unlike traditional software companies that might expand internationally after establishing domestic market leadership, Internet companies could potentially serve global markets from their initial launch. However, this global reach also created competitive pressures and regulatory complexities that domestic software companies could avoid.

The Browser Wars Begin: Microsoft's Competitive Response

Netscape's early success in the browser market attracted immediate competitive attention from Microsoft, initiating what would become known as the "browser wars." Microsoft's response to Netscape's challenge illustrated both the defensive advantages of established platform companies and the disruptive potential of Internet technologies that could bypass traditional software distribution models.

Microsoft's Internet Explorer development represented a fundamental shift in the company's strategic priorities. While Microsoft had initially dismissed the Internet's commercial significance, Netscape's rapid growth and media attention forced a comprehensive reevaluation of Internet opportunities and competitive threats. Bill Gates' famous "Internet Tidal Wave" memo in May 1995 acknowledged that Internet technologies posed existential challenges to Microsoft's desktop software dominance.

The competitive battle between Netscape and Microsoft involved more than traditional software feature competition. Microsoft's ability to bundle Internet Explorer with Windows provided distribution advantages that independent software companies couldn't match. This bundling strategy threatened to commoditize browser software while potentially extending Microsoft's platform control into Internet applications.

From a venture capital perspective, the Microsoft competitive threat validated both the opportunity and risks associated with Internet investing. Microsoft's aggressive response confirmed that Internet technologies represented significant market opportunities worth defending. However, Microsoft's platform advantages also demonstrated the challenges that startup companies faced when competing against established technology giants.

Netscape's competitive strategy emphasized innovation velocity and market development rather than attempting to match Microsoft's distribution capabilities directly. The company focused on advanced browser features, server software development, and emerging Internet standards that could differentiate its offerings beyond basic web browsing functionality.

The IPO Strategy: Public Markets and Internet Validation

The decision to take Netscape public less than two years after its founding reflected both the company's capital requirements and venture capital's confidence in Internet market potential. Traditional software companies typically achieved substantial revenue levels and profitability before considering public offerings, but Internet companies operated under different assumptions about growth trajectories and market opportunities.

Netscape's IPO prospectus revealed the challenges of valuing Internet companies using traditional financial metrics. The company had minimal revenues and substantial losses, but exponential user growth and enormous market potential that conventional valuation models couldn't adequately capture. The offering required educating public market investors about Internet business models and competitive dynamics that had no historical precedent.

The venture capital syndicate's decision to proceed with the IPO despite uncertain financial metrics reflected their confidence in Internet adoption trends and Netscape's competitive positioning. John Doerr and other board members believed that public market access would provide both the capital and strategic flexibility necessary for competing effectively against Microsoft's aggressive response.

The IPO pricing and marketing process also established precedents for subsequent Internet public offerings. The decision to price shares at $28 despite enormous demand reflected careful balance between maximizing proceeds and ensuring successful aftermarket performance. The resulting first-day price appreciation created substantial wealth for employees and investors while generating media attention that enhanced Netscape's competitive positioning.

Market Validation: The Internet Economy Emerges

Netscape's IPO success provided crucial validation for Internet commercial potential that extended far beyond the company's specific business prospects. The public market's enthusiastic reception of an unprofitable Internet company signaled fundamental changes in how investors evaluated technology opportunities and business model innovation.

The market validation also attracted entrepreneurial and investment attention to Internet applications across numerous industry categories. Companies developing Internet-based commerce, communication, entertainment, and information services began receiving venture capital backing based on growth potential rather than immediate profitability. This shift in investment criteria would accelerate Internet industry development while creating new categories of venture capital opportunities.

The public market success also established Internet companies as attractive acquisition targets for established technology and media companies seeking Internet capabilities. The acquisition activity created additional exit opportunities for venture capital investors while providing strategic alternatives for portfolio companies facing competitive challenges.

Platform Dynamics: The Browser as Internet Gateway

Netscape's browser success illustrated the strategic importance of platform control in technology markets. Web browsers served as the primary interface between users and Internet applications, potentially providing influence over user behavior and application development similar to operating systems' role in desktop computing.

This platform potential attracted both venture capital investment and competitive attention from established technology companies. Control over Internet access could provide advantages in adjacent markets like Internet commerce, online advertising, and web-based applications. Companies that controlled Internet platforms could potentially extract value from the broader Internet economy growth.

However, the browser platform also demonstrated the challenges of maintaining platform control in rapidly evolving technology markets. Unlike desktop operating systems that required substantial switching costs, Internet users could easily experiment with alternative browsers and web services. This reduced switching costs made Internet platforms more contestable than traditional technology platforms.

Developer Ecosystems: Enabling Internet Innovation

Netscape's browser and server software created development platforms that enabled thousands of entrepreneurs to build Internet-based applications and services. The company's commitment to open Internet standards facilitated innovation by reducing barriers to entry for web-based application development.

This ecosystem approach proved crucial for Internet market development by creating positive feedback loops between platform adoption and application availability. As more developers created web applications, browsers became more valuable to users. Increased user adoption attracted additional developer attention, accelerating Internet application innovation.

The developer ecosystem strategy also provided competitive advantages against Microsoft's proprietary platform approach. While Microsoft emphasized integration with Windows-specific technologies, Netscape supported cross-platform development that could reach users regardless of their operating system preferences.

International Markets: The Global Internet

Netscape's international expansion demonstrated Internet technologies' inherent global reach while revealing regulatory and cultural challenges that traditional software companies typically encountered gradually. Internet applications could potentially serve global markets from initial launch, but effective international competition required understanding diverse regulatory environments and user preferences.

The global nature of Internet markets also created competitive advantages for early market leaders like Netscape. International users often adopted the same Internet applications and standards as American users, providing scale advantages for companies that achieved early leadership in the United States market.

However, international expansion also exposed Internet companies to regulatory risks and competitive challenges from local companies with superior knowledge of regional markets and user preferences. Successful international expansion required balancing global platform consistency with local market adaptation.

Conclusion: The Internet Revolution Begins

Netscape's venture capital-backed success marked the beginning of the Internet revolution that would transform commerce, communication, and social interaction worldwide. The company's IPO validated Internet commercial potential while establishing venture capital as the primary funding source for Internet innovation.

The Netscape phenomenon also demonstrated venture capital's ability to identify and develop paradigm-shifting technologies before their impact became obvious to mainstream investors. John Doerr's early recognition of Internet potential positioned Kleiner Perkins to benefit from one of the greatest technology investment cycles in history.

Perhaps most importantly, Netscape's success established the template for Internet company development that would guide venture capital investing for the next two decades. The emphasis on rapid user growth, network effects, and platform dynamics rather than immediate profitability became standard practice for Internet venture investing.

The browser wars initiated by Netscape's challenge to Microsoft also established competitive dynamics that would characterize Internet markets: rapid innovation cycles, platform competition, and winner-take-all outcomes that rewarded early market leaders with sustainable competitive advantages.

Looking forward, Netscape's legacy extended far beyond its ultimate fate as a company. The Internet economy that emerged from Netscape's pioneering efforts would create trillions of dollars in market value while fundamentally reshaping how businesses operated and people lived. The venture capitalists who recognized this transformation early positioned themselves to guide and benefit from one of the most significant economic developments in modern history.

Chapter 11

The Dot-Com Boom

"The internet changes everything. Get big fast. Revenue doesn't matter, what matters is eyeballs and market share."

These mantras echoed through Sand Hill Road and startup offices across Silicon Valley as the 1990s drew to a close. What began as genuine excitement about the transformative potential of the World Wide Web had morphed into something far more dangerous: a speculative frenzy that would come to define one of the most spectacular boom-and-bust cycles in American economic history.

The dot-com boom of the late 1990s represented both venture capital's greatest triumph and its most humbling lesson. In the span of just five years, from 1995 to 2000, venture capitalists would deploy unprecedented amounts of capital, create paper wealth on a scale never before seen, and ultimately preside over one of the most dramatic market corrections in modern history. The stories of companies like Pets.com, Webvan, and eToys would become cautionary tales, while the underlying transformation they were attempting to capture, the digitization of commerce and communication would prove prescient, if premature.

The Perfect Storm

The dot-com boom didn't emerge in a vacuum. It was the confluence of multiple powerful forces that created conditions ripe for both innovation and speculation. The Netscape IPO in August 1995 had demonstrated that internet companies could command extraordinary public market valuations, but that was merely the spark. The fuel for the coming conflagration had been accumulating for years.

The Telecommunications Act of 1996 deregulated the telecommunications industry, spurring massive infrastructure investment in fiber optic cables and network capacity. This "build it and they will come" mentality created the physical foundation for the internet economy, even as demand lagged behind supply. Meanwhile, the Year 2000 problem drove corporations to upgrade their computer systems en masse, creating a technology spending boom that benefited both established companies and startups.

Perhaps most importantly, a generation of investors who had missed the personal computer revolution were determined not to repeat that mistake with the internet. As John Doerr of Kleiner Perkins famously declared, the internet represented "the largest legal creation of wealth in the history of the planet." This fear of missing out (FOMO) would drive investment decisions throughout the boom years.

The venture capital industry itself had been transformed by its earlier successes. The number of venture capital firms had grown dramatically, and the size of funds had expanded exponentially. In 1990, the entire venture capital industry raised $2.9 billion across all funds. By 1999, that figure had exploded to $54.5 billion, with much of that capital specifically earmarked for internet investments.

The Metrics Revolution

Traditional venture capital had always been about building sustainable businesses with clear paths to profitability. Companies were expected to demonstrate unit economics, sustainable competitive advantages, and reasonable capital requirements. The internet changed all of that, or so the conventional wisdom went.

The new gospel preached that internet businesses were fundamentally different. They exhibited network effects, where each additional user made the service more valuable for all users. They had marginal costs approaching zero for serving additional customers. Most importantly, they could achieve global scale with unprecedented speed. In this new paradigm, traditional metrics like revenue and profit were not just irrelevant, they were counterproductive distractions from the real goal of capturing market share.

Instead, entrepreneurs and investors focused on new metrics: page views, unique visitors, registered users, and market share. The theory was sound in principle, in winner-take-all markets, establishing dominance early was crucial, even if it required operating at a loss. The problem was that this logic was applied indiscriminately to businesses that weren't actually winner-take-all markets, or where network effects were weak or nonexistent.

Amazon.com, founded by Jeff Bezos in 1994, became the poster child for this "get big fast" strategy. Bezos famously said he wanted to build "an everything store" and was willing to operate at a loss for years to achieve scale. The company's focus on revenue growth over profitability was initially met with skepticism from Wall Street analysts who dubbed it "Amazon.bomb." But as the company's stock price soared, other entrepreneurs and investors took note.

The success of Amazon, along with other early internet pioneers like eBay and Yahoo!, created a template that countless startups attempted to replicate. The formula seemed simple: identify a traditional business model, add ".com" to the name, raise venture capital, spend aggressively on marketing to acquire customers, and go public as quickly as possible.

The Marketing Wars

Perhaps no aspect of the dot-com boom was more emblematic of its excesses than the marketing wars. Companies that had never generated meaningful revenue spent millions on television advertisements during premium time slots. The Super Bowl became ground zero for dot-com marketing, with startup after startup paying millions for thirty-second spots to build "brand awareness."

The 2000 Super Bowl was particularly notorious, featuring seventeen dot-com advertisers who collectively spent over $44 million on commercials. Companies like E*Trade, Monster.com, and Pets.com used humor, celebrity endorsements, and memorable jingles to try to break through the clutter. The Pets.com sock puppet became a cultural phenomenon, but the company behind it would be defunct within eighteen months.

This marketing frenzy was enabled by the unprecedented amounts of capital flowing into the internet sector. Venture capitalists, flush with cash from successful fundraising, encouraged entrepreneurs to spend aggressively to build market share before competitors could establish themselves. The logic was that customer acquisition costs would decline over time as brands became established and word-of-mouth marketing took effect.

The reality was far more complex. Many dot-com companies discovered that acquiring customers was expensive, but retaining them was even more challenging. Customer lifetime values often fell short of acquisition costs, creating a fundamental economic problem that no amount of additional funding could solve.

The IPO Machine

The public markets played a crucial role in perpetuating the dot-com boom. Investment banks, led by firms like Goldman Sachs, Morgan Stanley, and the boutique internet specialists at Robertson Stephens and Hambrecht & Quist, couldn't bring companies public fast enough to meet demand from individual and institutional investors.

The traditional requirements for going public, sustained profitability, proven business models, experienced management teams were relaxed or abandoned entirely for internet companies. Companies with minimal revenues and no profits were able to raise hundreds of millions of dollars in initial public offerings, creating instant paper wealth for their venture capital backers.

The IPO process itself became a marketing vehicle. Companies would embark on "roadshows" where they presented their vision to institutional investors across the country. These presentations often focused more on market opportunity and growth potential than on current financial performance. Phrases like "first-mover advantage," "network effects," and "viral marketing" became standard elements of every pitch deck.

The pop in stock prices on the first day of trading became a key metric of success. Companies whose stocks doubled or tripled on their first day of trading were celebrated in the business press, creating a self-reinforcing cycle that attracted even more capital to the sector.

Priceline.com exemplified both the promise and the peril of dot-com IPOs. The company, which allowed consumers to "name their own price" for airline tickets and hotel rooms, went public in March 1999 at $16 per share. The stock closed at $69 on its first day of trading, giving the company a market capitalization of nearly $10 billion, more than the combined value of Continental Airlines, Northwest Airlines, and US Airways.

The Venture Capital Feeding Frenzy

For venture capitalists, the late 1990s represented both unprecedented opportunity and unprecedented pressure. The traditional venture capital model of carefully nurturing companies over several years was being challenged by entrepreneurs who demanded faster decisions and larger initial investments.

Established firms like Kleiner Perkins, Sequoia Capital, and Benchmark Capital found themselves competing not just with each other, but with a new generation of venture funds created specifically to capitalize on the internet boom. Firms like Flatiron Partners in New York, Hummer Winblad in San Francisco, and Internet Capital Group in Philadelphia raised massive funds with the explicit goal of backing internet companies.

The competitive pressure led to a phenomenon known as "tourist investing," where venture capitalists would invest in deals outside their areas of expertise simply to gain exposure to the internet sector. Traditional enterprise software investors found themselves backing consumer e-commerce sites. Healthcare-focused funds invested in business-to-business marketplaces. The fear of missing out on the next Amazon or eBay drove otherwise rational investors to make increasingly speculative bets.

The speed of investment decisions accelerated dramatically. While traditional venture investments might take months of due diligence, internet deals were often completed in weeks or even days. Term sheets were issued based on PowerPoint presentations rather than detailed business plans. The mantra "ready, fire, aim" became an unofficial motto for many venture investors.

This urgency was driven partly by genuine competitive dynamics—truly innovative companies could be funded by competitors if existing investors moved too slowly. But it was also driven by the fear that the window of opportunity might close. Many venture capitalists believed they were witnessing a once-in-a-generation transformation and that normal investment processes were too slow to capitalize on the opportunity.

The Business Model Maze

One of the most striking aspects of the dot-com boom was the proliferation of business models that seemed to defy economic logic. Companies were valued based on their potential to "monetize" traffic or users at some undefined point in the future, even when the path to monetization was unclear.

The advertising-supported model dominated much of the consumer internet. Companies like TheGlobe.com, Geocities, and Tripod built large audiences of users who could create personal web pages, chat with friends, or access content. The theory was that these users represented valuable demographic data that could be sold to advertisers willing to pay premium rates for targeted online advertising.

The problem was that online advertising rates remained stubbornly low compared to traditional media, and users proved resistant to the banner advertisements and pop-ups that dominated early internet advertising. Companies that had projected millions in advertising revenue found themselves generating thousands.

Business-to-business marketplaces represented another popular model. Companies like VerticalNet, Commerce One, and Ariba promised to revolutionize how businesses bought and sold goods by creating online exchanges for everything from steel to chemicals to agricultural products. These "B2B" companies attracted massive venture investments based on projections that they would capture small percentages of enormous existing markets.

The reality proved more complex. Established business relationships, complex procurement processes, and industry-specific requirements made it difficult for generic online marketplaces to gain traction. Many B2B companies discovered that their target customers were satisfied with existing purchasing methods and saw little value in switching to online alternatives.

The subscription model showed more promise but faced its own challenges. Companies like Webvan and Kozmo.com attempted to create convenient delivery services for groceries and consumer goods. The unit economics were challenging, delivery costs often exceeded the gross profit on individual orders but investors hoped that scale and operational efficiency would eventually make these models profitable.

Spectacular Failures

The dot-com boom produced failures on a scale commensurate with its ambitions. These weren't quiet bankruptcies or modest write-offs, they were spectacular implosions that destroyed hundreds of millions of dollars in invested capital and became cautionary tales for future generations of entrepreneurs and investors.

Pets.com became the most notorious symbol of dot-com excess. Founded in 1998 to sell pet supplies online, the company raised over $82 million in venture capital and completed an IPO that valued the company at nearly $300 million. The company's sock puppet mascot became a cultural icon, appearing in Super Bowl commercials and even ringing the opening bell at the NASDAQ stock exchange.

But behind the marketing glitz, Pets.com faced fundamental business model problems. The company was selling low-margin products (pet food, toys) that were expensive to ship relative to their value. Customer acquisition costs were astronomical, the company was spending $82 to acquire each customer who generated an average of only $24 in gross profit. When the public markets turned against internet stocks in early 2000, Pets.com couldn't raise additional capital and liquidated in November 2000, just nine months after its IPO.

Webvan represented an even more ambitious failure. The online grocery delivery company raised over $800 million from investors including Kleiner Perkins, Sequoia Capital, and Goldman Sachs. The company's vision was compelling: consumers could order groceries online and have them delivered within a 30-minute window of their choosing.

To execute this vision, Webvan built enormous automated warehouses and hired thousands of employees. The company went public in 1999 with a market capitalization of over $1 billion and announced plans to expand to 26 cities within two years. But the unit economics never worked. The cost of building infrastructure, hiring employees, and delivering orders exceeded the gross profit margins on grocery sales. When the company finally shut down in July 2001, it had burned through nearly $1 billion in capital.

Kozmo.com offered an even more extreme version of convenience. The company promised to deliver everything from movies to ice cream to electronics within one hour in major cities, with no delivery fees and no minimum orders. The service was popular with consumers, particularly in urban areas like Manhattan but the business model was fundamentally flawed. The company was losing money on every delivery, hoping to make it up through volume and eventual scale efficiencies that never materialized.

These failures weren't isolated incidents but symptoms of a broader problem with dot-com business models. Many companies were attempting to use technology to solve problems that customers didn't know they had, or to improve processes that weren't actually broken. The convenience of online ordering was often offset by longer delivery times, higher costs, or reduced selection compared to traditional alternatives.

The B2B Bubble Within the Bubble

While consumer-focused dot-coms attracted the most media attention, some of the largest venture investments during the boom went to business-to-business companies that promised to revolutionize how corporations operated. These B2B companies often had more defensible business models than their consumer counterparts, but they also faced unique challenges.

Commerce One, which went public in 1999, created software platforms that enabled companies to conduct procurement activities online. The company's vision was that businesses would replace their manual purchasing processes with automated systems that could source suppliers, negotiate prices, and execute transactions electronically. At its peak, Commerce One had a market capitalization of over $21 billion.

The company's downfall came from a combination of factors. The enterprise sales cycle proved longer than expected, as large corporations were reluctant to change established procurement processes. The implementation costs were high, and the return on investment was often unclear. When the dot-com crash reduced corporate technology spending, Commerce One's pipeline of potential customers evaporated.

Ariba, another procurement software company, followed a similar trajectory. The company went public in 1999 and reached a market capitalization of over $40 billion at its peak. But like Commerce One, Ariba discovered that changing corporate behavior was more difficult than changing consumer behavior. The company survived the crash by refocusing on a smaller set of core products and customers, but its valuation fell by over 99% from its peak.

The B2B marketplace companies faced even greater challenges. Ventures like VerticalNet attempted to create online exchanges for specific industries, taking small commissions on transactions between buyers and sellers. The theory was that these marketplaces would increase efficiency by providing better price discovery and reducing transaction costs.

In practice, many industries already had efficient distribution mechanisms that provided value beyond simple price matching. Relationships, credit terms, technical support, and other services were often more important than getting the lowest possible price. Online marketplaces found it difficult to replicate these value-added services, and many buyers and sellers preferred to stick with established partners.

International Expansion and Global Mania

The dot-com boom wasn't limited to the United States. American venture capital firms expanded internationally, and local venture ecosystems emerged in Europe, Asia, and other regions. This globalization of the internet investment thesis created both opportunities and additional complexity.

In Europe, companies like Boo.com and LetsBuyIt.com raised hundreds of millions of dollars to create online fashion and group purchasing sites. Boo.com, backed by investors including LVMH and J.P. Morgan, spent over $130 million in eighteen months attempting to create a global online fashion retailer. The company's ambitious technology platform and international expansion proved too expensive to sustain, and it shut down in May 2000.

In Asia, the internet boom took on different characteristics but produced similar excesses. Companies like China.com and Pacific Century CyberWorks commanded enormous valuations based on their potential to serve the massive Chinese and Asian markets. However, the infrastructure and regulatory environment in many Asian countries wasn't ready to support the business models these companies were attempting to execute.

The globalization of dot-com investing also created arbitrage opportunities and increased complexity for venture investors. Companies could shop for capital across multiple markets, playing American venture capitalists against European or Asian investors. This competition drove up valuations and reduced the leverage that individual investors had in structuring deals.

The Role of Investment Banks

Investment banks played a crucial enabling role in the dot-com boom, serving as both advisors to companies and distributors of stock to public investors. The traditional gatekeeping function that investment banks had historically served, ensuring that only viable companies went public was largely abandoned in favor of maximizing deal volume and fees.

The lead underwriters for internet IPOs, Goldman Sachs, Morgan Stanley, Credit Suisse First Boston, and the boutique technology banks developed specialized internet banking groups that could process companies through the IPO pipeline with unprecedented speed. The roadshow process was streamlined, regulatory requirements were minimized, and the typical waiting period between filing and pricing was compressed.

This efficiency came at a cost. Many companies went public before they had proven their business models or achieved sustainable operations. The prospectuses for internet IPOs contained increasingly prominent risk disclosures, but these warnings were often ignored by investors caught up in the excitement of potential returns.

The investment banks also played a role in perpetuating unsustainable valuations through their research coverage. Internet analysts like Mary Meeker at Morgan Stanley and Henry Blodget at Merrill Lynch became celebrities in their own right, with their stock recommendations moving markets and their research reports serving as validation for both companies and investors.

The conflicts of interest were obvious but widely ignored during the boom. Investment banks were earning enormous fees from underwriting IPOs and follow-on offerings, while their research analysts were expected to provide objective analysis of the same companies. The pressure to maintain positive relationships with corporate clients made it difficult for analysts to issue negative recommendations, even when companies were clearly overvalued.

Lessons in Market Timing and Business Model Validation

The dot-com boom provided valuable lessons about the importance of market timing and business model validation, though these lessons would only become clear in retrospect. Many of the ideas pursued during the boom were fundamentally sound, they were simply too early for the market conditions that existed at the time.

Online grocery delivery, for example, made perfect sense in theory. Consumers would benefit from the convenience of shopping from home, and retailers would benefit from reduced real estate costs and more efficient inventory management. Companies like Webvan and Peapod raised hundreds of millions of dollars to execute this vision.

The problem wasn't the vision, it was the timing. In 1999, internet penetration was still limited, consumer comfort with online commerce was nascent, and the logistics infrastructure required to support efficient delivery didn't exist. Twenty years later, companies like Instacart, Amazon Fresh, and DoorDash would successfully implement similar models, benefiting from higher internet adoption, better logistics technology, and changed consumer behavior.

Similarly, the idea of online marketplaces for business-to-business commerce was prescient. Companies like Alibaba would eventually build massive B2B platforms that transformed global trade. But the early B2B marketplace companies like Commerce One and Ariba were attempting to change entrenched corporate behaviors without offering compelling enough value propositions to overcome switching costs.

The dot-com boom also demonstrated the danger of assuming that all internet businesses would exhibit network effects and winner-take-all dynamics. While this was true for some categories, search engines, social networks, and certain marketplaces it wasn't true for others. Online pet supplies, for example, didn't become more valuable as more people used the service. There were no meaningful network effects, and customers had little loyalty to specific brands.

The Venture Capital Industry's Response

As valuations soared and competition intensified, different venture capital firms responded in different ways. Some embraced the new paradigm wholeheartedly, raising larger funds and making bigger initial investments.

Others remained skeptical of the valuations and business models they were seeing and reduced their activity in internet investing.

Kleiner Perkins, led by John Doerr, was one of the most aggressive investors in internet companies. The firm's portfolio included Amazon, Netscape, Excite@Home, and dozens of other internet ventures. Doerr became the face of Silicon Valley's internet boom, preaching the gospel of "get big fast" and encouraging entrepreneurs to think globally from day one.

Sequoia Capital, under the leadership of Mike Moritz and Don Valentine, was more selective but still made significant investments in internet companies including Yahoo!, Google (though that investment came later), and PayPal. The firm's approach emphasized the importance of exceptional founding teams and sustainable competitive advantages, even in the fast-moving internet sector.

Some firms, however, remained skeptical of the internet boom. Warren Buffett famously avoided technology investments during this period, arguing that he couldn't understand the businesses or predict their long-term prospects. Similarly, some venture capital firms reduced their internet investing or focused on more traditional technology categories.

The firms that remained disciplined during the boom years often outperformed in the long run, though they suffered from short-term underperformance as their more aggressive competitors reported spectacular returns on paper. The challenge for venture investors was distinguishing between sustainable businesses and unsustainable bubbles in real time, when the ultimate outcomes were still uncertain.

The Psychology of Bubbles

The dot-com boom provided a real-time case study in bubble psychology and the behavioral factors that drive speculative manias. The combination of technological change, easy capital, and social validation created conditions where normal risk assessment processes broke down.

The "fear of missing out" (FOMO) was perhaps the most powerful psychological driver of the boom. Investors who had missed earlier technology waves were determined not to miss the internet revolution. This fear was amplified by the very public success stories of early internet investors and the equally public ridicule of skeptics who questioned internet valuations.

Social proof played a crucial role as well. When respected venture capitalists like John Doerr and Mike Moritz were making large investments in internet companies, it became easier for other investors to justify similar investments. The presence of prestigious investors in funding rounds served as a form of validation that reduced perceived risk.

The availability heuristic, the tendency to overweight recent, memorable examples also contributed to bubble psychology. The success stories of Amazon, eBay, and Yahoo! were widely publicized and discussed, while the failures of earlier internet companies were forgotten or dismissed as execution problems rather than fundamental business model issues.

Perhaps most importantly, the normal feedback mechanisms that might have corrected investor behavior were delayed or distorted. Public market valuations continued to rise throughout the boom, providing positive reinforcement for venture investment decisions. The ultimate test of business model viability, sustainable profitability was pushed into the future, allowing unsustainable companies to continue raising capital.

Setting the Stage for Crash

By early 2000, several warning signs were becoming apparent to careful observers. The number of internet IPOs had reached unsustainable levels, with companies going public at earlier and earlier stages of development.

Many public internet companies were burning through cash at alarming rates with no clear path to profitability.

The competition for deals had driven venture capital valuations to unprecedented levels. Companies that might have been valued at $10 million in earlier eras were raising initial venture rounds at $50 million or $100 million valuations. The mathematical reality was that very few companies would be able to justify these valuations through their ultimate exit values.

The infrastructure investments that had enabled the internet boom were also creating oversupply in many categories. Telecommunications companies had installed far more fiber optic capacity than could be utilized in the near term. Data centers were being built faster than demand was growing. The supply of internet infrastructure was outpacing demand, creating deflationary pressure on the costs of internet services.

Most ominously, the Federal Reserve had begun raising interest rates in response to concerns about inflation and economic overheating. Higher interest rates made alternative investments more attractive compared to speculative technology stocks, and they increased the discount rates used to value future cash flows, a particular problem for companies that were promising profits years in the future.

The stage was set for a dramatic correction. The only question was what would serve as the catalyst for the broader market realization that many internet companies were fundamentally overvalued. That catalyst would come in March 2000, when the NASDAQ composite index would peak at over 5,000 before beginning a devastating decline that would ultimately wipe out trillions of dollars in market value.

The dot-com boom had demonstrated both the transformative power of venture capital and its potential for destructive excess. The companies that emerged from this period, Amazon, eBay, Google, and others would indeed change the world. But the path to that transformation would be littered with the wreckage of hundreds of companies that promised similar impact but failed to deliver sustainable business models.

The lessons from this period would reshape venture capital for the next decade, leading to more disciplined investment practices, greater emphasis on business model validation, and more realistic expectations about the timeline required to build transformative companies. But those lessons would only be learned after the industry survived the coming crash, a correction so severe that it would test the very foundations of the venture capital model itself.

Chapter 12

Crash and Recovery

"When the tide goes out, you see who's been swimming naked."

Warren Buffett's famous observation would prove prophetic as the new millennium dawned. After years of unprecedented growth and speculation, the venture capital industry was about to face its most severe test since its inception. What began as a gradual cooling in public market sentiment would evolve into a complete collapse of confidence in internet and technology companies, wiping out trillions of dollars in market value and forcing a fundamental reassessment of business models, valuations, and investment strategies.

The crash that began in March 2000 would last nearly three years, destroying not just paper wealth but entire companies, careers, and the venture capital industry's carefully cultivated mythology of inevitable success. Yet from this devastation would emerge a more mature, disciplined, and ultimately more successful venture capital ecosystem, one that had learned hard lessons about market timing, business fundamentals, and the dangers of speculative excess.

The Beginning of the End

The NASDAQ Composite Index reached its all-time high of 5,048.62 on March 10, 2000. It was a Friday, and the market seemed to be celebrating another week of technology stock gains. That weekend, few investors could have imagined that they had just witnessed the peak of the greatest speculative bubble in technology investing history.

The initial trigger for the crash was surprisingly mundane. On March 13, 2000, just three days after the peak, a federal judge ruled that Microsoft had violated antitrust laws, a decision that sent shockwaves through the technology sector. While Microsoft had been battling the Department of Justice for years, the ruling crystallized growing concerns about regulatory scrutiny of technology companies and their business models.

But the Microsoft ruling was merely the match that lit a much larger powder keg. The fuel had been accumulating for months as warning signs mounted. The Federal Reserve had raised interest rates six times between June 1999 and May 2000, making risk-free investments more attractive and increasing the discount rates used to value future cash flows, a particular problem for companies promising profits years in the future.

More fundamentally, many public internet companies were beginning to report quarterly results that fell short of the optimistic projections that had supported their sky-high valuations. The gap between promise and reality was becoming impossible to ignore, even for the most enthusiastic technology investors.

The sell-off began gradually. The NASDAQ fell 4% on March 13, then another 3.2% the following day. For investors who had grown accustomed to viewing any decline as a buying opportunity, these initial drops seemed like typical market volatility. But as days turned to weeks, it became clear that something more fundamental was happening.

By April 14, 2000, exactly five weeks after the peak, the NASDAQ had fallen 34%, the fastest decline from a market peak in the index's history. Technology stocks were being indiscriminately sold regardless of their individual fundamentals. Companies with strong balance sheets and growing revenues fell alongside speculative startups with no clear path to profitability.

The Domino Effect

The public market crash quickly cascaded through the venture capital ecosystem. Companies that had been preparing for IPOs found that the public markets had effectively closed to all but the most profitable technology companies. The IPO pipeline, which had been the primary exit mechanism for venture-backed companies, suddenly dried up.

This created an immediate crisis for venture capitalists and their portfolio companies. The venture capital model depended on regular exits through IPOs and acquisitions to generate returns and free up capital for new investments. When the IPO market closed, it created a bottleneck that affected every aspect of the venture ecosystem.

Companies that had raised money with the expectation of going public within 12-18 months found themselves trapped in private markets with valuations that no longer reflected public market realities. Many had business models that required continuous capital infusions to support growth, and their burn rates were predicated on the assumption that additional funding would be readily available.

The psychology of venture investing changed overnight. Investors who had been competing aggressively for deals suddenly became highly selective. The "spray and pray" investment strategies that had characterized the boom years were replaced by intense scrutiny of business models, unit economics, and paths to profitability.

Perhaps most tellingly, the vocabulary of venture capital began to change. Terms like "runway" (how long a company's cash would last at current burn rates) and "bridge financing" (short-term funding to extend runway) entered the mainstream venture lexicon. The optimistic mantras of the boom, "get big fast" and "revenue doesn't matter" were replaced by more sober assessments focused on fundamentals.

Portfolio Company Carnage

For venture capitalists, the crash wasn't just about declining portfolio valuations, it was about watching portfolio companies fail in real time. Companies that had seemed promising just months earlier were suddenly unable to raise additional capital and were forced to shut down or dramatically restructure their operations.

The statistics were sobering. Of the 457 internet companies that went public between 1995 and 2000, more than half would ultimately fail or be acquired at prices below their IPO valuations. Many of the high-profile venture-backed companies that had symbolized the boom would not survive the crash.

Pets.com, perhaps the most iconic symbol of dot-com excess, shut down in November 2000 after burning through $300 million in funding. The company's sock puppet mascot, which had appeared in Super Bowl commercials and become a cultural phenomenon, was sold at liquidation along with the company's other assets. For venture investors, Pets.com represented everything that had gone wrong during the boom: a fundamentally flawed business model, excessive marketing spending, and valuations that bore no relationship to economic reality.

Webvan's collapse was even more spectacular. The online grocery delivery company had raised nearly $800 million from investors including Kleiner Perkins, Sequoia Capital, and Goldman Sachs. At its peak, the company was valued at over $1 billion and operated in multiple cities with plans for aggressive expansion.

But Webvan's unit economics never made sense. The company was losing money on every delivery while spending hundreds of millions on automated warehouses and logistics infrastructure. When the public markets crashed and additional capital became unavailable, Webvan quickly burned through its remaining cash. The company shut down in July 2001, laying off 2,000 employees and leaving customers with unused credits and venture investors with total losses.

The casualties weren't limited to consumer internet companies. Business-to-business companies, which had been considered more defensible during the boom, also faced severe challenges. Commerce One, which had reached a market capitalization of over $21 billion at its peak, saw its value collapse as corporate customers delayed technology purchases and questioned the value proposition of online procurement systems.

VerticalNet, which operated online marketplaces for various industries, faced similar challenges. The company had gone public in 1999 and used its high stock price to acquire dozens of smaller companies in a roll-up strategy. But when the crash hit, the underlying business model proved unsustainable. The company's advertising revenues collapsed, and many of the marketplaces it operated failed to gain traction with industry participants.

The Death of Easy Money

One of the most immediate and dramatic changes following the crash was the end of easy capital for startups. During the boom years, promising companies had been able to raise multiple rounds of financing in rapid succession, often at increasing valuations. This abundance of capital had allowed companies to experiment with business models, invest heavily in customer acquisition, and delay difficult decisions about profitability.

The crash changed all of that. Venture capitalists became much more selective about new investments and much more demanding about the terms of those investments. Valuations fell dramatically across all sectors and stages of investment. Companies that might have commanded $100 million valuations in 1999 were struggling to raise money at $10 million valuations in 2001.

The shift wasn't just about valuation levels, it was about the entire approach to building companies. The "get big fast" mentality was replaced by an emphasis on capital efficiency and sustainable growth. Venture investors began demanding that companies demonstrate unit economics and paths to profitability before investing additional capital.

This new discipline had profound effects on how startups operated. Marketing budgets were slashed, hiring was frozen or reversed, and companies were forced to focus on core products and services rather than expansive visions of market domination. The freewheeling culture of many dot-com companies was replaced by a more sober, metrics-driven approach to business building.

The changes were particularly dramatic in Silicon Valley, where the boom had created a culture of excess that extended far beyond the workplace. The expensive restaurants, lavish parties, and conspicuous consumption that had characterized the boom years quickly disappeared. Office buildings that had commanded premium rents sat partially vacant as companies downsized or shut down entirely.

Venture Capital Firm Struggles

The crash didn't just affect portfolio companies, it also created existential challenges for venture capital firms themselves. The industry's business model was predicated on generating returns through exits, and when the exit markets closed, it created a cascade of problems for venture investors.

The most immediate challenge was the marking down of portfolio valuations. Venture firms are required to provide periodic valuations of their investments to their limited partners, and the public market crash made it impossible to maintain the optimistic valuations that had characterized the boom years. Firms that had reported spectacular paper returns in 1999 were forced to write down their portfolios by 50%, 70%, or even more.

These write-downs had several effects. First, they reduced the management fees that venture firms could charge, since these fees were often calculated as a percentage of assets under management. Second, they made it more difficult to raise new funds, since limited partners could see the unrealized losses in existing funds. Third, they created psychological stress for venture partners who had never experienced losses of this magnitude.

The fund-raising environment for venture capital firms became dramatically more challenging. During the boom years, successful venture firms had been able to raise larger and larger funds with relative ease. Limited partners, pension funds, endowments, and wealthy individuals had been eager to increase their allocations to venture capital based on the spectacular returns of the 1990s.

After the crash, limited partners became much more selective. Many had their own portfolios decimated by the technology stock collapse and were in no position to make new venture capital commitments. Others became skeptical about the venture capital asset class entirely, questioning whether the returns of the 1990s had been sustainable or merely the result of a speculative bubble.

The result was a dramatic contraction in venture capital fundraising. According to the National Venture Capital Association, the industry raised $100 billion across all funds in 2000, the peak year for fundraising. By 2002, that figure had fallen to $21 billion, a decline of nearly 80%. Many established firms found themselves unable to raise follow-on funds, and dozens of venture firms shut down entirely.

Industry Consolidation and Strategy Refinement

The crash forced a fundamental reassessment of venture capital strategy and operations. Firms that survived the downturn did so by adapting their investment approaches, refining their portfolio management practices, and returning to the fundamental principles that had made venture capital successful in earlier eras.

One of the most significant changes was a return to stage-appropriate investing. During the boom, the lines between seed, early-stage, and late-stage investing had become blurred as firms competed for deals at every stage. After the crash, firms became more disciplined about focusing on their areas of expertise and competitive advantage.

Kleiner Perkins, which had been one of the most aggressive investors during the boom, refined its strategy to focus more heavily on companies with proven business models and experienced management teams. The firm's partners became more hands-on with portfolio companies, providing operational guidance and helping companies navigate the challenging post-crash environment.

Sequoia Capital, led by Mike Moritz and Don Valentine, had remained relatively disciplined during the boom and was better positioned to weather the crash. The firm used the downturn as an opportunity to invest in high-quality companies at attractive valuations, including Google, which would become one of the most successful venture investments of all time.

New firms also emerged during this period with investment strategies specifically designed for the post-crash environment. Firms like Foundry Group and First Round Capital were created by veteran investors who believed that the crash had created opportunities to build great companies with less capital and more disciplined approaches.

The crash also led to innovations in venture capital operations. Firms began investing more heavily in portfolio services, operational support for their companies that went beyond just providing capital. This included recruiting services, business development support, financial planning assistance, and strategic guidance.

The concept of "venture debt" also gained traction during this period. Companies like Silicon Valley Bank and Square 1 Bank began providing debt financing to venture-backed companies as an alternative to equity financing. This allowed companies to extend their runway without diluting existing shareholders and provided venture firms with more flexibility in managing their portfolios.

The Long Road Back

The recovery from the crash was neither quick nor uniform. While the public markets began to stabilize in 2002 and 2003, the venture capital ecosystem took much longer to recover. The combination of reduced fundraising, portfolio company struggles, and limited exit opportunities created a challenging environment that persisted for several years.

The IPO market remained effectively closed to all but the most profitable technology companies for nearly three years. Companies that had been preparing to go public in 2000 found themselves waiting until 2003 or 2004 for market conditions to improve. This extended timeline put pressure on both companies and their investors, as cash reserves dwindled and growth strategies had to be repeatedly revised.

The acquisition market provided some relief, but at much lower valuations than had been typical during the boom. Strategic acquirers became much more selective and price-sensitive, focusing on companies with clear strategic value rather than speculative growth potential. Many acquisitions during this period were effectively rescue transactions, allowing companies to avoid bankruptcy but providing minimal returns to investors.

Despite these challenges, some companies and investors found opportunities in the post-crash environment. The reduced competition for deals meant that high-quality companies could be funded at attractive valuations. The focus on fundamentals led to the creation of more sustainable businesses with clearer paths to profitability.

Companies like Google, which was founded in 1998 but didn't go public until 2004, benefited from the more disciplined investment environment. The company was able to focus on building a sustainable business model, advertising-supported search without the pressure to pursue rapid expansion at the expense of profitability.

Similarly, companies in sectors that had been overlooked during the internet boom began to attract venture investment. Clean technology, biotechnology, and enterprise software companies found it easier to compete for investor attention once the internet sector was no longer dominating the venture capital landscape.

Lessons Learned and New Principles

The crash and subsequent recovery period forced the venture capital industry to confront fundamental questions about investment strategy, risk management, and business model validation. The lessons learned during this period would shape venture capital practices for the next decade and beyond.

Perhaps the most important lesson was the danger of ignoring business fundamentals in favor of growth metrics. The boom years had created a culture where revenue growth, user acquisition, and market share were valued above profitability and sustainable competitive advantages. The crash demonstrated that companies without viable paths to profitability were ultimately unsustainable, regardless of their growth rates or market positions.

This led to a renewed emphasis on unit economics, the fundamental math underlying each customer relationship or transaction. Venture investors became much more focused on metrics like customer acquisition cost, lifetime value, gross margins, and payback periods. Companies were expected to demonstrate that they could generate more value from each customer than it cost to acquire and serve that customer.

The importance of capital efficiency also became clear. During the boom, many companies had raised large amounts of capital with the assumption that more funding would always be available. The crash demonstrated that capital markets could close quickly and unpredictably, making it essential for companies to achieve sustainability before running out of money.

This led to the popularization of concepts like "minimum viable product" and "lean startup methodology," though these terms wouldn't become widespread until later in the decade. The underlying principle, that companies should test and validate their business models with minimal capital before scaling became central to post-crash venture investing.

Risk management also became more sophisticated. Venture firms began to pay more attention to portfolio construction, diversification across sectors and stages, and the timing of investments relative to market cycles. The boom years had taught investors that even the most promising sectors could experience severe downturns, making diversification essential for long-term success.

The Role of Limited Partners

The crash had profound effects on the limited partners who provided capital to venture funds. Pension funds, endowments, and other institutional investors had significantly increased their allocations to venture capital during the 1990s based on the strong returns the asset class had generated. The crash forced these investors to reassess both their venture capital allocations and their selection criteria for venture fund investments.

Many limited partners found that their venture capital investments, which they had hoped would provide diversification from public market volatility, were actually highly correlated with public technology stocks. The crash demonstrated that venture capital was not immune to broader market cycles and that the illiquidity of venture investments could actually make them riskier than public market alternatives during downturns.

This realization led to several changes in how limited partners approached venture capital investing. First, many reduced their overall allocations to the asset class, recognizing that the extraordinary returns of the 1990s were unlikely to be sustainable. Second, they became much more selective about which venture firms they would back, focusing on firms with long track records and disciplined investment approaches.

Third, limited partners began to demand more transparency and accountability from venture firms. The boom years had created a seller's market where successful venture firms could dictate terms to their investors. After the crash, the balance of power shifted somewhat back toward limited partners, who began negotiating for better terms and more extensive reporting requirements.

The crash also led to innovations in limited partner strategies. Some institutional investors began making direct investments in companies alongside venture funds, allowing them to have more control over their venture exposure. Others began investing in secondary markets, purchasing existing venture fund stakes from other investors who needed liquidity.

Regulatory and Tax Implications

The crash had significant regulatory and tax implications that would affect the venture capital industry for years to come. The Sarbanes-Oxley Act, passed in 2002 in response to corporate scandals at companies like Enron and WorldCom, created new compliance requirements that made going public more expensive and time-consuming for venture-backed companies.

These new requirements particularly affected smaller companies that were typical IPO candidates from the venture capital world. The additional costs and complexity of Sarbanes-Oxley compliance created a higher bar for going public, which contributed to the longer timeline for venture-backed companies to achieve liquidity.

Tax policy also became more important as the industry worked to recover from the crash. The capital gains tax treatment of venture investments remained favorable, but there were ongoing policy debates about whether this treatment was appropriate given the losses that many investors had experienced.

The crash also highlighted the importance of carried interest taxation, which allowed venture capital partners to treat their share of fund profits as capital gains rather than ordinary income. This tax treatment became more controversial as the public became more aware of the wealth that had been created (and destroyed) in the venture capital industry.

Technology Evolution During the Recovery

While the crash was devastating for many internet and technology companies, the underlying technology trends that had driven the boom continued to evolve during the recovery period. This technological progress would ultimately create the foundation for the next wave of venture capital investment and company creation.

Broadband internet adoption accelerated during this period, creating better infrastructure for internet-based services. The cost of computing power continued to decline following Moore's Law, making it cheaper for startups to build technology products. Open-source software became more prevalent, reducing the cost of software development.

Perhaps most importantly, the crash cleared away many of the marginal companies that had been consuming market attention and resources during the boom. This allowed genuinely innovative companies to gain market traction without competing against dozens of well-funded but poorly conceived competitors.

Companies like Google, which had been founded during the boom but refined their business models during the crash, were able to emerge from the downturn as dominant market leaders. The company's focus on algorithmic search and advertising-supported business models proved to be much more sustainable than many of the e-commerce and content strategies that had dominated the boom years.

The Psychology of Recovery

The psychological aspects of the crash and recovery were as important as the financial and strategic elements. The venture capital industry, which had grown accustomed to success and positive media coverage during the boom years, had to adapt to a new environment characterized by skepticism, scrutiny, and much more modest expectations.

This psychological adjustment was particularly challenging for venture capitalists who had entered the industry during the boom years and had never experienced a prolonged downturn. Many young partners who had been celebrated as visionaries during the boom found themselves questioned and criticized as their portfolio companies failed or struggled.

The industry's relationship with entrepreneurs also changed. During the boom, venture capitalists had been courted by entrepreneurs who had multiple funding options and significant leverage in negotiations. After the crash, the balance of power shifted dramatically. Entrepreneurs found themselves competing for limited capital and accepting terms that would have been unthinkable during the boom years.

This shift in psychology had long-term benefits for the industry. It forced both venture capitalists and entrepreneurs to focus more heavily on building sustainable businesses rather than chasing market trends or pursuing growth at any cost. The discipline imposed by the crash created a foundation for more sustainable growth in subsequent years.

Setting the Stage for Renaissance

By 2003, the worst of the crash was behind the venture capital industry, though the recovery would continue for several more years. The combination of reduced competition, disciplined investment approaches, and improving technology infrastructure was creating conditions for a new wave of innovation and investment.

The companies that emerged from the crash, Google, PayPal, Salesforce.com, and others would prove that the internet revolution was far from over. These companies had learned the lessons of the crash and built sustainable business models that could thrive even in challenging market conditions.

The venture capital firms that survived the crash were also stronger and more disciplined than their predecessors. They had learned hard lessons about risk management, portfolio construction, and business model validation that would serve them well in future investment cycles.

Perhaps most importantly, the crash had reset expectations about what venture capital could and should achieve. The unrealistic expectations of the boom years, that every investment would generate spectacular returns and that growth was always preferable to profitability had been replaced by a more mature understanding of the challenges and opportunities in building transformative companies.

The stage was set for what would become known as the "Web 2.0" era, a period of renewed innovation and investment that would be characterized by more sustainable business models, better technology infrastructure, and more disciplined approaches to company building. The crash had been devastating, but it had also cleared the way for a more mature and ultimately more successful venture capital ecosystem.

The lessons learned during the crash and recovery would prove invaluable as the industry entered its next phase of growth. The companies and investors who had survived the downturn would be better equipped to navigate future challenges and build lasting value in an increasingly complex and competitive technology landscape.

Part V: The Modern Era (2000s-Present)

Chapter 13

Google's Algorithm for Success

"We want to build technology that everybody loves using, and that affects everyone. We want to create beautiful, intuitive services and technologies that are so incredibly useful that people use them twice a day. Like they use a toothbrush. There aren't that many things people use twice a day."

Larry Page's ambitious vision, articulated in the early days of Google, seemed almost impossibly grandiose to venture capitalists who had just witnessed the spectacular collapse of the dot-com bubble. Yet this audacious goal, to create technology as essential as a toothbrush would prove prophetic. Google wouldn't just survive the post-crash environment; it would emerge as the defining success story of venture capital's recovery, demonstrating that transformative companies could still be built even in the ruins of the internet bubble.

The Google story represents venture capital at its finest: patient capital supporting brilliant entrepreneurs who were solving real problems with innovative technology. But it also illustrates the challenges of timing, market development, and the delicate balance between vision and execution that separates world-changing companies from well-intentioned failures.

Academic Origins and the PageRank Revolution

The Google story began not in a garage or dorm room, but in the halls of Stanford University's computer science department. Larry Page arrived at Stanford in 1995 as a doctoral student with an unconventional background, his father was a computer science professor at Michigan State, and Page had grown up immersed in the early culture of computing and artificial intelligence.

Page's dissertation advisor, Terry Winograd, encouraged him to explore the emerging World Wide Web as a research topic. This was prescient timing: the web was growing explosively, but the existing tools for finding information were primitive and increasingly inadequate. Popular search engines like AltaVista, Excite, and Lycos relied primarily on keyword matching and were easily manipulated by website owners who wanted to game the system.

Page's insight was borrowed from academic citation analysis. Just as the importance of academic papers could be measured by how often other papers cited them, the importance of web pages could be measured by how many other pages linked to them. But Page's algorithm, which he initially called BackRub, was more sophisticated than simple link counting. It weighted links based on the importance of the linking page, a link from a highly-regarded site was worth more than a link from an obscure one.

The mathematical elegance of this approach was undeniable, but it required enormous computational resources. Analyzing the link structure of the entire web and calculating the relative importance of billions of pages was a massive undertaking that pushed the limits of available technology. Page and his collaborator Sergey Brin, a fellow Stanford PhD student who brought expertise in data mining and pattern recognition, spent months building the infrastructure needed to implement their vision.

The results were remarkable. Their search engine, which they named Google after the mathematical term "googol" (representing a 1 followed by 100 zeros), returned dramatically more relevant results than existing alternatives. Users who tried Google often had the same reaction: amazement at how much better it was at finding what they were actually looking for.

The Venture Capital Courtship

By 1998, Page and Brin faced a crucial decision. Their search engine was gaining popularity among Stanford students and faculty, but scaling it to serve the entire web would require significant capital investment. The server farm they had cobbled together in their dorm rooms was already straining Stanford's network capacity, and university administrators were beginning to ask pointed questions about their commercial activities.

The timing seemed inauspicious for raising venture capital. The dot-com boom was still in full swing, but search engines were considered a mature category with several well-funded incumbents. Yahoo!, the most valuable internet company, had started as a directory service but was positioning itself as a media company rather than focusing on search technology. Other search engines were pursuing advertising-supported models with mixed success.

More fundamentally, it wasn't clear that search could be a standalone business. Most observers saw search as a commodity service, important for attracting users to websites, but not valuable enough to support independent companies. The prevailing wisdom was that search would eventually be integrated into larger internet portals or provided free as a loss-leader service.

Page and Brin initially tried to license their technology to existing companies rather than start their own venture. They approached Yahoo!, Excite, and other internet companies with offers to sell or license PageRank. The response was lukewarm at best. Yahoo!'s executives were focused on building a media company and saw search as just one of many services they offered. Excite's leadership was similarly uninterested in dramatically improving their search technology.

This rejection forced Page and Brin to consider starting their own company. But they were academics, not entrepreneurs, and the prospect of leaving their doctoral programs to start a business was daunting. They began reaching out to the Stanford network of entrepreneurs and investors for advice on how to proceed.

Andy Bechtolsheim's Prescient Investment

The breakthrough came through Stanford's entrepreneurial ecosystem. Page and Brin were introduced to Andy Bechtolsheim, the co-founder of Sun Microsystems and a legendary figure in Silicon Valley. Bechtolsheim had a reputation for quickly identifying promising technologies and had made several successful angel investments in Stanford spin-offs.

The meeting took place in August 1998 on the front porch of Stanford faculty member David Cheriton's home. Page and Brin gave Bechtolsheim a demonstration of their search engine, showing how it could find relevant information faster and more accurately than existing alternatives. Bechtolsheim immediately grasped the significance of what he was seeing.

After a brief discussion about the technology and market opportunity, Bechtolsheim made a decision that would become legendary in venture capital circles. He wrote a check for $100,000 made out to "Google Inc.", even though the company didn't yet legally exist. This investment, completed in less than an hour without due diligence or formal documentation, demonstrated the kind of quick decision-making and technical insight that characterized the best angel investors.

Bechtolsheim's investment served multiple purposes beyond providing capital. It gave Page and Brin external validation that their technology was commercially viable. It forced them to actually incorporate their company and begin thinking seriously about business strategy. Most importantly, it connected them to Silicon Valley's network of investors and entrepreneurs who could help them scale their vision.

The Kleiner Perkins and Sequoia Partnership

Bechtolsheim's investment opened doors to institutional venture capital, but Google's founders faced a unique challenge: the two most prestigious venture capital firms in Silicon Valley, Kleiner Perkins and Sequoia Capital, were both interested in leading the company's first institutional round. Rather than choosing between them, Page and Brin proposed something unprecedented: a co-investment where both firms would participate equally.

This decision reflected both naivety and sophistication. It was naive because it meant Google would have twice as many board members and potentially conflicting strategic advice. But it was sophisticated because it gave the company access to the combined networks, expertise, and credibility of Silicon Valley's two most successful venture firms.

John Doerr from Kleiner Perkins and Mike Moritz from Sequoia Capital initially resisted the co-investment structure. Both firms preferred to lead investments and control board dynamics. But the quality of Google's technology and the founders' determination eventually convinced them to accept the unusual arrangement.

The $25 million Series A round was completed in June 1999, valuing Google at approximately $100 million. This was a substantial valuation for a company with minimal revenue, but it reflected the investors' belief that Google's superior search technology could eventually be monetized at scale.

The involvement of Kleiner Perkins and Sequoia brought more than just capital. Both firms had extensive experience helping technology companies navigate growth challenges, recruit executive talent, and develop business strategies. This would prove crucial as Google faced the complex challenge of building a sustainable business model around search.

The Business Model Evolution

When Google raised its venture capital, the company's business model was far from clear. Search engines in 1999 typically made money through banner advertising, licensing deals, or by charging users for premium services. None of these models seemed particularly well-suited to Google's approach, which emphasized clean, fast, and uncluttered search results.

The breakthrough came from an unlikely source: a small company called GoTo.com (later renamed Overture) that had pioneered paid search advertising. GoTo's model was simple: advertisers could bid for keywords, and their ads would appear when users searched for those terms. The highest bidders got the most prominent placement.

Page and Brin initially resisted this model. They were concerned that paid advertising would compromise the integrity of their search results and create conflicts between user interests and advertiser demands. Their academic backgrounds had instilled a commitment to providing the most relevant results possible, regardless of commercial considerations.

However, the realities of business eventually forced them to reconsider. Google was burning through cash rapidly as it scaled its infrastructure to handle growing search volume. The company needed revenue, and advertising seemed like the most viable path forward.

The key innovation was Google's approach to advertising quality and relevance. Rather than simply displaying ads from the highest bidders, Google developed an algorithm that considered both bid amount and ad relevance. Ads that users clicked on more frequently were given higher placement, creating incentives for advertisers to create genuinely useful advertisements.

This "AdWords" system, launched in 2000, represented a fundamental shift in online advertising. Instead of the intrusive banner ads and pop-ups that had characterized the dot-com era, Google's text-based ads were subtle, relevant, and closely integrated with search results. Users often found the ads genuinely helpful, which created a virtuous cycle of engagement and revenue.

Surviving the Crash

Google's timing was both fortunate and challenging. The company's venture funding was completed just before the dot-com crash began in earnest, providing capital to weather the storm. But Google was launching its business during the worst downturn in internet company history, when online advertising spending was collapsing and investors had lost faith in internet business models.

The crash actually provided some advantages for Google. Many competitors were forced to reduce their spending on technology development and marketing, creating opportunities for Google to gain market share. The failure of numerous dot-com companies also freed up engineering talent that Google could recruit at reasonable salaries.

More fundamentally, the post-crash environment favored companies with strong technology and sustainable business models. Google's superior search results and growing advertising revenue stood out in a landscape littered with failed companies that had prioritized growth over fundamentals.

The company's conservative culture, influenced by its academic origins, also served it well during the downturn. Unlike many dot-com companies that had spent extravagantly on marketing and perks, Google maintained relatively modest spending and focused on building its core technology and business operations.

By 2001, Google was profitable and growing rapidly. The company's advertising revenue was increasing month over month as more businesses discovered the effectiveness of search advertising. This financial stability was remarkable for an internet company during the post-crash period and validated the investors' belief in Google's business model.

Executive Leadership and Corporate Culture

One of the most important contributions of Google's venture investors was helping recruit executive leadership. Page and Brin were brilliant technologists, but they lacked experience managing large organizations or navigating complex business challenges. The company needed seasoned leadership to complement the founders' technical vision.

The search for a CEO was complicated by the founders' desire to maintain control over Google's direction and culture. They wanted someone who could provide operational expertise without interfering with their technical decisions or compromising their long-term vision.

After an extensive search process, Eric Schmidt was recruited as CEO in 2001. Schmidt brought a unique combination of technical credibility and business experience. He had previously served as CEO of Novell and had held senior positions at Sun Microsystems, giving him deep understanding of both technology markets and enterprise customers.

The arrangement that emerged, with Schmidt as CEO and Page and Brin as Presidents created an unusual but effective leadership structure. Schmidt handled day-to-day operations, business development, and external relationships, while the founders focused on product development and long-term strategy.

This leadership structure was supported by a corporate culture that emphasized technical excellence, data-driven decision making, and long-term thinking. Google's famous "20 percent time" policy, which allowed engineers to spend one day a week on personal projects, reflected the company's commitment to innovation and creative exploration.

The company's hiring practices also reflected its academic origins. Google recruited heavily from top universities and research institutions, looking for candidates with strong analytical skills and the ability to work on complex technical problems. This created a workforce that was exceptionally capable but also deeply committed to the company's mission of organizing the world's information.

The IPO Decision and Preparation

By 2003, Google faced growing pressure to go public. The company was profitable and growing rapidly, making it an attractive IPO candidate. Investment bankers were actively courting Google's leadership, and competitors like Yahoo! and Microsoft were beginning to take notice of Google's success.

However, Page, Brin, and Schmidt were reluctant to go public. They worried that the quarterly reporting requirements and short-term pressures of public markets would interfere with their long-term vision. They had seen how public market pressures had affected other technology companies and wanted to avoid similar constraints.

The decision was ultimately forced by SEC regulations requiring companies with more than 500 shareholders to file public financial reports. Google's employee stock option program had created hundreds of shareholders, and the company would soon cross the threshold requiring public disclosure regardless of whether it completed an IPO.

Faced with this regulatory requirement, Google's leadership decided to go public on their own terms. They structured the IPO using a Dutch auction process that was designed to democratize access to shares and reduce the influence of investment banks. This unconventional approach reflected the founders' desire to maintain control over their company's destiny.

The IPO prospectus, filed in April 2004, revealed the extraordinary success of Google's business model. The company had generated $1.5 billion in revenue in 2003, with profit margins that were unprecedented for an internet company. The filing also included a candid letter from Page and Brin explaining their philosophy and long-term vision.

Going Public and Market Validation

Google's IPO in August 2004 was one of the most closely watched public offerings in technology history. The Dutch auction process was controversial and complex, creating uncertainty about investor demand and appropriate pricing. Many Wall Street analysts were skeptical about Google's long-term prospects, questioning whether the company could maintain its growth rate and market position.

The initial price range of $108-135 per share was reduced to $85-95 just days before the offering, reflecting concerns about market conditions and investor appetite. When Google finally went public on August 19, 2004, the stock was priced at $85 per share, valuing the company at approximately $23 billion.

The market's initial response was mixed. The stock closed at $100.34 on its first day of trading, a respectable but not spectacular gain of 18%. Some observers interpreted the modest first-day pop as evidence that the Dutch auction had worked as intended, pricing shares closer to their fair value rather than creating artificial scarcity.

More importantly, Google's public market performance validated the venture capital investments that had made its success possible. Kleiner Perkins and Sequoia Capital saw their initial investments multiply by more than 100 times, generating returns that would rank among the most successful in venture capital history.

The IPO also demonstrated the evolution of the technology IPO market since the dot-com crash. Unlike the speculative offerings of the boom years, Google went public with a proven business model, strong financial performance, and clear competitive advantages. This represented the kind of fundamental-driven investing that had emerged from the ashes of the dot-com collapse.

The Platform Strategy Unfolds

Google's success as a public company validated not just its search business but its broader platform strategy. The company began leveraging its search technology and advertising infrastructure to launch new products and services that extended its reach and deepened user engagement.

Gmail, launched in 2004, demonstrated Google's ability to apply its technology expertise to new markets. The email service offered unprecedented storage capacity and integrated search functionality that made managing large email archives much easier. This wasn't just a new product, it was a strategic move to capture more user data and increase engagement with Google's ecosystem.

Google Maps, launched in 2005, represented another breakthrough in applying Google's technical capabilities to solve real user problems. The service provided interactive maps with satellite imagery and driving directions, capabilities that had previously required expensive specialized software. The integration with local search results created new advertising opportunities and further entrenched Google's position in users' daily routines.

These product launches illustrated Google's evolution from a search company to a platform company. Each new service created additional touchpoints with users, generated more data to improve Google's algorithms, and provided new opportunities for advertising revenue. This platform approach would become a template for many successful technology companies in subsequent years.

Competitive Response and Market Dynamics

Google's success inevitably attracted competitive responses from established technology companies. Microsoft, in particular, recognized that

Google's growing dominance in search and advertising represented a strategic threat to Microsoft's position in the technology industry.

Microsoft's response included launching its own search engine (MSN Search, later rebranded as Bing) and attempting to recruit Google employees with lucrative compensation packages. The company also explored potential acquisitions of Google competitors and invested heavily in search technology development.

Yahoo!, which had initially dismissed search as a commodity service, began refocusing on search technology and advertising. The company acquired several search-related companies and increased its investment in search algorithm development. However, these efforts were constrained by Yahoo!'s complex corporate structure and multiple competing priorities.

The competitive dynamics demonstrated the power of Google's early lead and focused execution. While competitors had larger resources and established customer relationships, Google's superior technology and specialized focus gave it sustained advantages that were difficult to replicate.

The Venture Capital Ecosystem Impact

Google's success had profound effects on the broader venture capital ecosystem. The company's extraordinary returns to Kleiner Perkins and Sequoia Capital validated the post-crash focus on fundamental business metrics and sustainable competitive advantages. It demonstrated that transformative companies could still be built and funded, even in challenging market conditions.

The success also influenced venture capital investment strategies. Firms began looking more seriously at companies with strong technical differentiation and potential for platform effects. The Google model, combining superior technology with scalable business models became a template that many venture investors sought to replicate.

Google's employee wealth creation also had significant effects on the venture ecosystem. Many Google employees used their stock options and equity gains to start their own companies or become angel investors. This created a new generation of entrepreneurs and investors who brought Google's culture of technical excellence and data-driven decision making to their new ventures.

The company's hiring practices also influenced the broader technology industry. Google's emphasis on recruiting top technical talent from universities created competitive pressure on other companies to upgrade their recruitment and retention practices. This contributed to the general rise in technology salaries and the increasing importance of stock options and equity compensation.

Long-term Strategic Vision

Perhaps the most important aspect of Google's success was the founders' commitment to long-term strategic thinking. Rather than optimizing for short-term financial performance, they consistently invested in research and development projects that might not generate returns for years or decades.

This long-term orientation was evident in projects like Google's digitization of library books, its investment in renewable energy infrastructure, and its early exploration of artificial intelligence and machine learning. These initiatives often seemed tangential to Google's core search business, but they reflected the founders' belief that organizing the world's information required continuous innovation and expansion into new domains.

The venture capital investors' support for this long-term vision was crucial. Both Kleiner Perkins and Sequoia Capital had experience with companies that required patient capital and sustained investment in research and development. Their willingness to support Google's ambitious projects, even when the commercial applications weren't immediately clear, enabled the company to build capabilities that would prove valuable years later.

Lessons for Venture Capital

Google's success story offered several important lessons for venture capitalists and entrepreneurs. First, it demonstrated the continued importance of technical differentiation in creating sustainable competitive advantages. Google's PageRank algorithm wasn't just incrementally better than existing search technologies, it was fundamentally superior in ways that were difficult for competitors to replicate.

Second, Google showed the power of focusing on solving real user problems rather than chasing market trends or financial metrics. The founders' commitment to providing the most relevant search results, even when it conflicted with short-term revenue opportunities, ultimately created a more valuable and defensible business.

Third, the company illustrated the importance of patience in building transformative businesses. Google's advertising business model took several years to develop and optimize, requiring sustained investment and experimentation during a period when the company could have pursued easier but less scalable revenue opportunities.

Finally, Google demonstrated the value of strong technical leadership combined with experienced business management. The partnership between the founders and Eric Schmidt created a leadership structure that balanced innovation with operational excellence, enabling the company to scale rapidly while maintaining its technical edge.

The Algorithm for Success

Google's extraordinary success wasn't the result of a single insight or decision, but rather the compound effect of many factors working in concert. Superior technology provided the foundation, but it was the combination of technical excellence, strategic vision, patient capital, experienced leadership, and favorable market timing that created one of the most valuable companies in history.

For the venture capital industry, Google represented validation that the discipline and focus imposed by the dot-com crash had created conditions for building more sustainable and valuable companies. The patient capital, rigorous due diligence, and emphasis on business fundamentals that characterized post-crash venture investing had enabled the creation of a company that would transform not just the internet, but the global economy.

As Google continued to expand its platform and explore new frontiers like artificial intelligence, autonomous vehicles, and space exploration, it became clear that the company's true algorithm for success was its commitment to ambitious long-term thinking supported by disciplined execution and sustained investment. This approach would inspire a new generation of entrepreneurs and investors who sought to build companies capable of tackling humanity's greatest challenges while generating extraordinary returns for all stakeholders.

Chapter 14

Facebook and Social Capital

"A squirrel dying in front of your house may be more relevant to your interests right now than people dying in Africa."

Mark Zuckerberg's blunt observation about human attention and social relevance, delivered to a room full of technology journalists in 2008, captured something profound about the social networking revolution he had unleashed. What began as a simple way for college students to connect with classmates had evolved into a global platform that would fundamentally reshape human communication, media consumption, and social interaction.

The Facebook story represents venture capital's ability to identify and nurture companies that don't just serve markets, they create entirely new categories of human behavior. But it also illustrates the complex challenges that arise when technological innovation outpaces social, regulatory, and ethical frameworks. The transformation of social relationships into digital capital would generate extraordinary financial returns while raising fundamental questions about privacy, democracy, and the nature of human connection in the digital age.

The Harvard Genesis

The story began in February 2004 in a Harvard University dormitory room, where nineteen-year-old Mark Zuckerberg was nursing both ambition and resentment. A computer science major with a reputation for building clever applications, Zuckerberg had recently been disciplined by Harvard's administration for creating Facemash, a website that allowed students to rate the attractiveness of their classmates by comparing photos scraped from dormitory directories.

While Facemash had been shut down within days, it had revealed something important: students had an intense appetite for digital tools that helped them navigate their social environment. The site had attracted 450 visitors and 22,000 photo views in its brief existence, crashing

Harvard's network in the process. More significantly, it had demonstrated that social comparison and connection could be digitized in ways that were both compelling and controversial.

The idea for "The Facebook", as it was initially known emerged from Zuckerberg's frustration with Harvard's reluctance to create an online directory of students. Many universities had "face books", physical directories with photos and basic information about students but Harvard had been slow to digitize this resource. Zuckerberg saw an opportunity to create something more dynamic and interactive than a simple online directory.

Working with his roommates Dustin Moskovitz and Chris Hughes, along with fellow student Eduardo Saverin who provided initial funding and business guidance, Zuckerberg spent several weeks in early 2004 building the initial version of Facebook. The concept was elegantly simple: students could create profiles with their photos and basic information, connect with friends, and share updates about their activities and interests.

The key innovation wasn't technological, it was social. Unlike existing social networking sites like Friendster and MySpace, which were open to anyone, Facebook required users to have verified college email addresses. This exclusivity created immediate social value: connections on Facebook corresponded to real-world relationships and social hierarchies. Users weren't connecting with strangers across the internet; they were digitizing their existing social networks.

The Viral Spread Across Campus

The response at Harvard was immediate and overwhelming. Within 24 hours of launch, more than 1,200 students had registered for Facebook. Within a month, more than half of Harvard's undergraduate population was actively using the service. The viral growth wasn't driven by marketing or advertising, it was powered by social dynamics and network effects that Zuckerberg had tapped into almost accidentally.

The exclusivity of the platform created a sense of urgency and social pressure to join. Students who weren't on Facebook found themselves excluded from social conversations and activities that were being organized on the platform. The "network effect", where each additional user made the service more valuable for existing users created a powerful growth dynamic that would become central to Facebook's expansion strategy.

More importantly, Facebook was solving real social problems for college students. It helped freshmen identify classmates and potential friends. It allowed students to maintain connections across different social circles, dormitories, classes, extracurricular activities. It provided a socially acceptable way to express interest in romantic connections. These weren't trivial conveniences; they addressed fundamental human needs for belonging, status, and connection.

The success at Harvard created a template for expansion. Zuckerberg and his co-founders began launching Facebook at other Ivy League schools, then expanded to other prestigious universities. The exclusivity was maintained, you could only join Facebook if you had an email address from a supported school which continued to drive demand and social pressure to join.

By the end of 2004, Facebook was active on over 30 college campuses and had attracted more than 100,000 users. The growth was entirely organic, driven by word-of-mouth and social dynamics rather than traditional marketing. This viral growth pattern would become one of Facebook's most important competitive advantages and a key factor in attracting venture capital investment.

The Move to Silicon Valley

The rapid growth at colleges created both opportunities and challenges for Facebook's founders. The company needed servers, bandwidth, and technical infrastructure to support its expanding user base. More fundamentally, it needed to develop a business model that could generate revenue from its growing social network.

In summer 2004, Zuckerberg made the crucial decision to move Facebook's operations to Silicon Valley, the epicenter of technology innovation and venture capital. This move represented a significant commitment to building Facebook into a major technology company rather than treating it as a college side project.

The relocation to Palo Alto brought Facebook into contact with Silicon Valley's ecosystem of entrepreneurs, investors, and technology professionals. The timing was fortuitous: the technology industry was recovering from the dot-com crash, and investors were beginning to show renewed interest in internet companies with strong user growth and engagement metrics.

Silicon Valley's culture also influenced Facebook's development in important ways. The emphasis on rapid growth, aggressive expansion, and long-term thinking that characterized successful technology companies became central to Facebook's strategy. The "move fast and break things" mentality that Zuckerberg would later articulate reflected Silicon Valley's bias toward speed and iteration over careful planning and risk avoidance.

Peter Thiel's Prescient Investment

The first major external investment in Facebook came from an unlikely source: Peter Thiel, the co-founder of PayPal who had recently established himself as an angel investor in Silicon Valley. Thiel's background in building online payment systems had given him insights into network effects and viral growth dynamics that would prove crucial in understanding Facebook's potential.

In September 2004, just seven months after Facebook's launch, Thiel invested $500,000 in the company for a 10.2% stake, valuing Facebook at approximately $4.9 million. This investment was remarkable not just for its size, $500,000 was a substantial angel investment in 2004 but for its timing and strategic insight.

Thiel's investment thesis was based on his understanding of network effects and winner-take-all dynamics in technology markets. He believed that social networking would exhibit strong network effects, where the value of the service increased exponentially with each additional user. In such markets, the first company to achieve critical mass and network density would be extremely difficult for competitors to dislodge.

More importantly, Thiel recognized that Facebook's focus on real identity and existing social relationships gave it fundamental advantages over competitors like Friendster and MySpace. While other social networking sites allowed users to create fictional personas and connect with strangers, Facebook was digitizing actual social networks. This created much stronger engagement and retention, as users' Facebook connections corresponded to their real-world relationships.

Thiel's investment also brought strategic value beyond capital. As a successful entrepreneur and PayPal co-founder, he provided credibility and connections that helped Facebook attract additional talent and investment. His involvement signaled to other Silicon Valley investors that Facebook was a serious company with significant potential.

Accel Partners and International Expansion

Facebook's rapid growth and increasing capital requirements soon attracted the attention of institutional venture capitalists. By early 2005, the company was expanding beyond college campuses and needed significant investment to support its technical infrastructure and business development.

Accel Partners, led by partner Jim Breyer, emerged as the lead investor in Facebook's Series A funding round. Breyer brought extensive experience investing in internet and software companies, having previously backed companies like RealNetworks and Foundry Networks. His partnership with Thiel, who remained involved as a board member created a powerful combination of angel and institutional investment expertise.

The $12.7 million Series A round, completed in May 2005, valued Facebook at approximately $98 million. This represented a 20x increase in valuation in just eight months, reflecting both Facebook's extraordinary growth and the venture capital market's renewed confidence in social networking companies.

Breyer's investment thesis emphasized Facebook's potential for international expansion and platform development. Unlike previous social networking sites that had struggled to expand beyond their initial markets, Facebook's focus on real identity and existing social relationships created a template that could be replicated globally. The company's technical infrastructure was also designed to scale efficiently, allowing it to serve millions of users without proportional increases in operational costs.

The Accel investment enabled Facebook to accelerate its expansion strategy. The company began launching in international markets, starting with English-speaking countries like the United Kingdom and Canada, then expanding to other regions. The exclusivity model was maintained, users needed verified email addresses from supported institutions but the geographic scope continued to expand rapidly.

More strategically, the venture funding allowed Facebook to begin developing its platform and advertising capabilities. The company launched Facebook Platform in 2007, allowing third-party developers to build applications that integrated with Facebook's social graph. This platform strategy created additional engagement and retention while providing new revenue opportunities through advertising and virtual goods.

The Business Model Evolution

Like many successful internet companies, Facebook's business model evolved significantly from its initial conception. The early focus was entirely on user growth and engagement, with little attention to revenue generation. The assumption was that a large, engaged user base would eventually support various monetization strategies, though the specific mechanisms weren't initially clear.

The first revenue experiments involved banner advertising and sponsored content, similar to other internet companies of the era. However, these approaches generated relatively modest revenues and didn't take full advantage of Facebook's unique social data and engagement patterns.

The breakthrough came with the development of targeted advertising based on user profile information and social connections. Facebook possessed unprecedented amounts of personal data about its users, demographic information, interests, social relationships, and behavioral patterns. This data could be used to target advertisements with remarkable precision, creating value for both advertisers and users.

The social aspect of Facebook's advertising was particularly innovative. Advertisements could be enhanced with social context, showing which friends had liked or engaged with particular brands or products. This "social proof" made advertisements more credible and engaging, improving click-through rates and advertiser return on investment.

The targeted advertising model also aligned well with Facebook's user experience philosophy. Rather than displaying irrelevant banner advertisements that interrupted social interactions, Facebook could show ads that were genuinely relevant to users' interests and social contexts. This created a more integrated and less intrusive advertising experience.

By 2007, Facebook's advertising revenue was growing rapidly, driven by both increasing user base and improving ad targeting capabilities. The company began attracting major brand advertisers who were interested in reaching Facebook's young, engaged user demographic. This revenue growth validated the venture capital investments and provided resources for continued expansion and product development.

The Platform Strategy and Developer Ecosystem

One of Facebook's most important strategic innovations was the launch of Facebook Platform in May 2007. This initiative allowed third-party developers to build applications that integrated with Facebook's social graph and could be distributed through Facebook's network.

The platform strategy was inspired by successful technology platforms like Microsoft Windows and the iPhone App Store (which wouldn't launch until the following year). By enabling developers to build on top of Facebook's infrastructure, the company could expand its functionality and user engagement without having to develop all applications internally.

The response from developers was extraordinary. Within months of the platform launch, thousands of applications had been built and deployed on Facebook. Games like FarmVille and Mafia Wars attracted millions of users and generated significant revenues through virtual goods and advertising. Utility applications helped users organize photos, plan events, and share content with friends.

This developer ecosystem created powerful network effects and competitive advantages for Facebook. As more developers built applications for the Facebook platform, the service became more valuable and engaging for users. As more users joined Facebook, it became more attractive for developers to build Facebook applications. This created a virtuous cycle that strengthened Facebook's position in the social networking market.

The platform strategy also had important implications for Facebook's business model. The company could generate revenue by taking a percentage of virtual goods sales and advertising revenue from platform applications. More importantly, the increased engagement from platform applications made Facebook's own advertising more valuable, as users spent more time on the site and provided more behavioral data for targeting.

Going Global and Cultural Adaptation

Facebook's international expansion required more than just technical scaling, it demanded cultural adaptation and localization that would test the company's ability to understand diverse global markets. Unlike Google's search engine, which could be relatively easily localized through language translation, Facebook's social networking required deep understanding of local social norms, communication patterns, and cultural sensitivities.

The expansion strategy began with English-speaking markets where cultural adaptation was minimal. Facebook launched in the United Kingdom, Canada, and Australia with great success, demonstrating that the core social networking concept translated well across similar cultures.

The real challenges came with expansion into non-English markets with different social structures and communication preferences. In some cultures, the explicit social connections and public sharing that characterized Facebook weren't aligned with local social norms. In others, competing local social networking services had already established strong positions.

Facebook's response was to develop sophisticated localization capabilities and cultural adaptation strategies. The company hired local teams in major markets who could understand cultural nuances and adapt product features accordingly. Translation tools were developed not just for language conversion but for cultural context adaptation.

More importantly, Facebook learned to navigate different regulatory and political environments. In some countries, government restrictions on internet content and social networking required careful compliance strategies. In others, privacy regulations were more stringent than those Facebook had encountered in the United States.

The international expansion was ultimately successful, but it required significant investment and strategic flexibility. Facebook's user base became increasingly global, with international users eventually representing the majority of the company's audience. This global reach would become one of Facebook's most important competitive advantages and a key driver of advertising revenue growth.

The Microsoft Partnership and Strategic Validation

In October 2007, Microsoft announced a strategic partnership with Facebook that included a $240 million investment for a 1.6% stake in the company. This investment valued Facebook at $15 billion, making it one of the most valuable private technology companies in the world.

The Microsoft partnership was significant for several reasons beyond the financial investment. Microsoft was competing aggressively with Google in online advertising and saw Facebook's social data and engagement as valuable assets in that competition. The partnership gave Microsoft exclusive rights to provide search and display advertising on Facebook internationally, creating a significant revenue stream for both companies.

More importantly, Microsoft's investment provided external validation of Facebook's business model and growth potential. Microsoft was a sophisticated technology company with extensive experience in online services and advertising markets. Their willingness to invest at a $15 billion valuation signaled to other investors and potential partners that Facebook had achieved sustainable competitive advantages and significant business value.

The partnership also demonstrated Facebook's strategic importance in the broader technology industry. Google had dominated online advertising through its search engine and contextual advertising platform. Facebook's social advertising represented a different approach that could potentially challenge Google's market position by providing access to social context and behavioral data that search couldn't capture.

However, the Microsoft partnership also highlighted some of the challenges Facebook faced in developing its business model. The company was still heavily dependent on advertising revenue, and competition with Google and other technology giants would require continuous innovation and significant investment in advertising technology and sales capabilities.

Privacy Challenges and Social Responsibility

As Facebook's user base grew and its data collection capabilities expanded, the company faced increasing scrutiny about privacy policies and data usage practices. The social networking model required users to share personal information and social connections, creating unprecedented databases of personal and social data.

Initial privacy concerns were relatively modest, focusing on issues like profile visibility and data sharing with third-party applications. However, as Facebook expanded its advertising capabilities and began using personal data for targeting, questions arose about user consent, data control, and the potential for misuse of personal information.

Facebook's response to these concerns evolved over time, often reactively rather than proactively. The company initially took a relatively permissive approach to data sharing and platform integration, prioritizing user engagement and developer ecosystem growth over strict privacy controls.

This approach created several high-profile controversies and regulatory challenges. Changes to privacy policies often generated user backlash and media criticism. Third-party applications sometimes accessed and used personal data in ways that users hadn't explicitly consented to. Advertising targeting raised questions about user awareness and control over how their personal information was being used.

These privacy challenges would become increasingly important as Facebook grew and as regulatory scrutiny of technology companies intensified. The company's ability to navigate privacy concerns while maintaining its business model would become a critical factor in its long-term success and social acceptability.

The Road to IPO

By 2009, Facebook had established itself as the dominant social networking platform globally, with hundreds of millions of users and rapidly growing advertising revenue. The company's venture capital investors were beginning to consider exit strategies, and an initial public offering seemed increasingly likely.

However, Facebook's leadership was ambivalent about going public. The company was generating substantial revenue and had access to private capital markets for growth funding. Going public would subject Facebook to quarterly earnings pressures and regulatory requirements that could constrain its long-term strategic flexibility.

The decision was ultimately forced by SEC regulations requiring companies with more than 500 shareholders to file public financial reports.

Facebook's employee stock option programs and secondary market trading had created hundreds of shareholders, making public disclosure inevitable regardless of whether the company completed an IPO.

The preparation for going public required Facebook to develop more sophisticated financial controls, governance structures, and business planning processes. The company had grown rapidly from a college startup to a global technology company, but its management systems and organizational structure needed to evolve to support public company requirements.

More fundamentally, going public would require Facebook to articulate its long-term vision and business model to public market investors who might have different perspectives on social networking and technology company valuations than private venture capitalists.

Network Effects and Competitive Dynamics

Facebook's success was built on network effects that created powerful competitive advantages and barriers to entry. As more users joined Facebook, the service became more valuable for existing users because they could connect with more of their friends, family members, and acquaintances.

These network effects were particularly strong because Facebook focused on real identity and existing social relationships rather than allowing users to create fictional personas or connect primarily with strangers. This meant that users' Facebook networks corresponded closely to their real-world social networks, creating strong switching costs and user retention.

The competitive dynamics in social networking reflected these network effects. Early competitors like Friendster and MySpace had struggled to maintain user engagement as Facebook grew. New entrants found it difficult to attract users away from Facebook because the value of social networking depended on where users' friends and family were already active.

However, Facebook's network effects also created responsibilities and challenges. The company's platform became a crucial piece of social infrastructure for billions of people, making reliability, security, and responsible governance essential. The power that came from controlling social connections and communication created both business opportunities and social obligations that would become increasingly important as Facebook matured.

The Transformation of Social Interaction

Facebook's impact extended far beyond creating a successful technology company, it fundamentally transformed how people communicate, share information, and maintain social relationships. The digitization of social networks created new forms of social capital and new mechanisms for social influence and information dissemination.

The concept of "social capital", the networks of relationships and social connections that provide individuals with access to resources and opportunities took on new meaning in the Facebook era. Digital social connections could be maintained more easily across geographic distances and time periods, but they might also be more superficial than traditional face-to-face relationships.

Facebook also changed the nature of privacy and personal information sharing. The platform encouraged users to share personal updates, photos, and thoughts with their social networks, creating new norms around transparency and self-disclosure. This shift had implications for both personal relationships and professional interactions.

The platform's influence on information consumption and news distribution was particularly significant. Facebook's News Feed algorithm determined which information users saw from their social networks, effectively becoming a personalized media filter. This gave Facebook enormous influence over information flow and public discourse, with implications for democracy, journalism, and social cohesion.

Venture Capital Returns and Industry Impact

Facebook's success generated extraordinary returns for its venture capital investors, validating investment strategies focused on network effects, viral growth, and platform development. Peter Thiel's initial $500,000 investment ultimately returned more than $1 billion, representing one of the most successful angel investments in technology history.

Accel Partners' Series A investment also generated spectacular returns, contributing significantly to the firm's reputation and fundraising capabilities. The success attracted attention from other venture capitalists and helped establish social networking and consumer internet services as important investment categories.

More broadly, Facebook's success influenced venture capital investment patterns and company-building strategies throughout the technology industry. The focus on viral growth, network effects, and user engagement became central to how investors evaluated consumer internet companies. The platform strategy and developer ecosystem model was replicated by numerous other companies seeking to create similar competitive advantages.

Facebook's employee wealth creation also had significant effects on the broader Silicon Valley ecosystem. Many Facebook employees used their stock options and equity gains to start their own companies or become angel investors, creating a new generation of entrepreneurs and investors who brought Facebook's culture of rapid growth and social product development to their new ventures.

Setting the Stage for Mobile and Beyond

By the early 2010s, Facebook had established itself as one of the world's most valuable and influential technology companies. The social networking revolution it had pioneered was reshaping human communication, media consumption, and social interaction on a global scale.

However, new challenges were emerging that would test Facebook's ability to adapt and evolve. The rise of mobile devices and smartphone adoption was creating new patterns of internet usage and social interaction. New social networking services like Instagram and Snapchat were attracting younger users with different communication preferences and social behaviors.

Facebook's response to these challenges would require continued innovation, strategic acquisitions, and adaptation to changing user preferences and regulatory environments. The company's venture capital origins had instilled a culture of rapid growth and strategic flexibility that would be essential for navigating these new challenges.

The transformation of social relationships into digital capital had created unprecedented opportunities for human connection and communication, but it had also raised fundamental questions about privacy, democracy, and the role of technology companies in society. Facebook's journey from Harvard dorm room to global platform illustrated both the power and the responsibility that came with venture capital's ability to identify and nurture transformative technologies.

The social capital that Facebook had created and monetized would continue to evolve, but the fundamental insight that human relationships could be digitized and scaled through technology platforms would influence the next generation of venture capital investments and technology innovation. The network effects and platform strategies pioneered by Facebook would become essential tools for building successful technology companies in an increasingly connected world.

Chapter 15

The Mobile Revolution

"Today, Apple is going to reinvent the phone."

Steve Jobs's confident declaration on January 9, 2007, would prove to be one of the most prescient statements in technology history. But the iPhone's impact would extend far beyond reinventing telephony, it would create an entirely new platform for innovation, entrepreneurship, and venture capital investment that would reshape the global economy and transform how billions of people interact with technology, commerce, and each other.

The mobile revolution represented venture capital's ability to identify and capitalize on platform shifts that create entirely new categories of business opportunity. Within just a few years of the iPhone's launch, venture investors would fund thousands of mobile applications, services, and infrastructure companies, creating new unicorns like Uber, Airbnb, Instagram, and WhatsApp that would fundamentally alter industries from transportation to hospitality to photography to communications.

The transformation wasn't just about putting existing services on smaller screens, it was about enabling entirely new behaviors, business models, and forms of human interaction that were only possible when powerful computing capabilities became ubiquitous, location-aware, and always-connected.

The Pre-iPhone Mobile Landscape

To understand the magnitude of the mobile revolution, it's essential to appreciate how primitive the mobile ecosystem was before the iPhone's arrival. In 2007, the mobile phone industry was dominated by companies like Nokia, BlackBerry, and Motorola, which focused primarily on voice communication with limited data capabilities.

The existing smartphone market was primarily oriented toward business users. BlackBerry devices were popular among corporate executives and government officials for their email capabilities and physical keyboards. Palm Pilots and Windows Mobile devices offered limited computing functionality but were clunky, slow, and difficult for average consumers to use effectively.

Mobile internet access was expensive, slow, and cumbersome. Most mobile websites were simplified, text-only versions of desktop sites that provided minimal functionality. The concept of mobile applications was limited to simple games like Snake or basic utility programs that came pre-installed on devices.

For venture capitalists, the mobile market in 2007 represented a challenging investment environment. The carriers, Verizon, AT&T, Sprint, and T-Mobile controlled distribution and customer relationships, making it difficult for independent software developers to reach consumers directly. The technical limitations of devices and networks meant that sophisticated applications weren't feasible for most use cases.

The few venture investments in mobile companies before the iPhone focused primarily on infrastructure, enterprise applications, or simple consumer services that worked within the constraints of existing devices and networks. Companies like Good Technology and Seven Networks built email and data synchronization services for business users, while mobile gaming companies like Jamdat created simple entertainment applications.

The iPhone changed everything by removing the technical and distribution barriers that had limited mobile innovation. Suddenly, developers could create sophisticated applications with rich user interfaces, and Apple's App Store provided direct access to consumers without carrier gatekeeping.

The iPhone as Platform Creation

The iPhone's significance for venture capital wasn't just its success as a consumer product, though that success was certainly remarkable. More importantly, the iPhone created an entirely new platform for software development and distribution that would enable thousands of venture-backed companies.

Apple's decision to allow third-party developers to create native applications for the iPhone was revolutionary. Previous mobile platforms had been closed ecosystems controlled by device manufacturers and wireless carriers. The iPhone's App Store, launched in July 2008, democratized mobile software distribution and created direct relationships between developers and consumers.

The technical capabilities of the iPhone were also transformative for venture-backed startups. The device included GPS location services, accelerometers, high-quality cameras, internet connectivity, and touchscreen interfaces that enabled entirely new categories of applications. These hardware capabilities, combined with Apple's intuitive user interface design, made it possible for software developers to create experiences that had never been feasible on mobile devices.

Perhaps most importantly, the iPhone established a new economic model for mobile applications. Instead of requiring complex carrier partnerships and revenue-sharing agreements, developers could sell applications directly to consumers through the App Store. Apple's 70-30 revenue split (70% to developers, 30% to Apple) was much more favorable than previous mobile distribution models and provided clear incentives for innovation.

The platform creation also included crucial infrastructure elements that venture capitalists would learn to recognize as essential for successful ecosystem development. Apple invested heavily in developer tools, documentation, and support programs that lowered the barriers to entry for application development. The company also created marketing and discovery mechanisms within the App Store that helped high-quality applications find audiences.

The Venture Capital Response

Venture capitalists were initially cautious about the iPhone's potential impact. The mobile market had disappointed investors before, and many VCs were skeptical about whether consumers would pay for mobile applications or whether the iPhone would achieve sufficient market penetration to support a viable ecosystem.

However, a few prescient investors recognized the platform opportunity early. Fred Wilson at Union Square Ventures became one of the most vocal advocates for mobile investing, arguing that the iPhone represented a fundamental shift comparable to the personal computer or the internet. His firm began actively seeking mobile application companies and became early investors in several successful mobile startups.

Kleiner Perkins, led by John Doerr and newly hired partner Bing Gordon, also recognized the mobile opportunity early. The firm created a $100 million iFund specifically focused on iPhone application development, providing both capital and strategic support for mobile entrepreneurs. This dedicated fund signaled to the market that mobile applications were a serious investment category worthy of institutional venture capital attention.

The early venture investments in mobile applications were modest by later standards but proved remarkably prescient. Companies like Ngmoco (mobile gaming), Shazam (music recognition), and Foursquare (location-based social networking) received venture funding in 2008 and 2009 when the iPhone was still establishing market traction.

More importantly, venture capitalists began to recognize that mobile wasn't just about applications, it was about enabling entirely new business models and user behaviors. The combination of ubiquitous internet connectivity, location awareness, and always-available computing created opportunities for companies that couldn't have existed in the desktop internet era.

Instagram: The Power of Mobile-Native Design

One of the most successful early examples of mobile-first venture investing was Instagram, though the company's path to success illustrated both the opportunities and challenges of the mobile revolution. Founded in 2010 by Kevin Systrom and Mike Krieger, Instagram began as a location-based social networking application called Burbn.

The original Burbn concept included check-ins, photo sharing, and social gaming elements, essentially trying to combine features from Foursquare, Facebook, and mobile gaming applications. However, user testing revealed that people were primarily interested in the photo-sharing functionality, leading Systrom and Krieger to pivot toward a focused photo-sharing application.

The decision to focus exclusively on photo sharing proved prescient. The iPhone's camera capabilities and the growing popularity of social media created perfect conditions for a mobile-native photo application. Instagram's filters and editing tools made it easy for users to create visually appealing photos, while the social networking features enabled sharing and discovery.

More importantly, Instagram was designed specifically for mobile devices rather than being adapted from desktop applications. The user interface was optimized for touchscreen interaction, the application was designed for quick loading on mobile networks, and the entire user experience assumed mobile connectivity and camera access.

The growth was extraordinary. Instagram launched in October 2010 and acquired 25,000 users on its first day. Within two months, the application had one million users. By September 2011, Instagram had 10 million users and was growing rapidly without any marketing spending, purely through word-of-mouth and viral sharing.

This growth attracted venture capital attention from firms including Baseline Ventures, Andreessen Horowitz, and Sequoia Capital. The company raised $7.5 million in Series A funding in February 2011, despite having only two full-time employees and no revenue model. The investment was based purely on user growth, engagement metrics, and the potential for mobile photo sharing.

Instagram's success validated several important principles for mobile venture investing. Mobile-native applications that were designed specifically for smartphone capabilities could achieve viral growth and user engagement that exceeded desktop applications. Consumer applications with strong network effects could scale rapidly without traditional marketing spending. Most importantly, mobile platforms enabled small teams to build applications that could reach global audiences with minimal infrastructure investment.

Uber: Reimagining Transportation Through Mobile

While Instagram demonstrated the power of mobile-native consumer applications, Uber illustrated how mobile platforms could transform traditional industries and business models. Founded in 2009 by Garrett Camp and Travis Kalanick, Uber began as a simple solution to the inconvenience of hailing taxis in San Francisco.

The original concept was straightforward: use mobile applications to connect passengers with drivers, enabling on-demand transportation that was more convenient and reliable than traditional taxi services. However, the execution required sophisticated technology, careful market development, and significant capital investment to achieve scale.

Uber's business model was only possible because of mobile platform capabilities. GPS location services enabled automatic passenger pickup without requiring complex address communication. Mobile payments allowed seamless transactions without cash or credit card processing. Real-time communication enabled coordination between passengers and drivers that wasn't feasible with traditional dispatch systems.

More fundamentally, Uber represented a new category of business model enabled by mobile platforms: on-demand services that connected supply and demand in real-time through technology intermediation. This model would be replicated across numerous industries, but transportation was an ideal starting point because existing taxi systems were inefficient and customer service was generally poor.

The venture capital response to Uber was initially mixed. The company's first institutional funding came from First Round Capital, which invested $1.25 million in a seed round in 2009. However, many investors were skeptical about whether Uber could navigate regulatory challenges from taxi commissions and whether the unit economics of the business would prove sustainable.

The breakthrough came when Benchmark Capital, led by Bill Gurley, invested $11 million in Uber's Series A round in 2011. Gurley's investment thesis focused on network effects and marketplace dynamics that would create sustainable competitive advantages as Uber scaled. More drivers would reduce wait times for passengers, which would attract more passengers, which would attract more drivers.

Uber's subsequent growth validated this network effects thesis while also demonstrating the capital requirements for building marketplace businesses. The company would raise multiple rounds of venture funding totaling billions of dollars as it expanded to new cities, developed new services, and competed with well-funded rivals like Lyft in the United States and numerous international competitors.

The Uber model also illustrated the regulatory and social challenges that could accompany mobile-enabled business model innovation. Traditional taxi companies and their regulatory supporters viewed Uber as unfair competition that circumvented existing rules and safety requirements. These conflicts would create ongoing challenges for Uber and other sharing economy companies throughout their development.

Airbnb: The Sharing Economy Platform

Airbnb's founding story paralleled Uber's in demonstrating how mobile platforms could enable new marketplace models, but the company's path to venture capital success was more circuitous and illustrated the challenges investors faced in recognizing transformative business models.

Founded in 2008 by Brian Chesky, Joe Gebbia, and Nathan Blecharczyk, Airbnb began as a way for people to rent air mattresses in their apartments to conference attendees who couldn't find hotel rooms. The concept seemed narrow and niche, a solution for specific events rather than a scalable business model.

The company's early fundraising attempts were largely unsuccessful. Many investors couldn't understand why people would stay in strangers' homes instead of hotels, or why property owners would rent to strangers instead of using existing rental platforms. The market size seemed limited, and the trust and safety challenges appeared insurmountable.

However, mobile platforms proved crucial for Airbnb's eventual success. Mobile applications made it possible for travelers to search for accommodations, communicate with hosts, and complete bookings while traveling. GPS and mapping services enabled location-based search and discovery that wasn't feasible with desktop-only platforms. Mobile cameras enabled hosts to easily photograph and list their properties.

More importantly, mobile platforms enabled the social features and user-generated content that addressed trust and safety concerns. Reviews and ratings systems, profile verification, and social network integration helped build trust between strangers in ways that weren't possible with traditional classified advertising or rental platforms.

The venture capital breakthrough came when Greylock Partners, led by Reid Hoffman, invested $7.2 million in Airbnb's Series A round in 2009. Hoffman's background with LinkedIn and PayPal had given him insights into how technology platforms could enable trust and transactions between strangers. He recognized that Airbnb was addressing a real market inefficiency, the underutilization of residential real estate through mobile-enabled technology.

Airbnb's subsequent growth demonstrated the global scalability of mobile-enabled marketplace models. The company expanded internationally much faster than traditional hospitality companies, leveraging mobile applications and internet infrastructure to enter new markets without requiring physical presence or local partnerships.

The sharing economy model pioneered by Airbnb would be replicated across numerous industries, from transportation (Uber, Lyft) to food delivery (DoorDash, Postmates) to freelance services (TaskRabbit, Fiverr). These companies shared common characteristics: they used mobile platforms to connect supply and demand, they relied on user-generated content and reviews for trust and safety, and they achieved global scale with relatively modest infrastructure investments.

The App Store Economy and New Business Models

The iPhone's App Store created an entirely new economy that would generate billions in revenue for developers and transform how software companies thought about distribution, monetization, and customer acquisition. For venture capitalists, the App Store represented both unprecedented opportunities and new challenges in evaluating and supporting portfolio companies.

The most immediate impact was the creation of paid application markets. For the first time, consumers were willing to pay small amounts ($0.99 to $9.99) for software applications, creating viable business models for simple utility applications, games, and productivity tools that couldn't have supported traditional software licensing models.

However, the most significant business model innovation was "freemium" applications that were free to download but generated revenue through in-app purchases, subscriptions, or advertising. This model enabled much broader user acquisition while still providing paths to monetization for successful applications.

Mobile gaming became particularly lucrative through freemium models. Companies like King Digital Entertainment (Candy Crush Saga), Supercell (Clash of Clans), and Zynga (FarmVille) demonstrated that mobile games could generate hundreds of millions in revenue through in-app purchases of virtual goods and game enhancements.

The success of mobile gaming attracted significant venture capital investment and created new specialized investment firms focused on mobile entertainment. Companies like DeNA, GREE, and Kabam raised hundreds of millions in venture funding to develop and publish mobile games, while infrastructure companies like Unity Technologies built development tools and platforms that enabled smaller developers to create sophisticated mobile applications.

Subscription-based mobile applications also proved successful for productivity, entertainment, and service applications. Companies like Netflix, Spotify, and Pandora adapted their services for mobile platforms and found that mobile access increased customer engagement and retention. New mobile-native companies like WhatsApp demonstrated that even simple communication applications could achieve massive scale and eventual billion-dollar valuations.

Location-Based Services and Geographic Commerce

One of the most distinctive capabilities of mobile platforms was GPS location awareness, which enabled entirely new categories of applications and business models. Location-based services became a major focus for venture capital investment as entrepreneurs explored how geographic information could create value for consumers and businesses.

Foursquare, founded by Dennis Crowley and Naveen Selvadurai in 2009, became the most prominent early example of location-based social networking. The application allowed users to "check in" at restaurants, bars, retail stores, and other locations, sharing their whereabouts with friends and earning rewards for frequent visits.

The venture capital response to Foursquare was enthusiastic, with firms including Union Square Ventures, Andreessen Horowitz, and Kleiner Perkins investing more than $70 million in the company by 2010. The investment thesis focused on the potential for location data to enable new forms of advertising and commerce, businesses could target customers who were physically nearby and offer incentives for visits and purchases.

However, Foursquare's consumer adoption was more limited than investors had hoped, and the company struggled to build sustainable revenue from location-based advertising. The check-in behavior that seemed natural to early smartphone adopters didn't scale to mainstream consumers, who were concerned about privacy and didn't see sufficient value in sharing their locations publicly.

More successful location-based applications focused on utility rather than social sharing. Yelp leveraged location awareness to provide restaurant and business reviews relevant to users' current locations. Google Maps and Apple Maps integrated location services with navigation and search functionality. Weather applications used location to provide locally relevant forecasts without requiring users to manually enter their locations.

The most transformative location-based applications were marketplace platforms like Uber and Airbnb that used geographic information to match supply and demand in real-time. These applications demonstrated that location awareness was most valuable when it enabled functional services rather than social features.

Mobile Commerce and Payment Innovation

Mobile platforms also enabled new approaches to commerce and payments that would transform retail and financial services industries. The combination of always-connected internet access, location awareness, and secure payment processing created opportunities for mobile-first commerce companies that couldn't have existed in the desktop era.

Square, founded by Jack Dorsey and Jim McKelvey in 2009, demonstrated how mobile platforms could democratize payment processing for small businesses. The company's small credit card reader that plugged into smartphone audio jacks enabled any business to accept credit card payments without expensive point-of-sale systems or complex merchant account setup processes.

Square's venture capital funding came from prominent investors including Kleiner Perkins, Sequoia Capital, and Visa, who recognized that mobile payment processing could transform small business commerce. The company's simple pricing, easy setup, and integration with mobile applications made credit card acceptance accessible to small retailers, food trucks, farmers markets, and service providers who had previously operated as cash-only businesses.

Mobile commerce applications also enabled new shopping experiences that took advantage of location awareness, camera functionality, and social features. Applications like Amazon's mobile app allowed consumers to scan product barcodes and compare prices while shopping in physical stores. Social commerce applications like Pinterest enabled discovery and purchasing of products through visual browsing and social recommendations.

The success of mobile commerce created new venture capital investment categories focused on mobile payments, point-of-sale systems, and commerce enablement. Companies like Stripe, Braintree, and PayPal adapted their payment processing services for mobile applications, while new startups like Venmo and Cash App created peer-to-peer payment applications designed specifically for mobile use.

The Rise of Mobile-First Venture Funds

The success of mobile applications and the distinctive characteristics of mobile markets led some venture capital firms to create specialized funds focused exclusively on mobile investing. These mobile-first funds developed expertise in mobile user acquisition, app store optimization, mobile advertising, and mobile-specific business models that generalist venture firms sometimes lacked.

Kleiner Perkins' iFund was one of the first dedicated mobile investment vehicles, but other firms followed with specialized mobile strategies. Flurry, a mobile analytics company, launched Flurry Ventures to invest in companies using their analytics platform. Google Ventures (now GV) created mobile-focused investment teams, while established firms like

Bessemer Venture Partners and General Catalyst developed mobile expertise within their broader investment strategies.

These mobile-focused investment approaches reflected several unique characteristics of mobile markets. Customer acquisition costs and lifetime values were different from desktop applications, requiring different financial modeling and business plan evaluation. App store dynamics and mobile advertising platforms created new marketing channels that required specialized knowledge. International expansion was often easier for mobile applications, but it also required understanding of different mobile platforms, payment systems, and regulatory environments across global markets.

The mobile-first investment approach also emphasized different metrics and success factors than traditional internet investing. Daily active users, session length, retention rates, and viral coefficients became more important than traditional web metrics like page views and unique visitors. Mobile applications needed to create habit-forming experiences that would survive in competitive app store environments where users had thousands of alternatives readily available.

Infrastructure and Developer Tools

The mobile revolution also created opportunities for venture investment in infrastructure and developer tools that enabled the broader mobile ecosystem. As thousands of developers began building mobile applications, they needed hosting services, analytics tools, push notification systems, and development frameworks that were optimized for mobile platforms.

Companies like Parse (mobile backend services), Twilio (communication APIs), and SendGrid (email services) provided infrastructure services that enabled mobile application developers to focus on user experience and business logic rather than building complex backend systems. These infrastructure companies often achieved high growth and attractive unit economics by serving the rapidly expanding population of mobile developers.

Development tool companies also attracted significant venture investment. Unity Technologies raised hundreds of millions in venture capital to build game development tools that enabled developers to create sophisticated mobile games without extensive programming expertise. Xamarin (later acquired by Microsoft) created cross-platform development tools that allowed developers to build applications for multiple mobile operating systems with shared code bases.

The success of mobile infrastructure companies demonstrated how platform shifts created investment opportunities throughout the technology stack. While consumer-facing mobile applications attracted the most media attention, the underlying infrastructure and tools required to support mobile development often proved to be more stable and profitable businesses with clearer paths to sustainable competitive advantages.

International Mobile Markets and Global Expansion

The mobile revolution was inherently global, with smartphone adoption proceeding rapidly in markets around the world. This created opportunities for venture capital firms to invest in mobile companies serving international markets, but it also created competition as successful mobile business models were replicated across different countries and regions.

In China, mobile platforms developed differently due to unique market conditions and regulatory environments. Companies like Tencent (WeChat), Alibaba (mobile commerce), and Baidu (mobile search) dominated Chinese mobile markets with applications and services that were often more advanced than their Western counterparts. Chinese mobile payment systems, led by Alipay and WeChat Pay, achieved higher adoption rates than mobile payments in the United States or Europe.

European mobile markets also developed distinctive characteristics, with companies like Skype (voice communication), Spotify (music streaming), and King Digital Entertainment (mobile gaming) achieving global success from European bases. Regulatory differences, consumer preferences, and competitive dynamics created opportunities for mobile companies that could navigate diverse international markets.

For venture capital firms, international mobile markets created both opportunities and challenges. Successful mobile business models could often be adapted for different markets, but execution required understanding local user preferences, regulatory requirements, and competitive landscapes. Some venture firms developed international investment strategies focused on mobile markets, while others partnered with local investors who provided market expertise and cultural knowledge.

The Platform Network Effects

The mobile revolution demonstrated the power of platform network effects at unprecedented scale. Successful mobile platforms like iOS and Android created virtuous cycles where more users attracted more developers, which created more applications, which attracted more users.

Apple's App Store and Google's Play Store became intermediaries for billions of dollars in commerce between developers and consumers. The platform owners collected 30% of all transactions while providing distribution, payment processing, and customer service that enabled developers to focus on application development and user experience.

These platform network effects also influenced venture capital investment strategies. Companies that could build platform businesses or leverage existing platforms for distribution and customer acquisition often achieved better growth and more defensible competitive positions than companies that relied solely on direct customer acquisition and retention.

The success of platform companies like Apple, Google, Facebook, and Amazon created new strategic considerations for venture-backed companies. Startups needed to consider how their strategies would interact with platform policies, revenue sharing models, and competitive dynamics with platform owners who might choose to compete directly with successful third-party applications.

Setting the Stage for the Next Platform Shift

By the early 2010s, the mobile revolution had fundamentally transformed the venture capital landscape. Mobile-first companies had achieved billion-dollar valuations, mobile business models had proven sustainable and scalable, and mobile platforms had become essential infrastructure for commerce, communication, and entertainment.

However, new platform shifts were already emerging that would create the next wave of venture capital opportunities. Cloud computing was enabling more sophisticated mobile applications and services. Social networking was evolving beyond simple status updates to include rich media and real-time communication. Artificial intelligence and machine learning were beginning to enable new categories of mobile applications that could understand and respond to user behavior in sophisticated ways.

The mobile revolution had also created new challenges and responsibilities for venture capital firms and their portfolio companies. Privacy concerns, regulatory scrutiny, and social impact considerations had become more prominent as mobile applications gained access to unprecedented amounts of personal data and influence over user behavior.

The lessons learned from mobile investing, the importance of network effects, the power of platform ecosystems, the global scalability of software-based business models, and the potential for technology to transform traditional industries would influence venture capital strategies for years to come. The mobile revolution had demonstrated once again that the most transformative investment opportunities often emerged from fundamental platform shifts that enabled entirely new categories of products, services, and business models.

As venture capitalists looked toward the future, they would apply the lessons of mobile investing to new platform opportunities including artificial intelligence, virtual and augmented reality, autonomous vehicles, and blockchain technologies. The mobile revolution had shown that patient capital, combined with entrepreneurial vision and technological innovation, could create companies that would reshape entire industries and generate extraordinary returns for investors willing to embrace transformative change.

Chapter 16

The Unicorn Era

"A unicorn is a startup valued at over $1 billion. As of this writing, there are 39 unicorns. That's a lot more than I expected when I first used the term."

Aileen Lee's 2013 blog post introducing the term "unicorn" to describe billion-dollar startups was intended to highlight how rare such companies were, as mythical as the legendary creatures for which she named them. Yet within just five years, there would be hundreds of unicorns, fundamentally transforming venture capital, reshaping global technology markets, and creating a new paradigm where billion-dollar valuations became not just common, but expected for successful startups.

The unicorn era, roughly spanning from 2010 to 2020, represented the most dramatic expansion of venture capital in history. Massive new funds, extended development timelines, global competition, and the emergence of "mega-rounds" worth hundreds of millions of dollars created an investment environment unlike anything the industry had previously experienced. This period would challenge every assumption about how venture capital worked, from fund sizes and investment stages to exit strategies and valuation methodologies.

The Origins of Unicorn Inflation

The unicorn phenomenon didn't emerge overnight, it was the result of several converging trends that had been building throughout the 2000s. The success of companies like Google, Facebook, and the mobile platform winners had demonstrated that technology companies could achieve unprecedented scale and market dominance. More importantly, these companies had shown that staying private longer while raising substantial capital could provide strategic advantages over going public too early.

The 2008 financial crisis paradoxically accelerated these trends. While public markets suffered severe volatility and regulatory oversight increased through legislation like Sarbanes-Oxley, private markets offered more stable capital sources and greater operational flexibility. Institutional investors, facing low yields in traditional asset classes, began increasing their allocations to alternative investments including venture capital.

At the same time, the global economy was becoming increasingly digital, creating larger addressable markets for technology companies. The internet and mobile platforms enabled startups to achieve global reach from their inception, while cloud computing infrastructure reduced the capital requirements for scaling technology services. These changes meant that successful technology companies could grow faster and achieve higher ultimate valuations than had been possible in previous eras.

The venture capital industry itself was also maturing and consolidating. Successful funds from the 1990s and 2000s had generated substantial returns, enabling them to raise increasingly large successor funds. Limited partners, pension funds, endowments, and sovereign wealth funds were becoming more sophisticated about venture investing and were willing to commit larger amounts of capital to top-performing funds.

Perhaps most importantly, the competitive dynamics of venture capital were intensifying. As the number of high-quality investment opportunities remained relatively constant while the amount of available capital increased dramatically, venture firms found themselves competing aggressively for access to the best entrepreneurs and companies. This competition drove up valuations and created pressure to differentiate through fund size, expertise, and value-added services.

The Emergence of Mega-Funds

The most visible manifestation of the changing venture capital landscape was the emergence of "mega-funds" worth $1 billion or more. Traditionally, even the most successful venture capital funds had raised $300-500 million, which was considered sufficient to make meaningful investments in early and growth-stage companies while maintaining focused portfolios.

The mega-fund trend began with established firms like Kleiner Perkins, Sequoia Capital, and Andreessen Horowitz raising funds that exceeded $1 billion for the first time. These firms argued that larger funds were necessary to support portfolio companies through longer development cycles and to compete with new classes of investors including hedge funds, mutual funds, and sovereign wealth funds that were entering the venture capital market.

Andreessen Horowitz, founded in 2009 by Marc Andreessen and Ben Horowitz, became particularly associated with the mega-fund approach. The firm's philosophy of "software eating the world" justified large investments in companies that were using technology to transform traditional industries. Their willingness to make $50-100 million investments in single companies, combined with extensive operational support services, represented a new model for venture capital that blurred the lines between venture investing and growth equity.

New entrants to the venture capital market also drove the mega-fund trend. SoftBank, the Japanese technology conglomerate led by Masayoshi Son, launched the $100 billion Vision Fund in 2017, by far the largest technology investment fund in history. The Vision Fund's approach was to make massive investments ($100 million to $1 billion per company) in later-stage companies, accelerating their growth and market dominance while generating returns through rapid scaling rather than traditional exit strategies.

Other international investors also created large technology investment funds. Chinese investors like Alibaba's Taobao Marketplace, Tencent, and various government-backed funds began making substantial investments in U.S. and global technology companies. Sovereign wealth funds from countries like Saudi Arabia, Singapore, and Norway allocated billions of dollars to technology investing, often through partnerships with established venture capital firms.

The availability of this capital had profound effects on the venture ecosystem. Companies that might have been forced to go public or seek acquisitions due to capital constraints could now raise successive private rounds worth hundreds of millions of dollars. This enabled them to pursue more ambitious growth strategies, invest more heavily in research and development, and delay exits until they had achieved greater scale and market position.

The Late-Stage Funding Explosion

The mega-fund trend was accompanied by a dramatic expansion of late-stage venture funding. Companies that had previously gone public with market capitalizations of $500 million to $1 billion were now raising private rounds at those valuations, pushing their eventual public market debuts to much higher levels.

This late-stage funding served several purposes for both companies and investors. For companies, private capital allowed them to invest in global expansion, product development, and market share capture without the quarterly earnings pressures and regulatory requirements of public markets. For investors, late-stage companies offered lower risk profiles than early-stage ventures while still providing exposure to high-growth technology sectors.

The late-stage funding also created new dynamics in venture capital fund management. Traditional venture funds with $100-300 million in capital could participate in early rounds but were often excluded from the large late-stage rounds that determined ultimate returns. This created pressure for venture firms to raise larger funds or develop partnerships with growth equity investors who could provide follow-on capital.

Companies like Uber, Airbnb, Palantir, and SpaceX became emblematic of the late-stage funding trend. These companies raised multiple rounds worth hundreds of millions of dollars each, achieving private market valuations that exceeded the market capitalizations of many established public companies. Uber alone raised more than $20 billion in private funding across multiple rounds, reaching a private valuation of $72 billion before going public.

The extended private market development also created new challenges for venture capital portfolio management. Traditional venture funds assumed that successful portfolio companies would go public or be acquired within 5-7 years, allowing investors to realize returns and reinvest capital. The unicorn era extended these timelines to 10-15 years or more, requiring different fund structures and investor expectations.

Valuation Methodology Evolution

The unicorn era forced venture capitalists to develop new approaches to company valuation that could handle unprecedented growth rates, market sizes, and competitive dynamics. Traditional valuation methods based on revenue multiples or comparable public companies often seemed inadequate for companies that were creating entirely new markets or achieving growth rates that had no historical precedent.

The concept of "total addressable market" (TAM) became central to unicorn valuations. Companies like Uber argued that their TAM included not just the existing taxi and limousine market, but all personal transportation, freight logistics, and food delivery. These expanded market definitions justified valuations that seemed enormous compared to existing market participants but reasonable when compared to the theoretical maximum market size.

Network effects and winner-take-all market dynamics also influenced valuation approaches. Companies that could demonstrate strong network effects, where each additional user made the service more valuable for all users were valued based on their potential to capture entire market categories rather than just market share within existing categories.

The concept of "blitzscaling", Reid Hoffman's term for prioritizing speed over efficiency in pursuit of market dominance became influential in venture capital valuation. Companies that could achieve rapid growth and market share capture were valued based on their ultimate monopoly potential rather than their current financial metrics.

International expansion potential also became a key valuation driver. Companies that could demonstrate success in multiple geographic markets were valued based on their global opportunity rather than just their domestic performance. This was particularly important for software and platform businesses that could scale internationally with relatively modest additional investment.

However, these new valuation approaches also created risks and challenges. Many unicorn valuations were based on assumptions about market development, competitive dynamics, and execution capabilities that would prove overly optimistic. The disconnect between private market valuations and public market expectations would create significant challenges when these companies eventually sought to go public.

The Delayed IPO Phenomenon

One of the most significant aspects of the unicorn era was the dramatic extension of the time between company formation and initial public offerings. While technology companies in the 1990s and early 2000s typically went public within 5-7 years of founding, unicorn-era companies often remained private for 10-15 years or more.

This delayed IPO phenomenon was driven by several factors. The availability of private capital meant that companies didn't need to access public markets for funding. The regulatory complexity and costs of being a public company had increased significantly since Sarbanes-Oxley, making private operation more attractive. Most importantly, many companies and their investors believed that staying private longer would enable them to achieve higher ultimate valuations by reaching greater scale and market maturity.

The delayed IPO strategy worked well for some companies but created challenges for others. Companies like Facebook, which went public in 2012 at a $104 billion valuation after eight years of private development, demonstrated that extended private market development could support massive public market success. However, other companies found that staying private too long led to inflated expectations that were difficult to meet in public markets.

The delayed IPO trend also created liquidity challenges for employees, early investors, and venture capital funds. Traditional venture capital fund structures assume 10-year fund lives with portfolio company exits occurring within 5-7 years. When successful companies remained private for 10-15 years, it created timing mismatches that required new fund structures and investor expectations.

Secondary markets for private company shares emerged to address some of these liquidity challenges. Companies like SecondMarket and EquityZen created platforms where employees and early investors could sell their shares to institutional investors, providing liquidity without requiring companies to go public. However, these secondary markets were limited in scale and often involved significant discounts to latest private round valuations.

Platform Companies and Winner-Take-All Markets

The unicorn era was characterized by the emergence of "platform" companies that created marketplaces, ecosystems, or infrastructure that other businesses could build upon. These platform companies often exhibited strong network effects and winner-take-all dynamics that justified extremely high valuations based on their potential market dominance.

Amazon exemplified the platform approach, expanding from online retail to cloud computing (AWS), advertising, and numerous other services. The company's platform strategy enabled it to enter new markets, cross-subsidize competitive activities, and create switching costs that made it difficult for customers to choose alternatives.

Google and Facebook also demonstrated platform strategies, leveraging their core services (search and social networking) to expand into advertising, mobile applications, and other technology services. These companies' ability to monetize their user bases across multiple services justified valuations that seemed enormous when compared to single-product companies.

New unicorn-era companies adopted similar platform strategies. Uber expanded from ride-sharing to food delivery (Uber Eats), freight logistics (Uber Freight), and other transportation-related services. Airbnb moved beyond home-sharing to experiences, business travel, and other hospitality services. These expansions were justified based on platform effects and customer lifetime value rather than profitability in individual business lines.

The platform approach also influenced venture capital investment strategies. Investors began looking for companies that could build platforms rather than just products, and they were willing to accept longer development timelines and higher capital requirements for companies that could demonstrate platform potential.

However, platform strategies also created execution risks and competitive vulnerabilities. Many companies that attempted to build platforms discovered that maintaining quality and focus across multiple business lines was more challenging than anticipated. Platform expansion also attracted competitive responses from established companies and new entrants who could focus on specific platform components.

The SoftBank Vision Fund Impact

No single investor had more impact on the unicorn era than SoftBank's Vision Fund, which raised $100 billion in 2017 with backing from Saudi Arabia's sovereign wealth fund, Abu Dhabi's Mubadala Investment Company, and other institutional investors. The Vision Fund's scale and investment approach fundamentally altered competitive dynamics in late-stage venture capital.

The Vision Fund's strategy was to make massive investments ($100 million to $1 billion) in companies that could achieve rapid global scale through aggressive spending on customer acquisition, market expansion, and competitive positioning. This approach prioritized growth and market share over profitability, betting that market dominance would eventually enable sustainable competitive advantages and strong financial returns.

The Vision Fund's investments included many of the era's most prominent unicorns: Uber ($8.1 billion invested), WeWork ($4.4 billion), Slack ($340 million), and dozens of others. These investments often represented the largest funding rounds in these companies' histories and enabled spending strategies that wouldn't have been feasible with traditional venture capital.

The Vision Fund's impact extended beyond its direct investments. The fund's willingness to make enormous investments at high valuations created competitive pressure on other investors to increase their investment sizes and accept higher valuations to win deals. This contributed to overall valuation inflation across the venture capital market.

More controversially, the Vision Fund's strategy raised questions about the sustainability of growth-at-all-costs approaches and the long-term viability of companies that achieved scale through subsidized customer acquisition rather than organic demand. Critics argued that the Vision Fund was distorting market dynamics and creating unsustainable business models that would eventually collapse when capital became less available.

The Vision Fund's mixed investment results, including major losses on WeWork and Uber would eventually validate some of these concerns. However, the fund's influence on unicorn-era investing patterns was undeniable, and its approach would be replicated by other large-scale technology investors.

Global Unicorn Expansion

The unicorn phenomenon wasn't limited to Silicon Valley or the United States. As global internet and mobile adoption accelerated, unicorn companies emerged in markets around the world, often adapting successful American business models for local conditions or creating entirely new approaches to technology and commerce.

China became particularly important in the global unicorn landscape, producing companies like Ant Financial (mobile payments), Didi Chuxing (ride-sharing), and ByteDance (social media and entertainment). These companies often achieved higher valuations than their American counterparts due to China's large domestic market, rapid growth rates, and unique competitive dynamics.

Chinese unicorns also demonstrated different approaches to business model development and monetization. Companies like Tencent and Alibaba integrated multiple services, social networking, e-commerce, payments, entertainment, and cloud computing in ways that created comprehensive digital ecosystems rather than focused single-product offerings.

European unicorns like Spotify (music streaming), Klarna (payments), and Adyen (payment processing) demonstrated that successful technology companies could emerge from markets with different regulatory environments, consumer preferences, and competitive landscapes. These companies often achieved global scale by focusing on specific market niches or technology capabilities rather than attempting to replicate broad platform strategies.

The global expansion of unicorns also created new challenges for venture capital firms, which needed to develop international investment capabilities and partnerships to access the best opportunities worldwide. Some American venture firms opened international offices or created separate funds for specific geographic markets, while others developed partnerships with local investors who provided market expertise and cultural knowledge.

The Direct Listing Innovation

As unicorn companies grew larger and more mature, some began exploring alternatives to traditional IPO processes that could provide liquidity for investors and employees while avoiding some of the costs and constraints of traditional public offerings. The "direct listing" approach, pioneered by Spotify in 2018, became an important innovation for large private companies.

Direct listings allowed companies to begin trading on public markets without raising new capital or using investment banks to underwrite and market their shares. Instead, existing shareholders could sell their shares directly to public market investors, providing liquidity without the dilution and expenses associated with traditional IPOs.

The direct listing approach was particularly attractive for companies that didn't need to raise additional capital and wanted to avoid the "IPO pop" that often occurred when investment banks priced shares below market-clearing levels. Companies like Slack and Palantir followed Spotify's example, demonstrating that direct listings could be viable alternatives for large, well-known companies.

However, direct listings also had limitations. They didn't provide companies with additional capital for growth or acquisitions, and they required companies to have sufficient existing shareholder bases to support liquid trading. The approach was most suitable for mature companies with strong financial performance and brand recognition rather than earlier-stage companies that needed capital for continued development.

The WeWork Cautionary Tale

Perhaps no single company better illustrated both the promise and the perils of the unicorn era than WeWork, the office space company that achieved a peak private valuation of $47 billion before its spectacular collapse during a failed IPO attempt in 2019.

WeWork's story embodied many characteristics of unicorn-era investing: a charismatic founder (Adam Neumann) with a bold vision, massive venture capital funding ($12.8 billion raised), aggressive global expansion, and a business model that prioritized growth over profitability. The company's "Space-as-a-Service" concept attracted investments from prestigious firms including Benchmark, JPMorgan Chase, and most notably, SoftBank's Vision Fund.

The company's valuation was justified based on its potential to transform commercial real estate through technology, flexible lease terms, and community-building among members. WeWork positioned itself as a technology company rather than a traditional real estate business, arguing that its software, data analytics, and member services created sustainable competitive advantages and justified high growth multiples.

However, WeWork's attempted IPO in 2019 exposed fundamental problems with its business model and governance. The company's S-1 filing revealed massive losses, questionable related-party transactions, and corporate governance practices that gave founder Adam Neumann extraordinary control over the company's direction. Public market investors were unwilling to accept the high valuation and governance structure that private investors had endorsed.

The failed IPO forced WeWork to withdraw its offering, accept a dramatic valuation reduction, and replace its CEO. The company's collapse became a cautionary tale about unicorn-era excess and the importance of sustainable business models, proper governance, and realistic valuations.

More broadly, the WeWork situation highlighted potential problems with late-stage venture capital investing. The company had raised enormous amounts of capital at increasing valuations without demonstrating sustainable unit economics or clear paths to profitability. The competitive dynamics among investors had created pressure to participate in financing rounds without adequate due diligence or valuation discipline.

The COVID-19 Acceleration

The COVID-19 pandemic, beginning in early 2020, had complex effects on the unicorn ecosystem. While many companies faced significant challenges due to economic disruption and changing consumer behavior, others experienced accelerated growth as digital transformation and remote work trends accelerated.

Companies focused on remote work, e-commerce, digital entertainment, and health technology saw dramatic increases in demand and valuation. Zoom, which had gone public in 2019, saw its market capitalization increase more than 10x as video conferencing became essential for business and social interaction. Similarly, companies like Peloton, DocuSign, and Shopify experienced rapid growth and valuation increases.

The pandemic also accelerated venture capital investment in certain sectors while reducing activity in others. Health technology, remote work tools, and e-commerce infrastructure attracted increased investment, while travel, hospitality, and physical retail-focused companies faced funding challenges.

More importantly, the pandemic demonstrated the importance of business model resilience and adaptability. Companies with strong balance sheets, diversified revenue streams, and flexible cost structures were better positioned to navigate the crisis than companies that depended on continuous growth and external funding.

Lessons and Evolution

The unicorn era fundamentally transformed venture capital, creating new possibilities for company building while also generating new risks and challenges. The availability of large amounts of patient capital enabled entrepreneurs to pursue more ambitious visions and achieve greater scale before going public, but it also created potential for valuation inflation and unsustainable business models.

The era demonstrated that technology companies could achieve unprecedented scale and market impact, but it also showed that growth-focused strategies needed to be balanced with sustainable unit economics and responsible governance. The most successful unicorns combined aggressive growth strategies with strong fundamentals and adaptable business models.

For venture capital firms, the unicorn era required new fund structures, investment approaches, and portfolio management strategies. The traditional venture capital model of small funds making relatively small investments in early-stage companies evolved to include mega-funds, growth equity strategies, and international investment capabilities.

The era also highlighted the importance of exit strategy planning and liquidity management. Extended private market development created opportunities for greater value creation but also increased risks related to valuation expectations, market timing, and investor liquidity needs.

As the unicorn era matured in the late 2010s and early 2020s, the venture capital industry began incorporating its lessons into more sophisticated investment approaches that balanced growth potential with business fundamentals, combined patient capital with performance accountability, and recognized both the opportunities and responsibilities that came with building companies at unprecedented scale.

The unicorn era had shown that venture capital could create companies capable of transforming entire industries and generating extraordinary returns, but it had also demonstrated that sustainable success required more than just ambitious vision and abundant capital. The most enduring unicorns would be those that combined transformative technology with sustainable business models, responsible governance, and long-term value creation for all stakeholders.

Part VI: Venture Capital's Evolution

Chapter 17

New Models, New Players

"The best way to predict the future is to invent it."

Alan Kay's famous observation about technological innovation could equally apply to the evolution of venture capital itself. By the 2000s and 2010s, the traditional venture capital model, established firms making carefully selected investments in promising startups was being challenged and complemented by an explosion of new approaches, new types of investors, and new mechanisms for connecting entrepreneurs with capital.

The emergence of accelerators, corporate venture capital, crowdfunding platforms, and international competitors didn't replace traditional venture capital so much as expand and democratize it. These new models reflected broader changes in technology, globalization, and capital markets that were lowering barriers to entry, increasing competition, and creating new opportunities for innovation in the venture capital industry itself.

The transformation was driven by several converging trends: the declining cost of starting technology companies, the globalization of entrepreneurship, the digitization of investment processes, and the recognition that venture capital's historical geographic and institutional constraints were limiting access to both entrepreneurs and capital sources. The result would be a more diverse, competitive, and globally distributed venture capital ecosystem that could support many more entrepreneurs while generating new forms of value creation and innovation.

The Accelerator Revolution

The modern startup accelerator model emerged from a simple observation: while venture capital was effective at funding promising companies, there was a significant gap in supporting the earliest stages of entrepreneurship. Traditional venture capitalists typically invested in companies that had already demonstrated some market traction, leaving a funding and mentorship gap for entrepreneurs who were just beginning to develop their ideas into viable businesses.

Y Combinator, founded in 2005 by Paul Graham, Jessica Livingston, Robert Morris, and Trevor Blackwell, pioneered the accelerator model that would be replicated hundreds of times around the world. The concept was elegantly simple: provide small amounts of capital ($6,000-20,000 per founder initially) combined with intensive mentorship, peer learning, and access to investor networks over a short, focused period (typically three months).

The Y Combinator model addressed several inefficiencies in the traditional venture capital ecosystem. It provided structure and deadlines that helped entrepreneurs focus their efforts and make rapid progress. The cohort-based approach created peer support and competitive dynamics that accelerated learning and development. Most importantly, the program culminated in "Demo Day", a presentation to investors that provided startups with access to venture capital networks that would have been difficult to reach independently.

The early success of Y Combinator alumni was remarkable. Companies like Airbnb, Dropbox, Stripe, and Reddit emerged from Y Combinator's early cohorts, demonstrating that the accelerator model could identify and nurture companies that would achieve billion-dollar valuations. This success attracted both entrepreneurs and investors to the accelerator model and validated the concept of systematic early-stage company development.

Techstars, founded in 2006 by David Cohen and Brad Feld, developed a similar but geographically distributed accelerator model. Rather than concentrating all activity in Silicon Valley, Techstars created accelerator programs in multiple cities, bringing mentorship and capital access to entrepreneurial communities that had been underserved by traditional venture capital. This geographic distribution proved that accelerator models could work outside traditional technology centers and could help develop local entrepreneurial ecosystems.

The accelerator model also evolved beyond technology companies to include specialized programs focused on specific industries, technologies, or social missions. Accelerators emerged for healthcare, clean technology, financial services, social impact, and numerous other sectors, each developing expertise and networks relevant to their focus areas.

Corporate accelerators became particularly important as large companies recognized that accelerator programs could provide access to innovative startups, emerging technologies, and entrepreneurial talent. Companies like Disney, Ford, Barclays, and Coca-Cola launched accelerator programs that combined startup mentorship with potential partnership and acquisition opportunities.

The success of accelerators also influenced traditional venture capital practices. Many venture firms began offering more extensive operational support, mentorship programs, and portfolio company services that resembled accelerator models. The lines between accelerators and early-stage venture capital became increasingly blurred as both models evolved to provide more comprehensive support for entrepreneurs.

Corporate Venture Capital Renaissance

Corporate venture capital, where established companies create investment arms to fund startups experienced dramatic growth during the 2000s and 2010s as corporations recognized that traditional research and development approaches were insufficient for keeping pace with technological change. Rather than trying to develop all innovations internally, companies could use venture investing to access external innovation while generating financial returns.

Intel Capital, one of the pioneers of corporate venture capital, demonstrated how strategic investing could serve multiple corporate objectives. Intel's investments in companies that used Intel processors created demand for Intel's core products while providing financial returns and market intelligence about emerging technologies and applications. This strategic alignment between investment activity and corporate objectives became a template for other corporate venture programs.

Google Ventures (later renamed GV), launched in 2009, represented a more sophisticated approach to corporate venture capital. Rather than focusing narrowly on companies that used Google's products, GV invested broadly in innovative technology companies across multiple sectors. The fund's independence from Google's core business operations allowed it to make investment decisions based on financial returns and strategic learning rather than immediate product integration.

The GV model also demonstrated how corporate venture capital could provide value to portfolio companies beyond just capital. Google's expertise in technology development, scaling operations, and navigating rapid growth could benefit startups in ways that financial investors couldn't replicate. This operational support became a key differentiator for many corporate venture programs.

Other technology companies followed Google's lead in creating substantial corporate venture arms. Apple's venture activities, while less publicized, focused on companies that could enhance Apple's ecosystem of products and services. Amazon's venture investments supported companies in e-commerce, cloud computing, and logistics that could benefit from Amazon's platform and infrastructure.

Traditional corporations outside the technology sector also embraced corporate venture capital as digital transformation accelerated across industries. General Electric's venture arm invested in industrial internet and energy technology companies. Johnson & Johnson's venture activities focused on healthcare and pharmaceutical innovations. Ford and other automotive companies created venture programs to access autonomous vehicle and mobility technology startups.

The growth of corporate venture capital created both opportunities and challenges for entrepreneurs and traditional venture capital firms. Corporate investors could provide strategic advantages, customer relationships, and operational expertise that financial investors couldn't match. However, corporate venture capital also introduced potential conflicts of interest, slower decision-making processes, and strategic constraints that could limit startup flexibility.

The most successful corporate venture programs learned to balance strategic objectives with financial returns, maintain investment independence while leveraging corporate resources, and provide value to portfolio companies without constraining their strategic options. This balance required sophisticated investment teams and corporate governance structures that could navigate the complex relationships between investment activities and core business operations.

The Crowdfunding Democratization

The emergence of crowdfunding platforms represented perhaps the most dramatic democratization of startup funding since the creation of venture capital itself. For the first time, entrepreneurs could raise capital directly from consumers, customers, and small investors without requiring approval from institutional venture capitalists.

Kickstarter, launched in 2009, pioneered the rewards-based crowdfunding model where entrepreneurs could pre-sell products to fund their development. This model was particularly effective for consumer products, creative projects, and hardware innovations that could benefit from market validation and customer engagement during the funding process.

The Kickstarter model demonstrated several advantages over traditional venture capital for certain types of companies. Product-focused companies could validate market demand before manufacturing, reducing the risk of product-market fit problems. Creative projects that might not meet venture capital return requirements could still access sufficient funding for development. Most importantly, the crowdfunding process itself provided marketing and customer acquisition benefits that traditional fundraising couldn't match.

Successful Kickstarter campaigns like Pebble smartwatches, Oculus VR headsets, and Exploding Kittens card games raised millions of dollars while building engaged customer communities and generating media attention. These successes demonstrated that crowdfunding could support substantial business development, not just small creative projects.

Indiegogo, launched in 2008, developed a more flexible crowdfunding platform that allowed both rewards-based and equity-based fundraising. The platform's international focus and lower barriers to entry made it accessible to entrepreneurs worldwide, further democratizing access to startup funding.

The JOBS Act of 2012 enabled equity crowdfunding in the United States, allowing non-accredited investors to purchase equity stakes in startups through online platforms. Companies like SeedInvest, EquityZen, and Republic created platforms where entrepreneurs could raise capital from retail investors while complying with securities regulations.

Equity crowdfunding addressed some limitations of rewards-based platforms by allowing companies to raise capital without requiring physical products or pre-sales. Service companies, software businesses, and other ventures that couldn't offer tangible rewards could access crowdfunding capital while building investor communities that could support future growth.

The crowdfunding model also evolved to include specialized platforms focused on specific industries or investor types. Real estate crowdfunding platforms like Fundrise and RealtyMogul enabled retail investors to participate in commercial real estate investments. Donation-based platforms like GoFundMe supported social causes and personal projects that couldn't provide financial returns.

However, crowdfunding also revealed challenges related to investor protection, due diligence, and company governance. Retail investors often lacked the expertise to evaluate startup investments effectively, leading to concerns about fraud and unsuitable investments. The democratization of startup investing required new regulatory frameworks and investor education programs to protect participants while preserving access to capital.

International Competition and Global Venture Capital

The globalization of venture capital accelerated dramatically during the 2000s and 2010s as entrepreneurial ecosystems developed worldwide and capital flows became increasingly international. Silicon Valley's dominance in venture capital, while still significant, was challenged by emerging venture centers in Asia, Europe, and other regions.

China's venture capital ecosystem experienced explosive growth, driven by the country's large domestic market, rapid internet adoption, and supportive government policies. Chinese venture firms like IDG Capital, Sequoia Capital China, and Hillhouse Capital developed expertise in local markets while also making international investments. Chinese technology companies like Alibaba, Tencent, and Baidu became major corporate venture investors, funding startups both domestically and internationally.

The success of Chinese internet companies also demonstrated that successful technology businesses could emerge from non-Western markets and achieve global scale. Companies like Alibaba's e-commerce platforms, Tencent's social networking and gaming services, and ByteDance's TikTok social media platform achieved user bases and valuations that rivaled or exceeded their American counterparts.

European venture capital also matured significantly, with countries like the United Kingdom, Germany, France, and the Nordic countries developing sophisticated venture ecosystems. European venture firms like Accel (London), Rocket Internet (Berlin), and Index Ventures (London/Geneva) achieved global recognition through successful investments in companies like Spotify, Skype, and numerous fintech companies.

The European venture capital ecosystem benefited from several unique characteristics, strong technical universities, favorable regulatory environments for certain technologies (particularly fintech and privacy-focused services), and cultural diversity that enabled companies to develop products for global markets from inception.

Israel became particularly important in venture capital due to its concentration of technical talent, military technology expertise, and government support for innovation. Israeli venture firms and startups attracted significant international investment, while Israeli entrepreneurs founded successful companies in Silicon Valley and other global technology centers.

Other regions also developed venture capital capabilities, often with support from government initiatives and international partnerships. Singapore, South Korea, Australia, Canada, and Brazil all created venture capital ecosystems that could support local entrepreneurs while attracting international investment.

The globalization of venture capital created both opportunities and challenges. Entrepreneurs gained access to larger pools of capital and could choose investors based on expertise and strategic fit rather than just geographic proximity. However, international venture investing also required sophisticated understanding of different regulatory environments, cultural contexts, and business practices.

Cross-border venture investing became increasingly common as firms sought to access the best opportunities regardless of location. American venture firms opened international offices, while international firms established presences in Silicon Valley. This global integration of venture capital markets increased competition while also expanding opportunities for entrepreneurs and investors.

The Rise of Solo Capitalists and Micro-VCs

The traditional venture capital model assumed that successful investing required teams of partners, extensive due diligence processes, and large funds capable of making substantial investments. However, the 2000s and 2010s saw the emergence of "solo capitalists" and "micro-VCs" who challenged these assumptions by creating smaller, more focused investment vehicles.

Solo capitalists like Chris Sacca (Lowercase Capital), Dave McClure (500 Startups), and Josh Kopelman (First Round Capital) demonstrated that individual investors with strong networks and investment expertise could achieve excellent returns without traditional venture firm structures. These investors often focused on early-stage companies where smaller investment amounts were sufficient and where personal relationships and quick decision-making could provide competitive advantages.

The micro-VC model was enabled by several trends: the declining cost of starting technology companies meant that smaller investments could support meaningful business development; the success of angel investors demonstrated that individual expertise could be as valuable as institutional resources; and the proliferation of entrepreneurial talent meant that promising opportunities existed beyond the deal flow of established venture firms.

Micro-VCs also benefited from operational advantages over larger funds. They could make investment decisions quickly without complex partnership approval processes. They could focus on specific sectors or stages without needing to diversify across multiple investment themes. Most importantly, they could provide more personalized attention to portfolio companies without the portfolio management constraints of larger funds.

First Round Capital, founded by Josh Kopelman, Howard Morgan, and Rob Hayes, became one of the most successful examples of the focused early-stage investment model. The firm's emphasis on seed-stage investments, operational support, and founder-friendly terms enabled it to participate in companies like Uber, Square, and Warby Parker from their earliest stages.

Dave McClure's 500 Startups took the micro-VC concept to its logical extreme by making very small investments ($25,000-100,000) in hundreds of companies per year. The "spray and pray" approach assumed that a few spectacular successes would generate returns that more than compensated for the inevitable high failure rates of early-stage investing.

The success of micro-VCs and solo capitalists influenced the broader venture capital industry by demonstrating the value of specialization, quick decision-making, and founder-focused approaches. Many established venture firms created smaller, faster-moving funds focused on seed-stage investing, while others modified their processes to compete more effectively with nimble micro-VC competitors.

AngelList and the Democratization of Angel Investing

AngelList, founded in 2010 by Naval Ravikant and Babak Nivi, created perhaps the most significant innovation in early-stage investing by building a platform that connected entrepreneurs with angel investors while reducing the friction and costs associated with early-stage fundraising.

The traditional angel investing process was highly relationship-dependent and geographically constrained. Entrepreneurs needed to know angel investors personally or obtain introductions through professional networks. Angel investors typically learned about opportunities through personal connections rather than systematic deal flow. The legal and administrative costs of angel investments were often disproportionate to the investment amounts, creating barriers for both entrepreneurs and investors.

AngelList addressed these inefficiencies by creating an online platform where entrepreneurs could create profiles for their companies and angel investors could browse opportunities, make investments, and coordinate syndicated deals. The platform's standardized legal documentation and streamlined investment processes reduced transaction costs while expanding access for both entrepreneurs and investors.

The AngelList model also introduced the concept of "syndicates," where experienced angel investors could lead investment rounds and allow other investors to participate alongside them. This approach provided newer angel investors with access to deal flow and expertise while enabling experienced investors to increase their investment capacity through other people's capital.

The success of AngelList demonstrated the potential for technology platforms to improve efficiency in venture capital markets. The platform's data about investment activity, company performance, and investor behavior provided transparency that had previously been unavailable in private markets. This transparency enabled better decision-making by both entrepreneurs and investors while also supporting academic research about venture capital effectiveness.

AngelList's evolution into a broader platform for startup services, including recruiting, fund administration, and secondary trading illustrated how technology platforms could address multiple inefficiencies in entrepreneurial ecosystems. The company's success encouraged other entrepreneurs to build technology solutions for venture capital and startup challenges.

Government-Backed Innovation Programs

Governments around the world recognized that venture capital and entrepreneurship were becoming increasingly important for economic competitiveness and began creating programs to support innovation ecosystems. These government initiatives took various forms, from direct investment funds to tax incentives to regulatory reforms that facilitated private investment.

The Small Business Innovation Research (SBIR) program in the United States, while predating the modern venture capital era, became an important complement to private venture capital by providing early-stage funding for technology development. SBIR grants enabled entrepreneurs to develop proof-of-concept technologies that could subsequently attract venture capital for commercialization.

Israel's government programs, including the Office of the Chief Scientist and various technology incubators, demonstrated how public sector support could catalyze private venture capital activity. Government co-investment programs reduced risk for private investors while ensuring that public resources were deployed alongside private capital and expertise.

The United Kingdom's Enterprise Investment Scheme and Seed Enterprise Investment Scheme provided tax incentives for angel investors, significantly increasing the pool of capital available for early-stage companies. These programs demonstrated how tax policy could be used to encourage private investment in innovation without requiring direct government spending.

Singapore's government created several venture capital programs, including direct investment funds and co-investment vehicles that partnered with private venture firms. The country's strategic focus on becoming a technology hub included substantial government resources for supporting entrepreneurship and attracting international venture capital.

China's government support for venture capital and innovation was particularly extensive, including direct investment through government funds, support for state-owned venture capital firms, and regulatory policies that favored domestic technology companies. This government involvement contributed to the rapid growth of China's venture capital ecosystem while also creating competitive advantages for Chinese companies.

However, government involvement in venture capital also created potential challenges and distortions. Political considerations might influence investment decisions in ways that reduced economic efficiency. Government funding might crowd out private capital or create dependencies that reduced entrepreneurial incentives. The most successful government programs learned to complement rather than replace private venture capital while maintaining focus on economic rather than political objectives.

The Evolution of Venture Capital Fund Structures

The emergence of new models and players also drove innovation in venture capital fund structures and terms. Traditional venture capital funds were organized as limited partnerships with 10-year terms, fixed management fees, and carried interest that aligned investor and manager incentives. While this structure remained dominant, new variations emerged to address different investment strategies and market conditions.

Rolling funds, pioneered by AngelList, allowed fund managers to raise capital continuously rather than in discrete fundraising cycles. This structure provided more flexibility for both managers and investors while reducing the time and costs associated with traditional fund formation. Rolling funds were particularly attractive for emerging managers and specialized investment strategies that might not support traditional fund structures.

Opportunity funds focused on later-stage investments in successful portfolio companies, providing additional capital for growth while generating returns for investors who wanted exposure to more mature venture-backed companies. These funds addressed the challenge of managing successful investments through extended private market development cycles.

Sector-specific funds became increasingly common as venture capital matured and specialized expertise became more important for success. Healthcare venture funds, fintech funds, enterprise software funds, and numerous other specialized investment vehicles emerged to serve entrepreneurs and investors with specific industry focus and expertise requirements.

Geographic funds also proliferated as venture capital became more globally distributed. Regional funds focused on specific countries or regions could provide local market expertise and relationships while accessing international capital sources. These funds were particularly important for developing entrepreneurial ecosystems in emerging markets.

Fund-of-funds vehicles allowed institutional investors to diversify their venture capital exposure across multiple fund managers and investment strategies. These vehicles were particularly attractive for smaller institutional investors who wanted venture capital exposure but lacked the resources to evaluate and manage relationships with multiple venture funds directly.

The evolution of fund structures reflected broader changes in venture capital markets, including increased competition, longer investment timelines, greater specialization, and more diverse sources of capital. These structural innovations enabled venture capital to serve a broader range of entrepreneurs and investors while maintaining alignment between economic incentives and successful company building.

The Impact of Technology on Venture Capital Operations

Technology platforms increasingly influenced how venture capital firms operated, from deal sourcing and due diligence to portfolio management and investor relations. Software tools and data analytics enabled venture firms to operate more efficiently while making better-informed investment decisions.

Deal sourcing platforms aggregated information about startup funding activity, enabling venture capitalists to identify promising companies earlier and more systematically. Services like PitchBook, Crunchbase, and CB Insights provided data about investment activity, company performance, and market trends that supported more informed investment decision-making.

Due diligence processes were enhanced by technology tools that could analyze large amounts of data about market opportunities, competitive dynamics, and company performance. Reference checking, background verification, and technical assessment could be conducted more efficiently through specialized software platforms and services.

Portfolio management platforms enabled venture firms to track portfolio company performance, provide operational support, and identify opportunities for value creation more systematically. These tools were particularly important for firms with large portfolios or complex operational support programs.

Investor relations and fund administration benefited from software platforms that automated reporting, compliance, and communication with limited partners. These tools reduced administrative costs while improving transparency and communication quality.

The use of artificial intelligence and machine learning in venture capital began emerging during this period, with some firms experimenting with algorithmic approaches to deal sourcing, due diligence, and investment decision-making. While human judgment remained central to venture capital success, technology tools increasingly augmented investor capabilities and operational efficiency.

Setting the Foundation for Future Innovation

The proliferation of new models and players in venture capital during the 2000s and 2010s created a more diverse, competitive, and accessible ecosystem for entrepreneurs and investors. Accelerators, corporate venture capital, crowdfunding, international competitors, and technology platforms all contributed to expanding opportunities while improving efficiency in venture capital markets.

These innovations didn't replace traditional venture capital but complemented and enhanced it. The best venture capital firms learned to work with accelerators, compete and partner with corporate investors, leverage technology platforms, and operate in increasingly global markets. The result was a venture capital ecosystem that could support more entrepreneurs, deploy more capital, and generate innovation across more industries and geographies than had previously been possible.

The diversity of models and players also created more pathways for entrepreneurial success. Companies could access capital and support through multiple channels, choosing the combination of investors and resources that best matched their specific needs and circumstances. This flexibility was particularly important as technology companies became more diverse in their business models, market focus, and capital requirements.

Looking forward, the continued evolution of venture capital models and the emergence of new players would be driven by ongoing changes in technology, globalization, and capital markets. The fundamental challenge would remain constant: connecting entrepreneurs with the capital, expertise, and networks they needed to build transformative companies. But the methods, mechanisms, and participants in this process would continue to evolve, creating new opportunities for innovation in the venture capital industry itself.

Chapter 18

The Climate Tech Revolution

"Climate change is the defining challenge of our time. It's also the greatest business opportunity of our time."

This declaration from venture capitalist John Doerr at the 2007 TED conference captured a fundamental shift in how the investment community was beginning to view environmental challenges. What had once been seen primarily as regulatory constraints or corporate social responsibility obligations was increasingly recognized as a massive market opportunity that could generate both significant financial returns and positive environmental impact.

The climate tech revolution in venture capital represented more than just a new investment sector, it embodied a transformation in how investors thought about risk, opportunity, and responsibility. As scientific consensus about climate change solidified and extreme weather events became more frequent and severe, venture capitalists began to recognize that environmental sustainability wasn't just morally imperative but economically inevitable.

The journey from niche environmental investing to mainstream climate tech would prove challenging, marked by early failures, technology breakthroughs, policy shifts, and ultimately the emergence of a new generation of companies that could compete on economics while delivering environmental benefits. This evolution would test venture capital's ability to balance patient capital with commercial returns, navigate complex regulatory environments, and support technologies that required longer development timelines than traditional software investments.

The Early Clean Tech Wave

The first major wave of venture investment in clean technology began in the early 2000s, driven by rising energy prices, concerns about energy security, and growing awareness of environmental challenges. However, this initial clean tech boom was characterized more by enthusiasm than by deep understanding of the unique challenges facing environmental technology companies.

Venture capitalists, fresh from the internet boom and bust, were attracted to clean technology by several compelling factors. The global energy market was enormous, trillions of dollars annually suggesting that even small market share gains could support billion-dollar companies. Government policies in the United States, Europe, and other regions were creating incentives for renewable energy and energy efficiency. Most importantly, clean technology seemed to offer the possibility of combining financial returns with positive environmental impact.

Kleiner Perkins became one of the most prominent early investors in clean technology, launching a $100 million clean tech fund in 2004 and eventually committing more than $1 billion to the sector. The firm's investments included solar companies like Miasole and Konarka, biofuel companies like Range Fuels and Mascoma, and battery companies like A123 Systems and Fisker Automotive.

Other established venture firms also entered the clean tech sector with substantial commitments. Khosla Ventures, founded by Sun Microsystems co-founder Vinod Khosla, focused heavily on clean technology with investments in biofuels, solar energy, and energy storage. New Enterprise Associates, Draper Fisher Jurvetson, and numerous other firms created clean tech investment programs and hired partners with relevant industry expertise.

The investment thesis underlying this first clean tech wave was compelling in theory but proved problematic in practice. Venture capitalists assumed that clean technology companies would follow similar development patterns to information technology companies, rapid iteration, asset-light business models, and network effects that created winner-take-all markets.

However, clean technology proved to have fundamentally different characteristics. Energy and environmental technologies often required substantial capital for manufacturing, long development timelines for technology validation, complex regulatory approval processes, and integration with existing infrastructure systems that changed slowly. These characteristics made clean tech investments more similar to traditional industrial or pharmaceutical investments than to the software companies that had driven venture capital returns in previous decades.

The Clean Tech 1.0 Disappointment

The first wave of clean tech venture investing, roughly from 2005 to 2012, produced disappointing results that would influence the sector's development for years to come. Despite more than $25 billion in venture capital investment, very few clean tech companies achieved the scale or returns that investors had expected.

Several high-profile failures illustrated the challenges facing clean tech investments. Solyndra, a solar panel manufacturer that received $535 million in government loan guarantees, filed for bankruptcy in 2011 as Chinese competitors achieved manufacturing scale and cost advantages that Solyndra couldn't match. Range Fuels, a biofuel company backed by Khosla Ventures and other prominent investors, shut down after failing to achieve commercial viability for its cellulosic ethanol technology.

A123 Systems, a battery manufacturer that went public in 2009 and was once valued at more than $2 billion, filed for bankruptcy in 2012 due to manufacturing defects and intense competition from Asian battery manufacturers. Fisker Automotive, an electric vehicle company backed by Kleiner Perkins, failed to achieve production scale and was eventually sold to a Chinese company for a fraction of its venture capital investment.

These failures revealed several structural challenges with the first generation of clean tech investing. Many companies were attempting to commercialize technologies that weren't sufficiently mature for large-scale deployment. The capital requirements for manufacturing and scaling clean tech companies were often much higher than venture capitalists had anticipated, leading to funding gaps that prevented companies from achieving commercial viability.

Competition from established players, particularly Chinese manufacturers with government support and lower labor costs, proved more intense than expected. Clean tech companies found themselves competing not just with other startups but with large, well-funded incumbents who could achieve manufacturing scale more quickly and efficiently.

Regulatory and policy risks also proved significant. Many clean tech business models depended on government incentives, tax credits, or regulatory mandates that could change unpredictably. When policy support was reduced or eliminated, many clean tech companies found their economic models unsustainable.

Perhaps most importantly, the first wave of clean tech investing revealed that environmental technology development followed different timelines and required different expertise than information technology. Venture capitalists who had succeeded with internet and software investments often lacked the technical knowledge, industry relationships, and patience required for successful clean tech investing.

Lessons Learned and Strategy Evolution

The disappointments of Clean Tech 1.0 led to significant reflection and strategy evolution within the venture capital community. Rather than abandoning environmental investing entirely, many investors began developing more sophisticated approaches that addressed the lessons learned from early failures.

The most important lesson was the recognition that clean technology investments required different evaluation criteria, investment structures, and portfolio management approaches than traditional venture capital. Successful clean tech investing required deeper technical due diligence, longer investment timelines, and often larger capital commitments than software investments.

Venture capitalists also learned to focus more carefully on market timing and competitive dynamics. Early clean tech investments had often assumed that environmental benefits alone would drive market adoption, but successful clean tech companies needed to compete on traditional business metrics like cost, performance, and reliability.

The importance of manufacturing and scaling capabilities became clear. Many clean tech companies that had promising laboratory results failed during the transition to commercial manufacturing. Successful clean tech investors began paying more attention to manufacturing partnerships, supply chain management, and the capital requirements for achieving production scale.

Policy risk analysis became more sophisticated. Rather than simply betting on continued government support for clean technology, investors began evaluating companies based on their ability to compete without subsidies and their resilience to policy changes.

Perhaps most importantly, venture capitalists began recognizing that successful clean tech investing required specialized expertise and industry knowledge. Firms began hiring partners with backgrounds in energy, environmental science, and industrial technology rather than relying solely on generalist investors with software and internet experience.

The Software-First Approach

One of the most significant developments in clean tech investing was the emergence of a "software-first" approach that applied digital technology to environmental challenges. This approach leveraged venture capital's core competencies in software and data analytics while addressing environmental problems in ways that didn't require the heavy capital investments and long development timelines that had characterized Clean Tech 1.0.

Companies like Opower (now Oracle Utilities) demonstrated how software could create environmental impact by helping utility customers reduce energy consumption through data analytics and behavioral insights. Rather than requiring new hardware or infrastructure, Opower's platform worked with existing utility systems to provide customers with detailed energy usage information and recommendations for reducing consumption.

Smart grid and energy management companies also attracted venture investment by focusing on software solutions that could optimize existing energy infrastructure. Companies like Tendril, Silver Spring Networks, and EnerNOC developed platforms that could reduce energy consumption and improve grid efficiency through better data collection and analysis.

The software-first approach proved attractive to venture investors because it offered more familiar investment characteristics: asset-light business models, scalable software platforms, and shorter development timelines. These companies could often achieve profitability and scale without the massive capital requirements that had challenged hardware-focused clean tech companies.

Building automation and energy efficiency software also emerged as attractive investment areas. Companies like BuildingIQ and Lucid Design Group developed platforms that could optimize energy usage in commercial buildings through data analytics and automated control systems. These solutions provided clear return on investment for customers while reducing environmental impact.

The success of software-focused environmental companies helped rehabilitate clean tech investing by demonstrating that environmental benefits and strong financial returns could be achieved simultaneously. This success encouraged broader venture capital participation in environmental technology while establishing new models for clean tech investment.

The Tesla Catalyst

Tesla's success as both a technology company and a clean tech investment became a crucial catalyst for renewed venture capital interest in environmental technology. Founded in 2003 by Martin Eberhard and Marc Tarpenning, and later led by Elon Musk, Tesla demonstrated that clean technology companies could achieve the scale, growth rates, and market valuations typically associated with software companies.

Tesla's early venture capital came from investors including Draper Fisher Jurvetson, VantagePoint Capital Partners, and Valor Equity Partners. These investments were notable for their size, Tesla raised more than $400 million in private funding and for the investors' willingness to support a hardware-intensive automotive company during a period when many venture capitalists were avoiding capital-intensive clean tech investments.

The company's approach differed significantly from other electric vehicle startups of the Clean Tech 1.0 era. Rather than trying to compete directly with internal combustion engine vehicles on cost, Tesla focused on creating premium electric vehicles that offered superior performance and technology integration. This strategy allowed the company to achieve positive margins while building the manufacturing capabilities and brand recognition needed for mass market expansion.

Tesla's initial public offering in 2010 was the first successful automotive IPO since Ford went public in 1956, demonstrating that public markets were willing to support innovative clean tech companies with strong technology and clear market traction. The company's subsequent growth and market capitalization expansion, reaching over $1 trillion at its peak validated the potential for clean tech companies to achieve extraordinary scale.

Perhaps more importantly, Tesla's success demonstrated that clean technology could be both environmentally beneficial and commercially successful without requiring ongoing subsidies or policy support. The company's ability to compete on performance, technology, and increasingly on cost, showed that clean tech companies could succeed through superior products rather than just environmental benefits.

Tesla's influence extended beyond its direct impact on electric vehicle markets. The company's success encouraged venture investment in related technologies including battery storage, electric vehicle charging infrastructure, and autonomous vehicle technology. It also demonstrated the importance of vertical integration, manufacturing excellence, and brand development for clean tech companies.

The Climate Crisis Urgency

By the mid-2010s, scientific evidence about climate change had become increasingly compelling and urgent. The Paris Climate Agreement in 2015 established global commitments to limit greenhouse gas emissions, while extreme weather events and their economic impacts made climate risks more tangible for businesses and investors.

This growing urgency began to influence venture capital investment decisions in several ways. Environmental, social, and governance (ESG) considerations became more important for institutional investors who provided capital to venture funds. Limited partners began asking venture firms about their climate-related investments and policies, creating market pressure for environmental investing.

The concept of "impact investing", investments intended to generate positive social or environmental impact alongside financial returns gained traction in venture capital. While impact investing had existed in various forms for decades, the climate crisis gave it new urgency and scale as investors recognized that environmental challenges represented both risks and opportunities.

Younger venture capitalists and entrepreneurs, particularly those from millennial and Generation Z demographics, brought heightened environmental awareness to investment decisions. This generational shift created cultural pressure within venture firms to consider environmental impact alongside financial returns.

The rise of benefit corporations (B-Corps) and other legal structures that explicitly recognized social and environmental objectives also influenced venture investing. Companies could now legally prioritize environmental impact alongside shareholder returns, reducing potential conflicts between profitability and sustainability.

Perhaps most importantly, the climate crisis created new market opportunities as governments, corporations, and consumers began prioritizing environmental solutions. Carbon pricing mechanisms, renewable energy mandates, and corporate sustainability commitments created economic incentives for clean technology adoption that didn't depend solely on environmental motivations.

Climate Tech 2.0: The New Wave

The second wave of climate tech investing, beginning around 2015, incorporated lessons from Clean Tech 1.0 failures while addressing the growing urgency of climate change. This new generation of climate tech companies and investors approached environmental challenges with more sophisticated strategies, better technology, and clearer paths to commercial viability.

One of the key differences in Climate Tech 2.0 was the focus on technologies that could compete economically without subsidies. Solar and wind energy had achieved cost parity with fossil fuels in many markets, creating opportunities for companies that could improve efficiency, reduce costs, or enable better integration with electrical grids.

Battery storage technology also reached inflection points that enabled new business models and investment opportunities. Companies like Tesla's energy division, Sonnen, and numerous other battery storage companies developed solutions that could store renewable energy, provide grid stability services, and reduce electricity costs for commercial and residential customers.

Electric transportation expanded beyond passenger vehicles to include commercial trucks, buses, delivery vehicles, and even aircraft. Companies like Rivian (electric trucks), Proterra (electric buses), and Wright Electric (electric aircraft) attracted substantial venture investment by focusing on specific transportation segments where electric vehicles offered clear operational advantages.

Alternative protein companies emerged as a major climate tech investment category, addressing the environmental impact of animal agriculture. Companies like Beyond Meat, Impossible Foods, and Memphis Meats developed plant-based and laboratory-grown alternatives to conventional meat products that could reduce greenhouse gas emissions while meeting growing global protein demand.

Carbon capture and removal technologies also attracted increased venture investment as governments and corporations made commitments to achieve carbon neutrality. Companies like Climeworks, Global

Thermostat, and Opus 12 developed technologies that could remove carbon dioxide from the atmosphere or industrial processes, creating new opportunities for environmental impact and revenue generation.

Specialized Climate Tech Funds

The evolution of climate tech investing led to the creation of specialized venture funds focused exclusively on environmental technology and impact. These funds brought deeper sector expertise, longer investment timelines, and more sophisticated approaches to the unique challenges of climate tech investing.

Breakthrough Energy Ventures, founded by Bill Gates in 2015 with more than $1 billion in committed capital, became one of the most prominent climate-focused venture funds. The fund's 20-year investment timeline and focus on breakthrough technologies that could achieve global scale reflected lessons learned from Clean Tech 1.0 about the patient capital requirements for environmental technology development.

Founders Fund, led by Peter Thiel, also made substantial investments in climate technology while maintaining focus on commercial viability and technological breakthroughs. The fund's investments included companies like Planet Labs (satellite imagery), Stripe (carbon removal), and various other environmental technology companies.

Lowercarbon Capital, founded by Chris Sacca and other investors, focused specifically on technologies that could reduce greenhouse gas emissions while generating strong financial returns. The fund's approach emphasized the economic opportunities created by climate change while maintaining rigorous investment criteria.

DCVC (Data Collective), Khosla Ventures, and numerous other established venture firms also developed specialized climate tech investment programs with dedicated partners, investment criteria, and portfolio support capabilities.

These specialized funds brought several advantages to climate tech investing. They developed deeper technical expertise in environmental technologies and market dynamics. They could provide more patient capital with longer investment timelines appropriate for clean tech development cycles. Perhaps most importantly, they created networks of entrepreneurs, technical experts, and industry participants that could support portfolio company development and success.

Corporate Climate Tech Investing

Large corporations also became significant participants in climate tech venture investing, driven by their own sustainability commitments and the recognition that environmental technologies could create competitive advantages or new business opportunities.

Energy companies like Shell, Chevron, and BP created venture capital arms focused on clean technology investments. These corporate venture programs provided access to industry expertise, potential customers, and strategic partnerships that could accelerate clean tech commercialization.

Technology companies also increased their climate tech investments. Google's venture arm invested in companies developing renewable energy, energy storage, and carbon removal technologies. Microsoft's climate investment initiatives supported companies working on carbon capture, sustainable materials, and environmental monitoring.

Automotive companies created venture programs focused on electric vehicle technologies, autonomous driving, and mobility services. Ford, GM, and other manufacturers recognized that transportation electrification represented both competitive threats and opportunities that required investment in new technologies and business models.

The success of corporate climate tech investing depended on balancing strategic objectives with financial returns, maintaining investment independence while leveraging corporate resources, and providing value to portfolio companies without constraining their strategic flexibility. The most successful corporate climate programs learned to operate more like financial investors while providing strategic advantages that pure financial investors couldn't match.

Policy and Regulatory Environment

Government policies played crucial roles in creating market opportunities for climate tech companies and influencing venture capital investment decisions. Unlike Clean Tech 1.0, which often depended on direct subsidies or tax credits, Climate Tech 2.0 benefited from more diverse and stable policy support mechanisms.

Carbon pricing systems in California, Europe, and other regions created economic incentives for companies to reduce greenhouse gas emissions, generating demand for clean technology solutions. Renewable energy mandates and portfolio standards created guaranteed markets for solar, wind, and energy storage technologies.

Electric vehicle policies, including purchase incentives, charging infrastructure investments, and internal combustion engine phase-out commitments, created large addressable markets for transportation electrification companies. These policies provided more predictable long-term demand than the fluctuating tax credits that had characterized earlier clean tech policy support.

Building energy efficiency standards and green building requirements created markets for companies developing smart building technologies, energy management systems, and sustainable materials. These regulatory requirements often provided clear return on investment calculations that made business cases more compelling.

International climate agreements and national commitments to carbon neutrality created global policy frameworks that supported climate tech investment. The Paris Agreement's national determined contributions and the increasing number of countries committing to net-zero emissions by 2050 provided policy stability and long-term market visibility.

However, venture capitalists also learned to evaluate climate tech investments based on their resilience to policy changes and their ability to compete without ongoing government support. The most successful Climate Tech 2.0 companies were those that could provide economic value independent of policy incentives while benefiting from supportive regulatory environments.

Measurement and Impact Assessment

The growth of climate tech investing also drove innovation in impact measurement and assessment methodologies. Investors needed ways to evaluate and compare the environmental benefits of different investments while maintaining focus on financial returns.

Life cycle assessment (LCA) techniques became more sophisticated and widely used to evaluate the total environmental impact of clean technology products and services. These assessments could account for manufacturing, operation, and disposal impacts to provide more complete pictures of environmental benefits.

Carbon accounting and greenhouse gas emission measurement became standard practices for climate tech companies and investors. Companies developed capabilities to measure and report their environmental impact using standardized methodologies that enabled comparison and verification.

Third-party verification and certification programs also emerged to provide independent validation of environmental impact claims.

Organizations like B Lab (B Corporation certification), the Global Reporting Initiative, and various carbon offset verification programs created standards that could be used to evaluate climate tech company performance.

The development of more sophisticated impact measurement capabilities enabled better investment decision-making while also providing marketing and credibility benefits for climate tech companies. Customers, partners, and investors increasingly demanded quantified environmental benefits alongside traditional business metrics.

Global Climate Tech Innovation

Climate tech innovation and investment became increasingly global phenomena as countries around the world recognized both the urgency of climate challenges and the economic opportunities they represented. Different regions developed specialized expertise and competitive advantages in various aspects of climate technology.

China emerged as a dominant force in renewable energy manufacturing, battery production, and electric vehicle development. Chinese companies achieved manufacturing scale and cost advantages in solar panels, wind turbines, and lithium-ion batteries that enabled global market leadership.

European countries developed strengths in offshore wind energy, energy storage, and sustainable transportation. Denmark's wind energy expertise, Norway's electric vehicle adoption, and Germany's energy storage development created regional clusters of climate tech innovation and investment.

Israel's technical expertise and entrepreneurial culture produced innovations in water technology, agricultural efficiency, and energy management. Israeli companies developed solutions for water scarcity, precision agriculture, and smart grid technologies that addressed both local needs and global markets.

The globalization of climate tech investing created opportunities for venture capitalists to access the best innovations regardless of location while also creating competitive pressure to develop international investment capabilities and partnerships.

The Future of Climate Tech Investing

By 2020, climate tech had evolved from a niche investment category to a mainstream venture capital sector with billions of dollars in annual investment and hundreds of companies developing solutions across multiple industries. The sector's maturation reflected both the growing urgency of climate challenges and the recognition that environmental technologies could generate significant financial returns while creating positive impact.

The COVID-19 pandemic and subsequent economic recovery programs also accelerated climate tech adoption as governments and corporations made substantial commitments to "build back better" with investments in clean energy, sustainable transportation, and environmental technology.

The success of companies like Tesla, Beyond Meat, and numerous renewable energy companies demonstrated that climate tech could achieve the scale, growth rates, and market impact that venture capitalists sought. These successes attracted broader venture capital participation while validating investment approaches that combined environmental impact with commercial viability.

Looking forward, climate tech investing would continue to evolve as new technologies matured, policy frameworks developed, and market opportunities expanded. The sector's combination of massive market opportunity, technological innovation potential, and positive environmental impact position it as a central theme in venture capital's next chapter of growth and development.

The climate tech revolution had shown that venture capital could address humanity's greatest challenges while generating strong financial returns, but it had also demonstrated that success required patience, expertise, and commitment to both commercial and environmental objectives. The continued evolution of climate tech investing would play a crucial role in determining both venture capital's future and the planet's environmental trajectory.

Part VII: Looking Forward

Chapter 19

Artificial Intelligence and the Future

"The development of full artificial intelligence could spell the end of the human race... It would take off on its own, and re-design itself at an ever-increasing rate."

Stephen Hawking's 2014 warning about artificial intelligence captured both the transformative potential and existential concerns that would come to define venture capital's approach to AI investing. Yet for venture capitalists, the emergence of practical artificial intelligence represented not just humanity's greatest technological challenge, but potentially its greatest business opportunity since the internet itself.

The AI revolution in venture capital began quietly in university laboratories and research institutions, where decades of incremental progress in machine learning, neural networks, and computational power were converging to create breakthrough capabilities. By 2010, these advances were beginning to enable new categories of products and services that could see, hear, understand, and learn in ways that had previously required human intelligence.

What followed was perhaps the most significant platform shift in venture capital history, one that would touch every industry, transform every business model, and create entirely new categories of companies while raising profound questions about the future of work, privacy, and human agency in an increasingly algorithmic world.

The Foundation Years: Machine Learning Emerges

The modern venture capital interest in artificial intelligence began not with dramatic breakthroughs, but with the quiet recognition that machine learning techniques were becoming practical tools for solving real business problems. Companies like Netflix were using recommendation algorithms to improve user engagement, Google was applying machine learning to search results and advertising, and financial services firms were using algorithmic trading and risk assessment systems.

The early venture investments in AI-adjacent companies focused primarily on data analytics and business intelligence applications that could extract insights from the growing volumes of digital data that companies were generating. Companies like Palantir, founded in 2003 with backing from In-Q-Tel and later Founders Fund, demonstrated that sophisticated data analysis could create substantial value for government and enterprise customers.

However, these early applications were primarily rule-based systems and statistical analysis rather than the adaptive, learning systems that would later define artificial intelligence. The venture capital community was still thinking about AI as an enhancement to existing software rather than as a transformative technology platform that could enable entirely new categories of products and services.

The breakthrough began with advances in deep learning, a subset of machine learning that used neural networks with multiple layers to recognize patterns in data. While the theoretical foundations of deep learning had existed for decades, the combination of increased computational power, larger datasets, and improved algorithms finally made these techniques practical for commercial applications.

The 2009 ImageNet challenge, which tasked computer vision systems with identifying objects in photographs, became a crucial milestone. When a deep learning system developed by Geoffrey Hinton's team achieved dramatically better performance than previous approaches, it demonstrated that artificial intelligence had reached a new level of capability that could have immediate practical applications.

This breakthrough attracted the attention of several prescient venture capitalists who recognized that improved pattern recognition capabilities could enable new categories of products and services. Companies that could automatically analyze images, understand speech, or extract insights from text could solve problems that had previously required human intelligence and manual labor.

The Deep Learning Revolution

The period from 2010 to 2015 saw the emergence of the first generation of venture-backed companies built specifically around deep learning and neural network technologies. These companies differed from earlier AI investments by focusing on applications that could learn and improve their performance through exposure to data rather than requiring explicit programming for each task.

Computer vision emerged as one of the first commercially viable deep learning applications. Companies like Clarifai, founded in 2013 with backing from Union Square Ventures, developed APIs that could automatically identify objects, scenes, and concepts in images. This capability enabled new applications in e-commerce, content moderation, medical imaging, and autonomous vehicles.

The practical applications were immediately compelling. E-commerce companies could automatically tag and categorize product images without manual labor. Social media platforms could identify inappropriate content at scale. Healthcare companies could assist radiologists in identifying abnormalities in medical scans. These use cases provided clear return on investment calculations that made venture capital funding decisions more straightforward.

Natural language processing also began achieving practical breakthrough capabilities. Companies like MonkeyLearn and Lexalytics developed platforms that could automatically analyze text for sentiment, extract key information, and categorize documents. While still limited compared to human language understanding, these systems could handle routine text analysis tasks with sufficient accuracy for commercial deployment.

Speech recognition technology, long a frustration for consumers who had experienced poor performance in earlier systems, achieved new levels of accuracy and reliability. Companies like Nuance Communications had been working on speech recognition for years, but the application of deep learning techniques enabled dramatic improvements in accuracy and natural language understanding.

The venture capital response to these early deep learning successes was initially cautious but increasingly enthusiastic as commercial traction became apparent. Investors who had been burned by previous AI hype cycles were initially skeptical, but the combination of technical breakthroughs and clear customer demand created compelling investment opportunities.

More importantly, the success of companies like Google, Facebook, and Amazon in applying machine learning to their core products demonstrated that AI could create sustainable competitive advantages and enormous business value. When Google's search results improved through machine learning, when Facebook's news feed became more engaging through algorithmic curation, and when Amazon's recommendations drove increased sales, it became clear that AI was not just a laboratory curiosity but a transformative business technology.

The Platform Companies Emerge

As deep learning techniques matured, several technology companies began positioning themselves as AI platform providers, offering tools and infrastructure that could enable other companies to incorporate artificial intelligence into their products and services without requiring extensive internal AI expertise.

Google's decision to open-source TensorFlow in 2015 was a pivotal moment that democratized access to advanced AI development tools. By providing a sophisticated machine learning framework for free, Google enabled thousands of developers and companies to experiment with AI applications while also creating an ecosystem of developers familiar with Google's tools and approaches.

Amazon Web Services launched a series of AI services, including image recognition, natural language processing, and speech synthesis, that could be accessed through simple APIs. These services allowed companies to incorporate AI capabilities into their applications without needing to develop machine learning expertise internally or hire expensive AI talent.

Microsoft Azure, IBM Watson, and other cloud computing platforms also developed comprehensive AI service offerings, creating a competitive marketplace for AI infrastructure and tools. This competition drove rapid improvement in capabilities while reducing costs and complexity for companies wanting to incorporate AI into their products.

The emergence of AI platforms created new dynamics in venture capital investing. Startups no longer needed to build fundamental AI capabilities from scratch, they could focus on application development while leveraging platform services for core AI functionality. This reduced development costs and timelines while enabling more entrepreneurs to build AI-powered companies.

However, the platform approach also created new strategic considerations. Companies that built their products on third-party AI platforms needed to consider vendor lock-in risks, data privacy implications, and the possibility that platform providers might compete directly with their applications. The most sophisticated AI startups learned to balance the efficiency of platform services with the strategic value of proprietary AI capabilities.

The Autonomous Vehicle Gold Rush

Perhaps no single application captured venture capital imagination more than autonomous vehicles, which promised to combine artificial intelligence with one of the world's largest industries while addressing fundamental challenges in transportation safety, efficiency, and accessibility.

The autonomous vehicle opportunity attracted venture investment from multiple angles. Traditional automotive companies like Ford and GM created venture capital arms focused on mobility technology. Technology companies like Google (through Waymo) and Apple invested billions in autonomous driving research and development. Most importantly, new startups emerged with the explicit goal of developing self-driving technology for various applications.

Uber's early investment in autonomous vehicle development illustrated both the opportunity and the challenges. The company spent billions acquiring autonomous vehicle startups and developing internal capabilities, arguing that self-driving technology would be essential for long-term competitiveness in ride-sharing markets. However, technical challenges proved more difficult than anticipated, and Uber eventually sold its autonomous driving division to focus on its core ride-sharing business.

Pure-play autonomous vehicle startups also attracted substantial venture investment. Companies like Cruise (acquired by GM), Zoox (acquired by Amazon), and Aurora raised hundreds of millions of dollars to develop autonomous driving technology for different market segments and use cases.

The venture capital investment thesis for autonomous vehicles was compelling: the global automotive market was worth trillions of dollars annually, autonomous vehicles could improve safety while reducing costs, and the winner-take-all dynamics of platform technologies could create enormous value for successful companies.

However, autonomous vehicles also illustrated the challenges of AI investments that required long development timelines, substantial capital requirements, and regulatory approval processes. Unlike software applications that could be deployed and iterated rapidly, autonomous vehicles needed to achieve extremely high reliability standards before commercial deployment was possible.

The technical challenges proved more complex than many investors initially anticipated. While controlled highway driving scenarios were achievable with existing technology, fully autonomous driving in complex urban environments required advances in perception, planning, and decision-making that pushed the boundaries of current AI capabilities.

Despite these challenges, autonomous vehicle investments continued to attract venture capital because of the enormous market opportunity and the potential for transformative impact on transportation, logistics, and urban planning. The long development timelines also meant that patient capital and sustained investment would be required, characteristics that aligned well with venture capital's ability to support breakthrough technologies through extended development cycles.

The Enterprise AI Transformation

While consumer applications like autonomous vehicles attracted media attention, some of the most successful AI investments focused on enterprise applications where artificial intelligence could improve business processes, reduce costs, and enable new capabilities for corporate customers.

Customer relationship management became an early area of AI adoption, with companies like Salesforce incorporating machine learning into their CRM platforms to provide predictive analytics, automated lead scoring, and intelligent recommendations for sales teams. These applications provided clear return on investment measurements that made adoption decisions straightforward for corporate buyers.

Cybersecurity emerged as another compelling application area for AI investment. Companies like Darktrace, CrowdStrike, and Cylance developed platforms that could automatically detect and respond to security threats using machine learning techniques that could identify patterns and anomalies that traditional rule-based systems might miss.

Human resources applications also attracted significant venture investment. Companies like HireVue developed AI-powered interviewing platforms, while others like Textio created systems that could improve job postings and recruitment communications using natural language processing and predictive analytics.

Financial services proved particularly receptive to AI applications. Fraud detection, algorithmic trading, credit risk assessment, and customer service automation all benefited from machine learning techniques that could process large amounts of data and identify patterns that human analysts might miss.

The success of enterprise AI applications reflected several advantages over consumer applications. Enterprise customers were often more tolerant of imperfect AI performance if the systems provided clear business value. B2B sales cycles allowed for extensive customization and training that could improve AI system performance. Most importantly, enterprise applications could often justify higher prices that supported venture capital return requirements.

The enterprise focus also aligned well with venture capital investment preferences for recurring revenue business models, defensible competitive positions, and scalable software platforms. Companies that could embed AI capabilities into mission-critical business processes often achieved high customer retention and expansion opportunities that created substantial long-term value.

The Talent Wars and Ecosystem Development

The rapid growth of AI investment created intense competition for technical talent, particularly machine learning researchers and engineers with experience in deep learning, computer vision, and natural language processing. The scarcity of AI talent became a major constraint on the industry's development and a key factor in venture capital investment decisions.

The competition for AI talent was driven by several factors. The number of people with advanced AI expertise was limited, concentrated primarily in leading university research programs and technology companies. The rapid growth of AI applications across multiple industries created demand that far exceeded the available supply of qualified professionals.

Technology companies began competing aggressively for AI talent, offering compensation packages that often exceeded traditional software engineering salaries by substantial margins. Google, Facebook, Amazon, and other platform companies hired prominent AI researchers from universities, often offering them the resources to continue their research while also contributing to commercial product development.

The talent shortage also created opportunities for venture capital investment in AI education and talent development. Companies like Coursera, Udacity, and others developed AI and machine learning courses that could help existing software engineers acquire AI skills. Specialized bootcamps and training programs emerged to address the specific needs of professionals wanting to transition into AI careers.

The talent constraints also influenced venture capital investment strategies. Investors began paying more attention to founding teams' AI expertise and access to technical talent. Companies with strong AI leadership and established relationships with AI research communities often commanded higher valuations and attracted more investor interest.

The development of AI research ecosystems also became important for regional economic development. Cities and regions began investing in AI research programs, corporate AI labs, and startup incubators focused on artificial intelligence. These ecosystem investments were intended to attract AI companies and talent while creating local competitive advantages in AI development.

The Ethics and Regulation Challenge

As AI applications became more widespread and sophisticated, concerns about ethical implications, privacy protection, and societal impact began influencing both technology development and venture capital investment decisions. The recognition that AI systems could exhibit bias, make errors with serious consequences, and impact employment raised questions about responsible AI development and deployment.

Algorithmic bias became a particular concern as AI systems were deployed in hiring, lending, criminal justice, and other applications that could significantly impact individuals' lives. When AI systems exhibited racial, gender, or other forms of bias, it created both ethical concerns and business risks for companies using these technologies.

Privacy and data protection also became more important as AI systems required large amounts of personal data for training and operation. The European Union's General Data Protection Regulation (GDPR) and similar privacy regulations in other jurisdictions created compliance requirements that AI companies needed to address in their product development and business models.

The potential impact of AI on employment created broader societal concerns about technological displacement and economic inequality. While venture capitalists typically focused on the business opportunities created by AI, they also began considering the social implications of funding technologies that could automate human work.

Some venture capital firms began developing explicit policies and evaluation criteria related to AI ethics and social impact. These approaches ranged from screening investments for potential negative impacts to actively seeking opportunities to fund AI applications that could create positive social outcomes.

The regulatory environment for AI also began evolving, with governments considering various approaches to oversight and governance of artificial intelligence systems. The uncertainty about future AI regulation created both risks and opportunities for venture capital investments, as regulatory decisions could significantly impact the commercial viability of different AI applications and business models.

The Foundation Model Revolution

The development of large language models like GPT-3, and later ChatGPT, represented a fundamental shift in AI capabilities that would transform venture capital investing in artificial intelligence. These "foundation models" demonstrated that AI systems could achieve human-level performance across a wide range of language tasks, from writing and summarization to coding and analysis.

OpenAI's development of increasingly sophisticated language models illustrated both the potential and the challenges of foundation model development. The company raised hundreds of millions of dollars from investors including Microsoft to fund the computational resources and research required for training large-scale AI models.

The breakthrough came with the recognition that large neural networks trained on vast amounts of text data could develop general language understanding capabilities that could be applied to many different tasks without task-specific training. This represented a shift from narrow AI systems designed for specific applications to more general-purpose AI capabilities.

The commercial implications were enormous. Rather than requiring separate AI systems for different language tasks, companies could potentially use foundation models as general-purpose tools for content generation, customer service, data analysis, and numerous other applications.

The venture capital response to foundation models was immediate and substantial. Investors recognized that general-purpose AI capabilities could enable new categories of products and services while also creating platform opportunities similar to those that had emerged with cloud computing and mobile platforms.

Companies like Anthropic, Cohere, and others raised substantial venture funding to develop foundation models and compete with OpenAI's capabilities. The competition drove rapid improvement in model performance while also raising concerns about the concentration of AI capabilities in a small number of well-funded companies.

The foundation model revolution also created new opportunities for application developers who could build products and services on top of general-purpose AI capabilities. Rather than requiring extensive AI expertise, entrepreneurs could focus on user experience, business model development, and market application while leveraging foundation models for core AI functionality.

The Generative AI Explosion

The public release of ChatGPT in late 2022 created unprecedented public awareness and excitement about artificial intelligence capabilities, triggering what would become known as the "generative AI" investment boom. The system's ability to engage in natural conversation, write coherently on complex topics, and assist with various cognitive tasks demonstrated AI capabilities that seemed to emerge overnight.

The venture capital response was immediate and massive. Investment in AI startups reached record levels as investors sought to identify companies that could capitalize on the new capabilities demonstrated by generative AI systems. The category became one of the hottest investment themes in venture capital history.

However, the generative AI boom also illustrated both the opportunities and challenges of investing in rapidly evolving AI technologies. While the capabilities were impressive, the underlying costs, reliability constraints, and competitive dynamics were still evolving rapidly.

Companies building applications on top of generative AI models faced questions about sustainable competitive advantages, as the underlying AI capabilities were increasingly commoditized through API access to foundation models. The most successful companies needed to create value through data, user experience, business model innovation, or specialized domain expertise rather than just leveraging general-purpose AI capabilities.

The generative AI explosion also raised new questions about intellectual property, content authenticity, and the economic impact of AI-generated content on creative industries. These concerns created both risks and opportunities for venture capital investments in generative AI applications and related technologies.

Global AI Competition and Strategic Implications

The development of artificial intelligence became increasingly recognized as a strategic competition between nations, particularly between the United States and China, with significant implications for venture capital investment patterns and technology development.

China's national AI strategy, announced in 2017, committed substantial government resources to AI research and development while also creating supportive policies for Chinese AI companies. Chinese AI companies like Baidu, Alibaba, and SenseTime achieved significant capabilities in computer vision, natural language processing, and other AI applications.

The strategic competition created new considerations for venture capital investment in AI companies. National security concerns about AI technology transfer led to increased government scrutiny of foreign investment in AI startups. Export controls and other trade restrictions affected international collaboration and technology sharing in AI development.

European AI development took a different approach, emphasizing privacy protection, ethical AI development, and regulatory frameworks that could ensure responsible AI deployment. The European Union's AI Act and other regulatory initiatives created different competitive dynamics and market opportunities for AI companies operating in European markets.

The global competition for AI leadership also influenced venture capital fundraising and investment strategies. Sovereign wealth funds and other government-backed investors increased their participation in AI venture capital, while private investors sought to identify AI companies that could compete effectively in global markets while navigating complex geopolitical dynamics.

The Future of AI and Venture Capital

As artificial intelligence continued to advance through the 2020s, several trends emerged that would likely shape the future relationship between AI and venture capital. The ongoing development of more sophisticated AI capabilities promised to create new categories of products and services while also raising fundamental questions about the role of human intelligence in an increasingly automated world.

The path toward artificial general intelligence (AGI), AI systems that could match or exceed human cognitive abilities across all domains remained uncertain but continued to attract substantial research investment and venture capital attention. Companies like OpenAI, DeepMind, and Anthropic pursued AGI research while also developing commercially viable AI applications that could fund continued research and development.

The infrastructure requirements for advanced AI systems also created new investment opportunities. Companies developing specialized AI hardware, cloud computing platforms optimized for AI workloads, and tools for AI model development and deployment attracted significant venture capital investment.

The application of AI to scientific research and discovery represented another frontier for venture capital investment. AI systems that could accelerate drug discovery, materials science, climate technology development, and other research domains offered the potential to address humanity's greatest challenges while generating substantial commercial returns.

However, the future of AI and venture capital also faced significant uncertainties. The potential for AI systems to automate cognitive work could impact the knowledge worker employment that had historically supported venture capital-backed companies. The concentration of AI capabilities in a small number of large technology companies could limit opportunities for venture capital investment in AI applications.

Regulatory developments, ethical considerations, and societal responses to AI deployment would also shape the investment landscape. The balance between innovation and responsible AI development would influence which AI applications could achieve commercial success and social acceptance.

Conclusion: Intelligence as the Ultimate Platform

The artificial intelligence revolution represented venture capital's encounter with perhaps the most transformative technology platform in human history. Unlike previous platform shifts that had connected people, digitized information, or mobilized computing, AI promised to augment and potentially replace human intelligence itself.

For venture capitalists, AI embodied both tremendous opportunity and profound responsibility. The companies they funded could create unprecedented value while solving humanity's greatest challenges, but they could also disrupt existing industries, displace workers, and concentrate power in ways that required careful consideration of social impact alongside financial returns.

The success of AI venture investing would ultimately depend on the industry's ability to balance innovation with responsibility, support breakthrough technologies while managing ethical implications, and create value for investors while contributing to broadly shared prosperity in an AI-transformed economy.

As artificial intelligence continues to evolve from narrow applications toward more general capabilities, venture capital's role in guiding its development and deployment would become increasingly important for determining not just financial returns, but the future trajectory of human civilization itself. The AI revolution had shown that venture capital could identify and nurture technologies capable of transforming the world, the question remaining was whether it could do so in ways that benefited all of humanity.

Chapter 20

Global Competition and Innovation

"Innovation is a global game. Today, knowledge and talent can be anywhere, and competitive advantage comes from being able to access the best of both, wherever they might be."

This observation from Michael Porter, the Harvard Business School strategy professor, captured a fundamental shift that had been transforming venture capital since the early 2000s. What began as a uniquely American phenomenon centered in Silicon Valley had evolved into a global ecosystem of innovation, with venture capital networks spanning continents and breakthrough technologies emerging from unexpected corners of the world.

The globalization of venture capital represented more than just geographic expansion, it reflected fundamental changes in how innovation occurs, how capital flows across borders, and how entrepreneurial ecosystems develop and compete. By 2020, venture capital was no longer an American export but a global language of innovation, with each region developing its own distinctive approaches, strengths, and competitive advantages.

This transformation would reshape not just the venture capital industry, but the global economy itself, as countries recognized that innovation ecosystems had become essential tools of national competitiveness and economic development.

The European Renaissance

Europe's emergence as a significant force in venture capital defied early skepticism about whether the continent's risk-averse culture and fragmented markets could support successful technology entrepreneurship. The transformation began in the late 1990s and accelerated through the 2000s as European entrepreneurs, investors, and governments recognized the strategic importance of building world-class innovation ecosystems.

The United Kingdom led Europe's venture capital development, building on its historical strengths in finance and its cultural connections to Silicon Valley. London's financial district provided access to capital and expertise that could be redirected toward technology investing, while the city's international orientation attracted entrepreneurs and investors from across Europe and beyond.

British venture capital firms like Index Ventures, Accel Partners London, and Atomico achieved global recognition through successful investments in companies like Skype, Supercell, and King Digital Entertainment. These successes demonstrated that European venture capitalists could identify and support companies that achieved global scale and impact.

The European success was built on several distinctive characteristics that differentiated it from Silicon Valley approaches. European entrepreneurs often focused more heavily on international expansion from inception, driven by the necessity of operating across multiple countries and languages within the European Union. This global perspective enabled European companies to achieve international scale more quickly than American companies that initially focused on large domestic markets.

European venture capital also benefited from the continent's strong technical universities and research institutions. The European Institute of Technology, various national research programs, and university-industry collaboration initiatives created pipelines of technical talent and breakthrough technologies that could support venture-backed companies.

Perhaps most importantly, European governments recognized the strategic importance of venture capital and entrepreneurship, implementing policies to support ecosystem development. Tax incentives for angel investors, government co-investment programs, and regulatory reforms to facilitate venture capital fundraising created more supportive environments for entrepreneurship and investing.

Germany's venture capital ecosystem developed around the country's engineering strengths and industrial expertise. Berlin emerged as a major startup hub, with companies like Rocket Internet systematically replicating successful business models across multiple geographic markets. The German approach emphasized operational excellence and systematic scaling that reflected the country's manufacturing heritage.

France's venture capital development was driven by government initiatives and the country's strong mathematical and engineering education systems. French entrepreneurs achieved particular success in enterprise software, artificial intelligence, and financial technology, with companies like BlaBlaCar and Criteo achieving global recognition.

The Nordic countries, Sweden, Denmark, Norway, and Finland developed venture capital ecosystems that punched above their weight relative to population and market size. Companies like Spotify, Skype, Supercell, and King demonstrated that small countries could produce globally successful technology companies through focus on international markets and technical excellence.

China's Venture Capital Revolution

China's transformation from a manufacturing-focused economy to a global innovation leader represented perhaps the most dramatic development in international venture capital. The country's venture ecosystem grew from virtually nothing in 2000 to become the world's second-largest source of venture capital by 2020, producing some of the most valuable technology companies in history.

The Chinese venture capital revolution was enabled by several converging factors. The country's large domestic market provided scale opportunities that could justify substantial venture investments. Rapid internet and mobile adoption created massive addressable markets for digital services. Most importantly, supportive government policies and substantial public investment in technology infrastructure created favorable conditions for entrepreneurship and innovation.

Chinese internet companies like Alibaba, Tencent, and Baidu demonstrated business models and growth strategies that were distinct from their American counterparts. Rather than focusing on single products or services, Chinese technology companies often built comprehensive ecosystems that integrated e-commerce, social networking, payments, entertainment, and other services into unified platforms.

Alibaba's ecosystem approach was particularly influential in demonstrating alternative models for technology company development. The company's integration of e-commerce (Taobao, Tmall), payments (Alipay), cloud computing (Alibaba Cloud), and logistics services created competitive advantages that were difficult for single-purpose competitors to replicate.

Tencent's evolution from a gaming and social networking company to a comprehensive technology platform also illustrated distinctly Chinese approaches to technology development. The company's WeChat platform became essential infrastructure for Chinese digital life, integrating messaging, payments, commerce, and government services in ways that had no equivalent in Western markets.

The success of Chinese technology giants also created vibrant ecosystems of entrepreneurs and investors. Former employees of Alibaba, Tencent, and Baidu founded numerous startups, while these companies' corporate venture arms invested in emerging technologies and business models.

Chinese venture capital firms like Sequoia Capital China, IDG Capital, and Hillhouse Capital achieved global recognition through investments in successful Chinese companies while also expanding internationally. These firms developed expertise in Chinese markets while also creating bridges between Chinese and international technology ecosystems.

The Chinese government's strategic focus on technology development also created unique dynamics in venture capital investing. National initiatives like the "Made in China 2025" plan and substantial government investment in artificial intelligence, electric vehicles, and semiconductor technologies created market opportunities and competitive advantages for Chinese companies.

However, the Chinese venture capital ecosystem also faced challenges related to international expansion, intellectual property protection, and geopolitical tensions that could affect access to global markets and technologies. The relationship between Chinese technology companies and the government also created concerns among international investors and partners about data security and political influence.

Israel: The Startup Nation

Israel's emergence as a global technology powerhouse demonstrated how small countries could create outsized impact in venture capital and innovation through focus on technical excellence, military technology transfer, and systematic entrepreneurship development.

The "Startup Nation" phenomenon was built on several unique advantages that Israel had developed through necessity and strategic focus. The country's military technology programs, particularly Unit 8200 (intelligence) and Talpiot (technology), created pipelines of technical talent with experience in cybersecurity, communications, and advanced computing.

Israeli entrepreneurs often brought unique perspectives on technology development shaped by the country's security challenges and resource constraints. This resulted in companies that focused on solving complex technical problems with practical, efficient solutions that could be applied globally.

The Israeli venture capital ecosystem was also characterized by strong government support and systematic approaches to technology commercialization. The Office of the Chief Scientist (later the Israel Innovation Authority) provided early-stage funding and support for technology development, while various incubator and accelerator programs helped entrepreneurs transition from research to commercial applications.

Israeli companies achieved particular success in cybersecurity, with firms like Check Point Software, CyberArk, and numerous other security companies becoming global leaders. The country's expertise in cybersecurity was driven by both military applications and the recognition that digital security was becoming essential for all organizations.

The Israeli approach to international expansion was also distinctive. Given the small domestic market, Israeli companies typically focused on global markets from inception, often establishing significant operations in the United States or Europe while maintaining research and development in Israel.

The success of Israeli technology companies attracted international venture capital investment and created a virtuous cycle of entrepreneurship and investing. American venture capital firms opened Israeli offices, while Israeli entrepreneurs and investors developed strong networks with Silicon Valley and other global technology centers.

Israeli venture capital firms like Bessemer Venture Partners Israel and JVP also achieved international recognition through successful investments in Israeli companies that achieved global impact. These firms developed expertise in identifying and supporting Israeli entrepreneurs while helping them navigate international expansion.

India's Innovation Emergence

India's venture capital ecosystem developed along a different trajectory, initially focused on services and outsourcing before evolving toward product companies and original innovation. The country's large domestic market, technical talent base, and cost advantages created unique opportunities for venture capital investment.

The Indian venture capital story began with the country's information technology services industry, which demonstrated Indian technical capabilities and created wealth and expertise that could be reinvested in entrepreneurship. Companies like Infosys, Wipro, and Tata Consultancy Services established India as a global technology hub while creating networks of experienced technologists and business leaders.

However, the transition from services to products required different skills and approaches. Indian entrepreneurs needed to develop expertise in product development, marketing, and customer acquisition that differed from the relationship-based service models that had initially driven the country's technology success.

The breakthrough came with companies that could leverage India's domestic market scale and unique characteristics. Flipkart's e-commerce platform, Ola's ride-sharing service, and Paytm's mobile payments system demonstrated that Indian entrepreneurs could build world-class technology companies serving Indian consumers.

These successes attracted international venture capital investment and validated the potential for Indian product companies. Firms like Sequoia Capital India, Accel Partners India, and various other international venture firms established significant presences in Indian markets.

Indian entrepreneurs also began developing expertise in mobile-first product development, driven by the country's rapid smartphone adoption and the need to serve customers with limited internet bandwidth and computing resources. This mobile-first approach created innovations that could be applied in other emerging markets with similar constraints.

The Indian government's Digital India initiatives and various startup support programs also contributed to ecosystem development. Policies supporting cashless payments, digital identity systems, and startup tax incentives created more favorable conditions for technology entrepreneurship.

However, the Indian venture capital ecosystem also faced challenges related to regulatory complexity, infrastructure limitations, and the need to develop more sophisticated capital markets that could support later-stage company development and public market exits.

Southeast Asia's Rising Markets

Southeast Asia emerged as an important region for venture capital investment as internet and mobile adoption accelerated and economic development created new market opportunities. Countries like Singapore, Indonesia, Thailand, Vietnam, and the Philippines developed venture ecosystems that attracted both local and international investment.

Singapore positioned itself as a regional hub for venture capital and technology companies, leveraging its strategic location, business-friendly policies, and financial sector expertise. The Singapore government created various programs to attract venture capital firms and technology companies while also supporting local entrepreneurship.

Indonesian companies like Gojek and Tokopedia demonstrated that Southeast Asian markets could support unicorn-scale technology companies. These companies often needed to adapt global business models to local conditions, including fragmented payment systems, logistics challenges, and diverse cultural and linguistic environments.

The Southeast Asian approach to technology entrepreneurship was often characterized by "super-app" strategies that integrated multiple services into comprehensive platforms. Companies like Grab expanded from ride-sharing to include food delivery, payments, and other services, while Gojek evolved into a comprehensive on-demand services platform.

International venture capital firms recognized Southeast Asia's potential and established regional presences to access investment opportunities. Firms like Sequoia Capital Southeast Asia, Golden Gate Ventures, and various other investors developed expertise in regional markets while connecting local entrepreneurs with global resources and networks.

The diversity of Southeast Asian markets also created challenges for venture capital investing. Different countries had different regulatory environments, cultural contexts, and competitive dynamics that required localized approaches rather than uniform regional strategies.

Africa's Entrepreneurial Awakening

Africa's venture capital ecosystem developed more gradually but showed significant potential as internet connectivity improved, mobile adoption accelerated, and economic development created new market opportunities. Countries like South Africa, Nigeria, Kenya, and Egypt emerged as centers for technology entrepreneurship and venture capital activity.

African entrepreneurs often focused on solving local problems through technology, creating innovations in mobile payments, agricultural technology, healthcare delivery, and financial services that addressed the specific challenges and opportunities of African markets.

Kenya's M-Pesa mobile payment system became a globally influential innovation that demonstrated how African entrepreneurs could create solutions that were later adopted worldwide. The success of mobile payments in Kenya was driven by the country's limited traditional banking infrastructure, which created opportunities for mobile-based financial services.

Nigerian companies in fintech, e-commerce, and digital media attracted increasing venture capital investment as the country's large population and growing middle class created market opportunities. Companies like Flutterwave, Paystack, and Jumia demonstrated that African markets could support significant technology companies.

South Africa's more developed financial markets and infrastructure provided a foundation for venture capital development, while the country's technical universities and established business sectors created pipelines of entrepreneurial talent and expertise.

International venture capital firms began developing African investment strategies, often in partnership with local investors who provided market knowledge and cultural expertise. Organizations like TLcom Capital, Partech Africa, and various other funds developed expertise in African markets while connecting local entrepreneurs with global resources.

However, African venture capital also faced significant challenges related to infrastructure limitations, regulatory complexity, currency volatility, and the need to develop more sophisticated capital markets and exit opportunities for venture-backed companies.

Government Strategies and National Competition

The recognition that venture capital and innovation ecosystems were becoming tools of national competitiveness led governments around the world to develop strategies for supporting entrepreneurship and attracting venture capital investment.

Different countries adopted different approaches based on their existing strengths and competitive positions. The United States focused on maintaining its leadership through continued investment in research universities, immigration policies that attracted global talent, and regulatory environments that supported innovation and risk-taking.

China's approach emphasized large-scale government investment in technology infrastructure, strategic industries, and research and development, combined with policies that favored domestic technology companies and protected emerging industries from international competition.

European countries typically focused on creating supportive regulatory environments, providing tax incentives for venture capital investment, and developing programs that connected research institutions with commercial applications. The European Union also worked to harmonize regulations and create single market opportunities that could support larger-scale technology companies.

Israel's strategy emphasized military technology transfer, systematic entrepreneurship education, and policies that encouraged international collaboration while maintaining domestic technology capabilities.

Other countries developed strategies that leveraged their specific advantages, Singapore's focus on becoming a regional hub, India's emphasis on leveraging its technical talent base, and various other approaches that reflected different economic conditions and competitive positions.

The competition between national innovation strategies created both opportunities and tensions in the global venture capital ecosystem. Countries competed to attract the best entrepreneurs and investors while also developing domestic capabilities that could compete internationally.

Cross-Border Investment and Global Networks

The globalization of venture capital led to increasing cross-border investment flows as investors sought access to the best opportunities regardless of location, while entrepreneurs looked for capital sources that could provide strategic value for international expansion.

American venture capital firms established international offices and developed global investment strategies that could access opportunities in major markets worldwide. Firms like Sequoia Capital, Accel Partners, and Andreessen Horowitz created separate regional funds with local expertise while maintaining connections to global networks and resources.

International venture capital firms also established presences in Silicon Valley and other major technology centers, creating networks that could support portfolio companies' global expansion while accessing American technology and talent resources.

The development of global venture capital networks created new opportunities for entrepreneurs who could access capital, expertise, and market relationships from multiple regions. However, it also created new complexities related to currency exchange, regulatory compliance, and cultural differences in business practices.

Cross-border venture capital investment also became subject to increasing government scrutiny as national security concerns about technology transfer and foreign investment in strategic industries led to new regulatory requirements and approval processes.

The Impact of Geopolitical Tensions

The rise of strategic competition between major powers, particularly the United States and China, created new challenges and considerations for global venture capital investment. Technology became increasingly viewed as a source of national competitive advantage, leading to policies that could restrict international collaboration and investment.

Trade tensions, export controls, and investment restrictions affected venture capital flows and forced investors and entrepreneurs to consider geopolitical factors in their strategic planning. Companies that had previously operated in global markets found themselves needing to navigate complex regulatory environments and potential restrictions on technology sharing and market access.

The technology industry's increasing importance for national security also led to greater government involvement in venture capital markets. Foreign investment review processes, export control regulations, and various other policies created new compliance requirements and strategic considerations for venture capital investors and their portfolio companies.

These tensions created both challenges and opportunities for venture capital investors. While some cross-border investments became more difficult, the focus on technological competitiveness also increased government support for domestic venture capital ecosystems and technology development.

Innovation Patterns and Global Collaboration

Despite geopolitical tensions, the globalization of venture capital continues to demonstrate that innovation benefits from international collaboration and the free flow of ideas, talent, and capital. Different regions developed distinctive strengths and approaches that could be combined to create more successful technology companies and solutions.

Silicon Valley's strength in software platforms and consumer technology complemented European expertise in enterprise solutions and privacy-focused technologies. Chinese innovations in mobile payments and super-app platforms provided models that could be adapted for other markets. Israeli cybersecurity expertise addressed global security challenges, while Indian mobile-first development approaches created solutions for emerging markets worldwide.

The most successful global technology companies often combined innovations and capabilities from multiple regions, with research and development in countries with strong technical capabilities, manufacturing in locations with cost advantages, and market development strategies adapted for different regional conditions and customer preferences.

Global venture capital networks also enabled the rapid diffusion of successful business models and technologies across different markets. Innovations that proved successful in one region could be quickly adapted and deployed in others, accelerating the pace of global technology development.

The Future of Global Venture Capital

As venture capital continued to globalize through the 2020s, several trends emerged that would likely shape the future of international innovation competition. The ongoing development of new technology centers, the increasing importance of government strategy and support, and the potential for continued geopolitical tensions would all influence how global venture capital networks evolved.

Emerging markets continued to develop their venture capital capabilities, creating new sources of innovation and competition. Countries in Africa, Latin America, and other regions showed potential for developing significant technology companies and venture ecosystems that could compete globally.

The increasing importance of sustainability and social impact in investment decisions also created opportunities for countries and regions that could develop expertise in climate technology, social innovation, and other areas where technology could address global challenges.

The potential for continued technological advancement in areas like artificial intelligence, biotechnology, and space technology would require global collaboration while also creating strategic competition between countries seeking to maintain or develop leadership in critical technologies.

The balance between collaboration and competition in global venture capital would likely continue evolving as countries sought to benefit from international innovation while also developing domestic capabilities and protecting strategic advantages. The most successful regions would likely be those that could effectively participate in global networks while also developing distinctive strengths and competitive advantages.

Conclusion: Innovation as a Global Commons

The globalization of venture capital had demonstrated that innovation was increasingly becoming a global commons, with breakthrough technologies and successful business models emerging from unexpected locations and spreading rapidly across international networks. While geopolitical tensions and national competition created challenges for international collaboration, the fundamental drivers of innovation, talent, capital, and market opportunities continued to transcend borders.

The future success of venture capital would likely depend on its ability to navigate the balance between global collaboration and national competition, supporting entrepreneurs and technologies that could create value for all stakeholders while respecting the legitimate interests and concerns of different countries and regions.

As venture capital continued to evolve as a global phenomenon, its impact would extend far beyond financial returns to influence how countries competed, how technologies developed, and how humanity addressed its greatest challenges through innovation and entrepreneurship. The global competition in innovation had made venture capital not just an investment strategy, but an essential tool of economic development and international competitiveness.

Chapter 21

The Next Generation

"We are at the very beginning of time for the human race. It is not unreasonable that we grapple with problems. But there are tens of thousands of years in the future. Our responsibility is to do what we can, learn what we can, improve the solutions, and pass them on."

Richard Feynman's perspective on humanity's long-term trajectory captures the essence of venture capital's next chapter. As the industry looks toward the 2020s and beyond, it faces a constellation of emerging technologies and paradigm shifts that promise to be as transformative as the personal computer, internet, and mobile revolutions that defined its past.

The next generation of venture capital will be characterized not by single breakthrough technologies, but by the convergence of multiple exponential technologies, artificial intelligence, blockchain, quantum computing, biotechnology, space technology, and others that together could reshape every aspect of human civilization. This convergence creates both unprecedented opportunities for value creation and complex challenges that will test venture capital's ability to navigate technological, ethical, and societal implications of the innovations it supports.

The companies and technologies that emerge from this next generation of venture investing may not just create new industries, they may fundamentally alter the relationship between humans and technology, redefine the nature of work and society, and determine humanity's trajectory as a space-faring, digitally enhanced, and potentially immortal species.

Blockchain and the Decentralized Future

The emergence of blockchain technology and cryptocurrency represented one of the most polarizing and potentially transformative areas for venture capital investment. What began with Bitcoin's creation in 2008 evolved into a broader vision of decentralized systems that could reshape finance, governance, and digital interactions.

The venture capital community's initial response to blockchain was mixed, with some investors dismissing cryptocurrency as speculative while others recognized its potential to enable entirely new categories of applications and business models. The volatility of cryptocurrency prices, regulatory uncertainty, and technical limitations created challenges for traditional venture capital evaluation methods.

However, the underlying blockchain technology demonstrated capabilities that extended far beyond digital currencies. Smart contracts, self-executing agreements with terms directly written into code enabled new forms of automated business logic and trustless transactions. Decentralized autonomous organizations (DAOs) explored new models of governance and coordination that could operate without traditional corporate structures.

The venture capital opportunity in blockchain emerged across multiple layers of the technology stack. Infrastructure companies developed blockchain platforms, development tools, and scaling solutions that could support widespread application adoption. Application companies built decentralized finance (DeFi) platforms, non-fungible token (NFT) marketplaces, and various other services that leveraged blockchain capabilities.

Andreessen Horowitz became one of the most prominent venture capital firms in blockchain investing, raising specialized funds and developing deep expertise in cryptocurrency and decentralized technologies. The firm's approach emphasized the potential for blockchain to enable new forms of ownership, governance, and value creation that could be as significant as previous platform shifts.

The investment thesis for blockchain technology was based on several key insights. Decentralized systems could reduce reliance on traditional intermediaries, potentially creating more efficient and transparent markets. Programmable money and smart contracts could enable new forms of financial services and business automation. Cryptographic tokens could create new models for incentivizing network participation and aligning stakeholder interests.

However, blockchain investing also revealed significant challenges. The technology's energy consumption, transaction processing limitations, and regulatory uncertainty created obstacles to widespread adoption. The speculative nature of many cryptocurrency projects made it difficult to distinguish between legitimate innovations and opportunistic schemes.

The emergence of "Web3", a vision of a decentralized internet built on blockchain infrastructure represented perhaps the most ambitious application of blockchain technology. Web3 proponents argued that decentralized systems could return control and value to users rather than concentrating power in large technology platforms.

The venture capital community's engagement with Web3 reflected broader questions about the future of digital platforms and user ownership. While some investors saw Web3 as the next major platform shift, others questioned whether decentralized systems could achieve the performance and user experience of centralized alternatives.

The regulatory environment for blockchain and cryptocurrency also evolved rapidly, with different countries taking varying approaches to oversight and compliance. These regulatory developments could significantly impact the commercial viability of blockchain-based business models and the risk-return profiles of venture capital investments in the sector.

Quantum Computing's Revolutionary Potential

Quantum computing represented perhaps the most scientifically ambitious area of venture capital investment, with the potential to solve computational problems that were intractable for classical computers while also threatening to disrupt existing cryptographic systems and business models.

The fundamental promise of quantum computing was based on quantum mechanical properties that allowed quantum bits (qubits) to exist in multiple states simultaneously, enabling parallel processing of exponentially larger problem spaces than classical computers could address.

The potential applications were transformative across multiple industries. Drug discovery could be accelerated by quantum simulations of molecular interactions. Financial modeling could be enhanced through quantum algorithms for optimization and risk assessment. Artificial intelligence could benefit from quantum machine learning approaches that could process larger datasets and identify patterns beyond classical AI capabilities.

However, quantum computing also presented unique challenges for venture capital investment. The technology required extreme technical expertise that was concentrated in a small number of research institutions and companies. The timelines for commercial application were uncertain and likely measured in decades rather than years. The capital requirements for quantum computing hardware were substantial, often exceeding traditional venture capital investment scales.

Several approaches to quantum computing emerged, each with different technical characteristics and commercial potential. Companies like IBM, Google, and Rigetti developed superconducting quantum processors, while others like IonQ focused on trapped ion systems. These different approaches represented technical bets on which quantum computing architectures would prove most viable for commercial applications.

The venture capital community's response to quantum computing was characterized by both excitement about the long-term potential and caution about near-term commercial viability. Early-stage investments focused primarily on software and applications that could run on near-term quantum systems, while hardware investments required longer-term perspectives and larger capital commitments.

Government investment also played a crucial role in quantum computing development, with countries including the United States, China, and various European nations investing billions of dollars in quantum research and development. This government support created both opportunities and competitive dynamics that venture capital investors needed to navigate.

The national security implications of quantum computing also influenced venture capital investment strategies. Quantum computers could potentially break existing cryptographic systems, creating both cybersecurity threats and opportunities for companies developing quantum-resistant security technologies.

Biotechnology and Human Enhancement

The convergence of biotechnology, artificial intelligence, and engineering was creating opportunities for venture capital investment in companies that could enhance human capabilities, extend lifespan, and address previously incurable diseases.

Gene editing technologies like CRISPR-Cas9 enabled precise modifications to DNA that could correct genetic diseases, enhance crop yields, and potentially improve human capabilities. The development of more sophisticated gene editing tools created opportunities for venture capital investment in therapeutics, agriculture, and various other applications.

Synthetic biology emerged as a platform technology that could engineer biological systems for manufacturing, environmental remediation, and novel product development. Companies like Ginkgo Bioworks developed automated platforms for designing and testing engineered organisms that could produce pharmaceuticals, chemicals, and materials.

The longevity and life extension sector attracted increasing venture capital investment as researchers identified biological mechanisms of aging and developed interventions that could potentially extend healthy human lifespan. Companies working on senolytics, cellular reprogramming, and various other longevity approaches raised hundreds of millions of dollars from investors including Jeff Bezos, Peter Thiel, and various specialized funds.

Brain-computer interfaces represented another frontier for biotechnology venture capital investment. Companies like Neuralink, backed by Elon Musk, developed technologies that could create direct connections between human brains and computers, potentially enabling treatment of neurological conditions and enhancement of human cognitive capabilities.

However, biotechnology investing also raised complex ethical and regulatory considerations. Gene editing technologies could potentially be used for human enhancement as well as therapeutic applications, raising questions about equality, safety, and the future of human evolution. The regulatory approval processes for biotechnology applications were typically longer and more complex than for software or hardware products.

The venture capital community's approach to biotechnology was influenced by the sector's unique characteristics, long development timelines, substantial regulatory requirements, and significant capital needs. Successful biotechnology investing required specialized expertise and often involved collaboration with academic researchers and established pharmaceutical companies.

Space Technology and the New Space Economy

The commercialization of space technology created new opportunities for venture capital investment as private companies began developing capabilities that had previously been the exclusive domain of government space agencies.

SpaceX's success in developing reusable rocket technology demonstrated that private companies could achieve significant cost reductions and performance improvements in space launch capabilities. The company's achievements attracted attention from venture capital investors and validated the potential for commercial space ventures.

The "New Space" economy encompassed multiple sectors including satellite manufacturing and deployment, space launch services, space mining, and various other applications. Companies like Planet Labs developed large constellations of small satellites for Earth observation, while others focused on space-based manufacturing, space tourism, and lunar exploration.

Venture capital investment in space technology was driven by several trends. The cost of launching payloads to space had declined dramatically due to reusable rocket technology and more efficient manufacturing approaches. The miniaturization of electronics enabled smaller, cheaper satellites that could be deployed in large constellations. Growing demand for satellite-based services including communications, navigation, and Earth observation created expanding markets for space-based capabilities.

However, space technology investment also presented unique challenges. The technical risks were high, with launch failures potentially destroying entire investments. The regulatory environment was complex, with international treaties and government oversight affecting commercial space activities. The capital requirements were often substantial, particularly for hardware development and manufacturing.

The strategic importance of space technology also attracted government attention and investment. National security considerations, economic competitiveness, and scientific advancement all depended on space capabilities, creating both opportunities and complications for venture capital investment in the sector.

Advanced Manufacturing and Materials Science

The development of new manufacturing technologies and advanced materials created opportunities for venture capital investment in companies that could transform how physical products were designed, produced, and distributed.

Additive manufacturing (3D printing) evolved from prototyping applications to production-scale manufacturing, enabling new approaches to product design and customization. Companies developing advanced 3D printing technologies, materials, and applications attracted venture capital investment as the technology's capabilities expanded.

Nanotechnology and advanced materials science enabled the development of materials with unprecedented properties, stronger, lighter, more conductive, or more durable than traditional alternatives. These materials could enable new applications in electronics, aerospace, automotive, and various other industries.

Robotics and automation technologies also evolved beyond traditional industrial applications to enable new forms of manufacturing, logistics, and service delivery. Companies developing collaborative robots, autonomous warehousing systems, and robotic manufacturing platforms attracted venture capital investment as labor costs increased and precision requirements became more demanding.

The convergence of digital design tools, advanced manufacturing, and on-demand production created opportunities for more distributed and responsive manufacturing systems. Companies could potentially manufacture products closer to customers, reduce inventory requirements, and enable greater customization than traditional mass production approaches.

However, advanced manufacturing investments also faced challenges related to capital requirements, technical risks, and competition from established manufacturing systems. The transition from laboratory demonstrations to commercial production often required substantial additional investment and expertise.

Digital Health and Personalized Medicine

The convergence of digital technology, biotechnology, and healthcare created opportunities for venture capital investment in companies that could improve health outcomes while reducing costs and increasing access to care.

Wearable devices and continuous monitoring systems enabled new approaches to preventive medicine and chronic disease management. Companies developing advanced sensors, data analytics, and intervention systems could potentially shift healthcare from reactive treatment to proactive prevention and management.

Artificial intelligence applications in healthcare included medical imaging analysis, drug discovery, personalized treatment recommendations, and various other applications that could augment or enhance human medical expertise. The combination of AI with large healthcare datasets created opportunities for more precise and effective medical interventions.

Telemedicine and digital health platforms also expanded rapidly, particularly accelerated by the COVID-19 pandemic, creating new models for healthcare delivery that could increase access while reducing costs.

Companies developing virtual care platforms, remote monitoring systems, and digital therapeutics attracted substantial venture capital investment.

Personalized medicine approaches that tailored treatments to individual genetic profiles, biomarkers, and other characteristics represented another major area of healthcare innovation. Companies developing companion diagnostics, precision therapies, and personalized treatment platforms could potentially improve treatment effectiveness while reducing side effects.

However, digital health investing also faced significant regulatory challenges. Healthcare applications typically required FDA approval or other regulatory clearances that could be time-consuming and expensive. Privacy and security requirements were also more stringent in healthcare than in other sectors.

Sustainable Technology and Circular Economy

The growing urgency of environmental challenges created opportunities for venture capital investment in technologies that could enable more sustainable economic systems and circular economy approaches.

Advanced recycling technologies that could break down complex materials and recover valuable components attracted venture capital investment as waste management became more expensive and resource scarcity increased. Companies developing chemical recycling, electronic waste processing, and various other recycling innovations could potentially create value while addressing environmental challenges.

Alternative protein technologies including plant-based meat substitutes, cultured meat, and insect protein attracted substantial venture capital investment as consumers and companies sought more sustainable protein sources. These technologies could potentially reduce the environmental impact of food production while meeting growing global protein demand.

Carbon capture and utilization technologies that could remove carbon dioxide from the atmosphere and convert it into useful products represented another area of sustainable technology investment. Companies developing direct air capture, carbon conversion, and various other carbon management technologies attracted investment as governments and corporations made commitments to carbon neutrality.

Renewable energy technology continued to evolve beyond solar panels and wind turbines to include energy storage, grid management, and various other applications that could enable higher renewable energy adoption. Companies developing advanced battery technologies, power electronics, and grid optimization systems could potentially accelerate the transition to renewable energy systems.

Regulatory Evolution and Societal Adaptation

The next generation of technologies also required new approaches to regulation and governance that could balance innovation with safety, privacy, and societal benefit. Venture capital investors increasingly needed to consider regulatory risks and societal impact alongside financial returns.

The European Union's approach to technology regulation, including GDPR privacy regulations and proposed AI governance frameworks, created new compliance requirements that could affect the commercial viability of technology ventures. The balance between innovation and regulation would likely continue evolving as governments sought to capture technology benefits while managing risks.

The societal impact of technology also became more important for venture capital investment decisions. Issues including job displacement, privacy protection, algorithmic bias, and wealth concentration created both risks and opportunities for technology companies and their investors.

The development of new governance models for technology platforms, including stakeholder governance approaches and various forms of distributed decision-making, represented potential alternatives to traditional corporate structures that could better align technology development with societal interests.

Investment Strategy Evolution

The next generation of technologies also required evolution in venture capital investment strategies, evaluation criteria, and portfolio management approaches. Traditional venture capital models developed for software and internet companies needed adaptation for longer development timelines, higher capital requirements, and more complex regulatory environments.

The emergence of new fund structures including evergreen funds, opportunity funds, and impact investing vehicles reflected attempts to better align venture capital with the characteristics of next-generation technologies. These structures could provide more patient capital and different risk-return profiles than traditional venture capital funds.

The increasing importance of technical expertise also influenced venture capital firm organization and recruitment. Firms needed partners with deep domain expertise in quantum physics, biotechnology, materials science, and various other technical areas that differed from traditional venture capital backgrounds.

The global nature of next-generation technology development also required more sophisticated international investment strategies and partnerships. The best opportunities might emerge from any geographic region, while regulatory and competitive considerations could affect investment viability and exit strategies.

The Convergence Effect

Perhaps the most significant characteristic of the next generation was the convergence between previously separate technology domains. Artificial intelligence enhanced biotechnology applications, quantum computing could accelerate materials science, blockchain enabled new models for space commerce, and various other combinations created emergent capabilities that exceeded the sum of their parts.

This convergence effect created both opportunities and challenges for venture capital investment. Companies that could successfully combine multiple next-generation technologies might achieve breakthrough capabilities and competitive advantages. However, the complexity of managing multiple technological risks and development timelines could also create execution challenges.

The convergence also required new forms of expertise and collaboration that crossed traditional disciplinary boundaries. Successful next-generation companies might need to integrate computer scientists, biologists, physicists, engineers, and various other specialists in ways that differed from traditional technology company organization.

Conclusion: Venture Capital's Next Frontier

The next generation of venture capital represented both continuity and transformation. The fundamental mission, identifying and supporting entrepreneurs who could build transformative companies remained constant, but the technologies, timelines, and impacts were evolving in ways that could reshape human civilization.

The venture capital industry's ability to navigate this next generation would determine not just financial returns, but potentially the trajectory of human technological development and its impact on society. The companies funded by next-generation venture capital could address humanity's greatest challenges while also creating entirely new categories of risks and opportunities.

The success of next-generation venture capital would require balancing technological optimism with ethical responsibility, supporting breakthrough innovations while considering their societal implications, and creating value for investors while contributing to broadly shared prosperity and human flourishing.

As venture capital entered its next chapter, it carried with it the accumulated wisdom of decades of innovation, the responsibility of stewardship over transformative technologies, and the opportunity to play a defining role in humanity's technological future. The next generation would test whether venture capital could evolve to meet these challenges while maintaining its essential function as a catalyst for innovation and entrepreneurship.

The story of venture capital was far from over, in many ways, its most important chapters are yet to be written.

Conclusion

Nothing Ventured, Everything Gained

"The reasonable man adapts himself to the world; the unreasonable man persists in trying to adapt the world to himself. Therefore, all progress depends on the unreasonable man."

George Bernard Shaw's observation about the nature of progress captures the essence of what venture capital has accomplished over the past eight decades. From its post-World War II origins in the offices of J.H. Whitney & Company to the global ecosystem of innovation it has become today, venture capital has been the financial engine of unreasonable ambition, supporting entrepreneurs who refused to accept the world as it was and instead insisted on building the world as it could be.

This journey from modest beginnings to global transformation reveals venture capital as more than just an investment strategy or asset class. It has become the primary mechanism through which modern societies translate scientific discovery into economic value, entrepreneurial vision into transformative companies, and human ingenuity into civilizational progress.

The Venture Capital Legacy

The numbers tell part of the story. Venture capital has created trillions of dollars in market value, funded thousands of companies that have become household names, and generated returns that have made it one of the most successful investment strategies in history. Companies backed by venture capital now represent more than 20% of the market capitalization of U.S. public markets and an even larger share of economic dynamism and job creation.

But the true legacy of venture capital extends far beyond financial metrics. The companies it has funded have fundamentally altered how humans live, work, communicate, and understand their place in the world. The personal computer revolution democratized access to information and computing power. The internet connected humanity in ways previously unimaginable. Mobile technology puts powerful computing capabilities in billions of hands. Social networks transformed human relationships and information flow. Search engines organized the world's knowledge. E-commerce revolutionized retail and distribution.

Each of these transformations was enabled by venture capital's unique ability to provide patient, risk-tolerant capital to entrepreneurs pursuing visions that seemed impossible to conventional thinkers. When established companies and traditional financing sources said no, venture capitalists said yes, not just with money, but with expertise, networks, and the kind of long-term commitment required to build transformative companies.

The venture capital approach proved particularly powerful because it aligned multiple incentives in service of innovation. Entrepreneurs gained access to capital and expertise. Investors achieved returns that compensated for the high risks of supporting unproven technologies and business models. Society benefited from innovations that improved productivity, created jobs, and solved previously intractable problems.

Perhaps most importantly, venture capital created a systematic approach to innovation that could be replicated, scaled, and improved over time. The venture capital model, combining financial capital with human capital, network effects with portfolio diversification, patient money with performance accountability became a technology for innovation itself.

The Evolution of Expertise

The story of venture capital is also a story of learning and adaptation. The industry that emerged from the wreckage of the dot-com crash was more sophisticated, disciplined, and effective than the one that had fueled the speculative excesses of the late 1990s. The climate tech investments of the 2010s incorporated hard lessons learned from the clean tech disappointments of the 2000s. The AI revolution of the 2020s built on decades of accumulated knowledge about platform shifts, network effects, and technology commercialization.

This evolution reflects venture capital's unique characteristic as a learning system. Unlike many other forms of investing that can rely on historical patterns and established metrics, venture capital operates at the frontier of what is known and possible. Success requires continuous learning, pattern recognition, and the ability to update beliefs based on new evidence.

The best venture capitalists have always been students of technology trends, market dynamics, human psychology, and the complex interplay between all three. They developed expertise not just in financial analysis, but in product development, market strategy, organizational behavior, and the myriad challenges that entrepreneurs face in building companies from ideas.

This expertise has become increasingly specialized and sophisticated over time. The generalist venture capitalist of the 1960s has evolved into specialist investors with deep domain knowledge in sectors like artificial intelligence, biotechnology, climate technology, and enterprise software. The simple financial support of early venture capital has expanded to include operational assistance, strategic guidance, and access to networks that can accelerate company development.

The professionalization of venture capital has also led to more systematic approaches to portfolio construction, risk management, and value creation. While venture investing will always involve irreducible uncertainties and the potential for spectacular failures, the industry has developed tools and frameworks that can improve the odds of success while managing downside risks.

The Democratization of Innovation

One of venture capital's most significant contributions has been the democratization of innovation opportunity. By creating systematic mechanisms for funding unproven companies and entrepreneurs, venture capital enabled individuals and small teams to pursue ambitious visions that would have been impossible without access to substantial financial resources.

This democratization has had profound implications for economic dynamism and social mobility. Entrepreneurs from diverse backgrounds, including many who lacked traditional credentials or family wealth could access the capital needed to build transformative companies. The venture-backed success stories include immigrants, college dropouts, and individuals from modest backgrounds who achieved extraordinary success through innovation and execution.

The geographic spread of venture capital has also democratized access to innovation funding. While Silicon Valley remains the epicenter of venture activity, thriving venture ecosystems have emerged around the world, from London and Berlin to Beijing and Bangalore. This geographic diversification has enabled more entrepreneurs to access venture capital without relocating to traditional technology centers.

The emergence of new models, accelerators, crowdfunding, corporate venture capital, and others has further democratized access to early-stage funding and support. These alternatives to traditional venture capital have lowered barriers to entry for entrepreneurs while creating more pathways to commercialize innovative ideas.

However, the democratization remains incomplete. Venture capital investment is still concentrated among a relatively small number of firms, sectors, and geographic regions. Women and underrepresented minorities continue to receive disproportionately small shares of venture funding.

The benefits of venture capital-funded innovation, while broadly distributed, have not been equally shared across all segments of society.

The Double-Edged Nature of Innovation

The venture capital story also illustrates the complex and sometimes contradictory nature of technological progress. The same innovations that have created enormous value and improved countless lives have also generated new forms of risk, inequality, and social challenge.

Social media platforms funded by venture capital have enabled global communication and democratic movements while also facilitating misinformation and political polarization. E-commerce has provided convenience and selection for consumers while disrupting traditional retail employment. Artificial intelligence promises to augment human capabilities while also raising concerns about job displacement and algorithmic bias.

These contradictions reflect the inherent nature of transformative innovation, it creates both opportunities and disruptions, winners and losers, intended and unintended consequences. Venture capital's role in funding these innovations has made it a participant in both their benefits and their risks.

The recognition of these dual effects has led to increasing focus on responsible innovation and impact investing within the venture capital community. More investors are considering the broader implications of their investments, beyond just financial returns. Environmental, social, and governance (ESG) factors have become more important in investment decision-making.

However, the challenge of balancing innovation benefits with potential risks remains complex. The same technologies that create societal challenges may also provide solutions to other problems. The process of innovation itself, with its inherent uncertainty and potential for unintended consequences makes it difficult to predict and manage all risks in advance.

Global Competition and Collaboration

The globalization of venture capital has created both opportunities and challenges for continued innovation leadership. The emergence of strong venture ecosystems in China, Europe, Israel, India, and other regions has increased competition while also expanding the global pool of entrepreneurial talent and innovative ideas.

This global competition has generally been beneficial for innovation, creating pressure for continued improvement in venture capital practices while increasing the resources available for funding breakthrough technologies. The diffusion of venture capital models and expertise has enabled more countries and regions to participate in the innovation economy.

However, increasing geopolitical tensions and concerns about technology transfer have created new challenges for international venture capital collaboration. The recognition that technological leadership has become a source of national competitive advantage has led to policies that can restrict cross-border investment and collaboration.

The future of global venture capital will likely require navigation of these competing pressures, maintaining the international collaboration that accelerates innovation while respecting legitimate national security and economic competitiveness concerns. The most successful approaches will likely be those that can balance openness with security, competition with collaboration.

The Responsibility of Success

As venture capital has become more powerful and influential, questions about its responsibilities and obligations have become more prominent. The industry that once operated in relative obscurity now shapes markets, employment, and social trends in ways that attract public attention and regulatory scrutiny.

The concentration of venture capital among a relatively small number of firms and investors has created concerns about the democratization of opportunity and the distribution of innovation benefits. The influence of venture capitalists over the companies they fund has raised questions about accountability and governance in an increasingly important sector of the economy.

The environmental and social impact of venture capital investments has also become more significant as the scale and influence of venture-backed companies have grown. Climate change, inequality, privacy, and other societal challenges are increasingly recognized as issues that venture capital can either help address or potentially exacerbate through its investment choices.

These responsibilities require venture capital to evolve beyond pure financial optimization toward more complex considerations that balance multiple stakeholder interests. The most successful venture capital firms of the future may be those that can generate strong financial returns while also creating positive environmental and social impact.

The Technology Convergence Horizon

Looking forward, venture capital faces perhaps its most significant opportunity and challenge in the convergence of multiple exponential technologies. Artificial intelligence, biotechnology, quantum computing, blockchain, space technology, and climate technology are all advancing simultaneously, creating potential for breakthrough innovations at their intersections.

This convergence could enable solutions to humanity's greatest challenges, climate change, disease, poverty, and resource scarcity while also creating new forms of value and opportunity. However, it also increases complexity, risk, and the potential for unintended consequences that could have far-reaching implications.

The venture capital industry's ability to navigate this convergence will require even greater sophistication in technical evaluation, risk assessment, and portfolio management. It will also require continued evolution in investment approaches, fund structures, and stakeholder relationships to match the characteristics of these emerging technologies.

The ethical dimensions of technology development will also become more prominent as the capabilities and potential impacts of emerging technologies increase. Venture capital's role in funding these developments will require careful consideration of not just commercial potential, but also societal implications and long-term consequences.

The Enduring Principles

Despite the dramatic changes in technology, markets, and society that have occurred over venture capital's eight-decade history, several core principles have proven enduring and essential for success.

The importance of supporting exceptional entrepreneurs remains fundamental. While technologies and markets change, the human element of entrepreneurship, vision, persistence, adaptability, and execution capability continues to be the most important factor in venture capital success.

The value of patient capital for breakthrough innovation has also proven consistent across different technological eras. Whether supporting the development of semiconductors in the 1960s, internet companies in the

1990s, or artificial intelligence in the 2020s, transformative innovations have required sustained investment over extended periods.

The power of network effects and ecosystem development has become even more important as technologies have become more complex and interconnected. The most successful venture capital firms have been those that could provide not just capital, but also access to expertise, customers, partners, and additional funding sources.

The discipline of focusing on business fundamentals, sustainable competitive advantages, scalable business models, and paths to profitability has repeatedly proven essential for long-term success, even during periods when speculative enthusiasm seemed to make such fundamentals less important.

The willingness to take intelligent risks on unproven technologies and business models remains central to venture capital's value creation. The ability to see potential where others see only uncertainty continues to differentiate successful venture capitalists from other types of investors.

The Future of Innovation

As we look toward the future, venture capital's role in enabling innovation seems likely to become even more important rather than less. The challenges facing humanity, climate change, aging populations, resource constraints, and inequality will require technological solutions that can only be developed through sustained innovation and entrepreneurship.

The increasing complexity and cost of breakthrough innovation will require the kind of patient, risk-tolerant capital that venture capital provides. The interdisciplinary nature of emerging technologies will require the kind of network effects and collaborative relationships that venture capital ecosystems create.

The global nature of both challenges and opportunities will require the kind of international cooperation and competition that has characterized venture capital's evolution from a Silicon Valley phenomenon to a worldwide system of innovation funding.

However, the future of venture capital will also require continued evolution and adaptation. The industry will need to develop new approaches to evaluation, support, and governance of the technologies it funds. It will need to balance financial returns with broader stakeholder interests and societal impact.

Most importantly, venture capital will need to maintain its essential character, the willingness to support unreasonable ambitions, to fund entrepreneurs who believe they can change the world, and to provide the patient capital required to turn visionary ideas into transformative companies.

Nothing Ventured, Everything Gained

The title of this book reflects both the risk inherent in venture capital, the reality that without venturing into the unknown, no progress is possible and its extraordinary success in creating value not just for investors and entrepreneurs, but for society as a whole.

The companies funded by venture capital have created millions of jobs, generated trillions of dollars in economic value, and improved the lives of billions of people through innovations in technology, healthcare, transportation, communication, and countless other areas. The venture capital industry itself has become a model for how patient capital, entrepreneurial vision, and systematic innovation can be combined to create transformative change.

But perhaps the greatest achievement of venture capital has been to demonstrate that the future is not predetermined, that through human ingenuity, technological innovation, and intelligent risk-taking, we can build a world that is better than the one we inherited. The entrepreneurs and investors who populate the venture capital ecosystem are united by a fundamental optimism about human potential and technological progress.

This optimism has been repeatedly vindicated by the innovations that venture capital has enabled. The personal computers that democratized access to information. The internet that connected humanity. The mobile devices that put powerful technology in everyone's hands. The medical advances that have extended and improved human life. The environmental technologies that offer hope for addressing climate change.

Each of these innovations required someone to believe in possibilities that others deemed impossible, to commit resources to uncertain outcomes, and to persist through the inevitable setbacks and failures that accompany breakthrough innovation. Venture capital provided not just the financial resources to support these efforts, but the institutional framework and cultural values that made sustained innovation possible.

As venture capital enters its next chapter, funding artificial intelligence, biotechnology, quantum computing, space technology, and other frontier innovations it carries with it the accumulated wisdom of decades of success and failure. The industry has learned to balance optimism with realism, ambition with discipline, risk-taking with responsibility.

The future will undoubtedly bring new challenges, new technologies, and new opportunities for both value creation and unintended consequences. But if the history of venture capital teaches us anything, it is that the combination of entrepreneurial vision, patient capital, and systematic innovation can overcome seemingly insurmountable obstacles and create transformations that improve the human condition.

In the end, venture capital's greatest contribution may be its demonstration that nothing is truly impossible for those bold enough to try, patient enough to persist, and wise enough to learn from both success and failure. By venturing into the unknown, supporting the unreasonable, and funding the impossible, venture capital has gained not just financial returns, but something far more valuable, the opportunity to shape the future itself.

The story of venture capital is far from over. The most important chapters may yet to be written, the greatest companies yet to be funded, the most transformative innovations yet to be imagined. But the foundation has been laid, the principles have been proven, and the stage has been set for continued innovation and entrepreneurship.

Nothing ventured, nothing gained. Everything ventured, everything possible. The future, as always, belongs to those unreasonable enough to insist on changing the world and to the venture capitalists wise enough to support them in that essential work.

www.ingramcontent.com/pod-product-compliance
Lightning Source LLC
LaVergne TN
LVHW052033200926
848481LV00005B/1658
* 9 7 9 8 2 3 2 2 2 2 2 1 5 *